THE GUARDIAN BOOK OF THE WELFARE STATE

The Guardian Book
of the
Welfare State

Edited by
R.A. Pearson

Series edited by
R.H. Haigh
D.S. Morris
A.R. Peters

WILDWOOD HOUSE

R.H. Haigh, D.S. Morris, A.R. Peters and Gemimi News
Service Ltd 1988

Published by
Wildwood House Limited
Gower House
Croft Road
Aldershot
Hants GU11 3HR
England

Distributed in the United States by
Gower Publishing Company
Old Post Road
Brookfield
Vermont 05036
USA

British Library Cataloguing in Publication Data

The Guardian Book of the Welfare State.
    —(Related Guardian books).
    1. Public Welfare—Great Britain
    —History—20th century
    I. Haigh, R.H.   II. Morris, D.S.
    III. Peters, A.R.   IV. Pearson, R.A.
    V. Manchester Guardian   VI. Series
361'941   HV245

The reports in this book, all from the pages of the *Manchester
Guardian*, were selected by an independent historian, who
also wrote the annotations, introduction and appendices.

ISBN 0 7045 3084 8

Printed and bound in Great Britain by
Billing and Sons Limited, Worcester.

Contents

Acknowledgements

A number of people have made our task in producing this book a great deal easier than would have otherwise been the case. Michael Harkin, Social Sciences Librarian at the Central Library in Manchester, responded most readily to our request for microfilmed copies of the *Manchester Guardian* and, by so doing, greatly reduced the time and effort expended on producing the manuscript. Roger Hines, Margot Madin, Ray Thompson and Laura Tolley of the Eric Mensforth Library, Sheffield City Polytechnic, all gave willingly of their time and never failed to meet the many arduous demands we made of them.

Finally our thanks are owed, as on many previous occasions, to our families. Without their tolerance and support, our task would have been that much more difficult. To them we dedicate this book.

R.H. Haigh
D.S. Morris
A.R. Peters
Series Editors
Sheffield 1987
R.A. Pearson
Editor 1987

Editors' Introduction
to Series

The historian is blessed with many advantages. He can assemble all of the available facts relevant to any particular past event, analyse each in turn, assemble his accumulated knowledge into a comprehensive and logically sequential pattern and present a rationally sound appraisal of all the elements which have contributed both directly and indirectly to a social phenomenon considered by him or by others to be worthy of special attention.

In marked contrast to the historian stands the journalist. Not for him the luxury of wide-ranging and detailed information; instead he is confronted by a complex blend of fact, rumour and innuendo which falls far short of being comprehensive in character or cohesive in format. Working from partial information he can at best offer his reader a rational assessment of what he has gleaned from a multiplicity of sources, with but little hope or opportunity of being able to verify and validate every element of his story by reference to other knowledgeable or accepted authorities and accounts.

Yet despite the advantages enjoyed by the historian and despite the disadvantages which beset the journalist, there is an immediacy about journalistic accounts which the historian can only try to capture in his own scholarly labours. Social events rarely happen in a causal sequence, decisions are invariably taken on the basis of limited knowledge, and the complexity of societal phenomena makes total comprehension and a fully rational response an impossibility. Perhaps, therefore, the historian may be not unreasonably accused of enforcing a rationality and order on to events which is largely his own, and of attributing motives which accord with his perceptions rather than being the motives which underlay human actions at the time of his chosen event.

In short the journalist offers a 'snap shot' of the world as he perceives it in the present, an assessment which has an immediacy even though it affords an interpretation which may well lack comprehensiveness. The historian working from accumulated past knowledge and enjoying the benefit of hindsight is able to offer a fuller account of past events but one which will almost inevitably fall short of conveying the immediacy which is a feature of the journalistic report.

Let it not be forgotton that the work of a journalist can, of itself, be a factor which influences the actions of others. Journalistic accounts are themselves elements which are capable of influencing the perceptions and behaviours of social actors and can, therefore, be an integral part of significant events in man's social activities. The historian may point to past 'errors' and may influence current and future events by so doing, but it is most unlikely that his work will ever, by its very nature, be as significant a determinant of current events as that of the journalist.

This is not to deny or denigrate the art of the historian. It is simply to state that in order to gain an understanding of a past event and to acquire an appreciation of it that was available to the majority of those living at the time it was unfolding, it may well be more fruitful to give consideration to journalistic accounts of the day rather than simply being restricted to the more academically oriented accounts of historians. Journalists offer living history, historians offer considered history. Neither is of itself better than the other, nor are the two mutually exclusive. This book has chosen to utilise the former in order to provide an insight into the creation of the Welfare State in the 1945 1950 post-war Labour Government and by so doing has consciously sought to offer a counterbalance to the many voluminous and more profound academic accounts which have been produced over the years.

Whether or not this has succeeded, indeed whether or not such an exercise should ever have been attempted, must be left to the judgement of the reader.

R.H. Haigh
D.S. Morris
A.R. Peters
(Series Editors)
Sheffield 1986

Editor's Introduction

In many respects it is misleading to characterise the period 1945–48 as one in which the Welfare State was created, since to do so is to neglect the contributions made to welfare theory and practice in the late nineteenth century and the first four decades of the twentieth century. Britain's experience as the first industrial nation and the accompanying problems of urbanisation, unemployment, and poverty amid plenty had forced the question of the role of the State in meeting these contingencies into a prominent position as early as the eighteenth century, when the Elizabethan Poor Law came under the scrutiny of the political economists. The nineteenth century produced no single answer to that question and the growth of welfare services did not follow any clearly defined path towards greater State involvement. Experience did not teach everyone the same lesson; competing ideologies, competing political organisations, vested interests, local traditions, all combined to produce advance in one area of welfare provision and reaction in others; progressive local authorities cheek by jowl with those who interpreted their duties in a fashion which would have drawn the highest praise from Samuel Smiles.

Although the last decade of the nineteenth century and the first twenty years of the twentieth had witnessed a heightening of political interest in welfare issues, in which imperialism and the First World War had played a significant role, the depression of the inter-war years illustrated the inability of Government to prevent the privations of unemployment and the failure of the welfare services to alleviate its effects. Ill health, bad housing, poverty and educational deprivation were still the lot of many of the population. However, the period should not be viewed entirely negatively since it was one in which the groups pressing for more positive State action were growing in strength and experience, accumulating evidence, producing policy alternatives, sharpening the cutting edge of their critiques of the piecemeal, *ad hoc* approach of successive governments. The idea of a national minimum standard of living embracing income maintenance, full employment, health care, housing and education became a sharper, more rigorous, more urgent policy proposal than its late nineteenth-century ancestor.[1] Supporters of this proposal were drawn mainly from the Labour Party and the Liberal Party but also included some progressive Tories.[2] Though also we can point to key individuals like J.M. Keynes and W. Beveridge it is important not to forget the growing importance of the 'welfare professions' and the administrators, civil servants, local government officials, members of the inspectorates, whose experience and empirical evidence fuelled the demand for change.

It was of course the Second World War which provided the opportunity for welfare policy to become the key domestic political issue, an opportunity which Sir William Beveridge seized enthusiastically in producing his Report on Social Insurance and Allied Services in 1942, which went far beyond his original brief.[3] At this point it may be tempting to go to the other extreme and to reduce the significance of the period 1945–48 under the Labour Government to that of merely implementing a blueprint for which a political consensus had already been won during the war.[4] Thus the Labour Government, far from making any distinctive contribution to the Welfare State, was simply the occupant of political office at a time when legislation was the natural, even inevitable, cumulation of a developmental process stretching back to the Poor Law of 1834. According to this view, key building blocks were already in place in the form of Coalition White Papers or legislation such as the Family Allowances Act and the Education Act, and the Labour Government, far from being the architect of the Welfare State, was simply the building gang which assembled it.

This is not the place in which to enter into the labyrinths of such a debate, though two very general points might be made. The first is that even if a consensus of some kind did exist one should not dismiss the role of the Labour Party in the formation of that consensus in the years preceding the Second World War.[5] Secondly, consensus may be more apparent than real particularly when there is no immediate risk of moving from policy proposals to legislation. The peculiar circumstances of war may heighten the tendency toward a public stance which displays solidarity and unity in government.

Thus proposals have to be translated into the details of legislation and it is at this point that the battles have to be fought. Nowhere is this better illustrated than in the protracted negotiations about the shape of the National Health Service.[6] The circumstances of the immediate post-war period were hardly the most congenial to the creation of an expensive network of national welfare services. It is true that a great deal of groundwork had been done by the Coalition Government but the Labour Government faced a period in which every conceivable raw material was in short supply and in which the demands for those materials exploded after the privations of the war years. The expectations of the people were high but the country faced a grave economic situation in which the Government was dependent on American aid. Welfare policies had to be 'sold' not only to the Treasury, the Civil Service, the professions and Parliament but also to the American Government. Even the weather appeared to oppose the Government's programme as the fuel crisis and the housing crisis were deepened by the severe winter of 1947. The problems of demobilisation, continuing military action in Greece, disengagement from India and the Palestinian crisis all provided possible distractions and excuses for inaction.

In these circumstances the Labour Government's legislative programme, which included not only the great spread of welfare services, but also the nationalisation of major industries, reveals an energy and commitment which had no precedent. It would be difficult to argue that that commitment did not stem from a belief in Socialist principles no matter how vaguely defined within the 'broad church' of the Labour Party. It is true that in many areas of legislation the Labour Government showed little imagination. One might even suggest that they were unprepared for power and for putting the flesh on the bones of their manifesto. In vital areas of welfare policy Labour did not find the answers because they did not raise the question of, for example, how to incorporate democratic control and accountability into the welfare services. The level of benefits and capital spending may have had to be restricted in the post-war economy, but where is the dynamic, participatory, democratic socialism which would allow the people to determine priorities and to develop the civic virtues on which the unilateral transfers of welfare services depend? All too often in Social Security, in Health, Education, and Housing, bureaucratic centralism was the dominant form of service provision and the profession and the full-time administrators were to be the judges of what was best for those who paid for and consumed the services. It is in areas such as these that it would perhaps be fair to criticise the Labour Government for failing to put its distinctive stamp on the Welfare State. However, to do this is certainly not to suggest that principles did not inform Labour's programme.

The purpose of this book is to provide the opportunity to gain insight into some of these questions through the perspective of the *Manchester Guardian* 1945–48. The *Guardian* is a particularly appropriate choice since it has a long tradition of a progressive liberal stance and a history of championing the cause of social reform. The *Guardian* also has a reputation of careful, balanced reporting and even-handed judgement in its editorial comment. The extracts which follow will, I believe, give greater weight to that reputation during this period. It is not my intention to give a detailed picture of all the appropriate legislation and the complex intertwining of welfare policy with other legislation and political events. The sheer volume of material from the *Guardian* would make this impossible and the detailed history of the Labour Government has already been covered extremely well by others.[7] It is rather to give an indication of how the debates and issues of welfare policy would have appeared to *Guardian* readers in the period 1945–48 and to give an impression of the newspaper's stance on the important issues of the day. It has proved to be an extremely rich seam in which to mine and a great deal of material has had to be excluded. In selecting material an attempt has been made to assess its relative importance as gauged by the *Guardian's* coverage, though obviously my own judgement may have distorted this.

The extracts are arranged both chronologically and thematically.[1] Each of the years 1945 to 1948 is dealt with in sequence but within each year the material is arranged around the themes of Housing, Health, Education, Social Security and Welfare Services. The exception is 1945, which is further subdivided into the periods before and after the General Election.

R.A. Pearson
Sheffield 1986

NOTE

1   There are exceptions to the chronological sequence on pp. 31-44 where it has made sense to place articles with others covering the same topic.

REFERENCES

[1] For a discussion of the idea of the national minimum in the late nineteenth century see R. Pearson and G. Williams, *Political Thought and Public Policy in the Nineteenth Century*, Longman 1984.

[2] See M. Beloff, *War and Welfare*, Arnold 1984.

[3] J. Harris, 'Some Aspects of Social Policy in Britain during the Second World War' in W.E. Mommsen (ed.), *The Emergence of the Welfare State in Britain and Germany*, Croom Helm 1981.

[4] On the 'consensus' of the war period see P. Addison, *The Road to 1945*, Quartet Books 1977, and J. Hess, 'The Social Policy of the Attlee Government' in W.E. Mommsen, op. cit.

[5] See A. Marwick, 'The Labour Party and the Welfare State in Britain 1900–1948', *American Historical Review* 1967.

[6] The clearest insight into these negotiations may be gained from M. Foot, *Aneurin Bevan 1945–1960*, Davis Poynter 1973.

[7] K.O. Morgan, *Labour in Power 1945–51*, Oxford 1985; H. Pelling, *The Labour Governments 1945–51*, Macmillan 1984.

(1945)

From the publication of the Beveridge Report in 1942 up to the election in 1945, social policy issues assumed a central role on the domestic political stage. The Coalition Government's response to Beveridge was somewhat belated: in 1944 White Papers on health and social insurance were published but these did not progress to legislation before the end of the Coalition. Major legislation was passed in the areas of education and family allowances but otherwise social policy remained unresolved.

As the war drew to a close and the possibility of an election increased the three main parties directed their attention to these questions, one of the most urgent of which was future housing policy.

Housing
PRE-ELECTION

16 January 1945 p.6

TORY HOUSING PLAN
Target of 750,000 in Two Years

A target of 750,000 houses within two years of the end of the war in Europe is one of the chief recommendations contained in the latest report of the Conservative Central Committee on Post-war Problems – 'A Policy for Housing in England and Wales,' prepared by the Sub-committee on Housing and published to-day.

The committee have proceeded on the assumption that 'make do and mend' and 'adapt' must be the watchwords in the emergency, and that the first consideration must be the housing of every homeless family, and in particular of the men returning from abroad and their families. 'We believe, that unless a reasonable degree of housing comfort is quickly afforded to every homeless family, discontent will spread through the country. 'The housing of the returning men and their families 'may take as long as two years, and in our view it would be intolerable if any such men remained ill-housed for longer than this.'

16 January 1945 p.4

Leader ## TORIES ON HOUSING

The prospect of a serious dearth of houseroom in the period of demobilisation is exercising the mind of the Conservative party with unwonted thoroughness. 'Unless a reasonable degree of housing comfort is quickly afforded to every homeless family,' says the Housing Sub-committee of its central organisation in a report issued to-day, 'discontent will spread throughout the country.' To forestall such a dangerous development it has done what it describes – for the most part with justice – as 'some straight thinking.' It divides the problem logically into the emergency need

3

for the speediest possible provision of independent shelter for the 750,000 family units who will otherwise have no homes of their own, the transitional need for as many permanent dwellings to replace slums and temporary make-shifts and to provide a margin for mobility, and the continuing need for the replacement of obsolescent houses.

The policy it puts forward to meet these needs differs little from that now being professed by the Government except in emphasis, but it is useful to have on record the party's support for the maintenance of controls over building prices and the allocation of labour and materials, its recognition of the need to develop new techniques, and its call for a higher proportion of houses to let.

29 January 1945   *p.4*

Leader   **REBUILDING BRITAIN**

'Nobody doubted that there were votes in housing, and in a democracy that means that things get done.' This comment on post-1918 conditions in Sir Ernest Simon's new book, 'Rebuilding Britain – a Twenty-year Plan,' will apply with increasing force in the years ahead; for no matter how energetically the job is tackled there is bound to be a shortage of houseroom of any kind for several years, while the shortage of dwellings that conform to modern standards must persist for a decade to come. Already enough has been done, in the face of this politically dangerous prospect, to ensure that we shall at least see some improvement on the performance of the last post-war reconstruction period. Already, too, the political parties are showing themselves anxiously aware that there are votes to be got by promising to do a great deal more. Labour and trade union spokesmen have made wild assertions about the capacity of the depleted building labour force to meet post-war needs without the aid of prefabrication; a Conservative policy committee, with a great show of hard-headed practicality, has outbid the official emergency target by a modest 50 per cent; now the Liberal party executive has capped all with a demand for four million permanent houses in the first five years of peace.

1 February 1945   *p.3*

TEMPORARY HOUSES
Steel Supply Difficulties

Mr. Duncan Sandys, Minister of Works, answering a number of questions in the House of Commons yesterday about prefabricated houses, said that his predecessor explained in the House

4

of Lords that the figure of £600 per house was a target to be aimed at. It applied only to steel houses, and it was based on the assumption that these would be mass-produced and that production would not begin until after the war in Europe.

Since then it had been decided not to wait until then before starting on a programme of temporary houses. Owing to the fact that material needed for the steel houses could not at present be made available, it had been necessary to adopt less highly pre-fabricated types which were not so well suited for mass-production methods.

24 February 1945   *p.3*

HOUSING SWITCH-OVER
Permanent Dwellings as Soon as Possible to Aid Town-Planning

The decision of the Government to switch over as soon as practicable from the construction of temporary to permanent houses was announced in the House of Commons yesterday by Mr. Duncan Sandys (Minister of Works) in a statement on the Government's housing programme.

The Housing (Temporary Accommodation) Act, 1944 envisaged a production of some 200,000 temporary houses during the first two years following the end of hostilities in Europe, but, he said, much of the factory capacity and labour on which this programme had been based could not yet be released from munitions production, and in addition choice of design was restricted by shortages of timber and sheet steel.

'We have in consequence been obliged to turn to the less highly pre-fabricated type of house involving an increased number of man-hours on the site, and this is one of the reasons why the cost appears likely to work out considerably higher than was originally estimated for the pressed-steel house,' he said. 'At the same time some local authorities are finding serious difficulty in providing sites for temporary bungalows without encroaching on sites which have been prepared for permanent houses and so running the risk of compromising their long-term building programme.

'The Government have therefore decided in the interests of economy and of town planning to switch over as soon as is practicable to the construction of permanent dwellings which can be built on normal sites and which will not have to be pulled down in a few years' time.'

5

Leader **A CHANGE OF POLICY?**

Yesterday's statement by Mr. Duncan Sandys on housing policy was hardly calculated to clear up the muddle created in the public mind by the conflicting pronouncements of Government, party, and trade spokesmen. An early debate is desirable, if only to give the Minister an opportunity to find less ambiguous expressions. Whatever fresh decision has been taken, it is certainly not intelligibly conveyed in the phrase 'to switch over as soon as is practicable to the construction of permanent dwellings.' It always has been   and evidently still is – the Government's policy to start the permanent-housing programme as soon as building labour can be spared from defence and repair work and to expand it as rapidly as the release and training of more building labour will make possible. But the biggest building labour force that can be made available cannot possibly make good the immediate deficiency of houseroom for several years. Accordingly, it was (and is) the Government's policy 'to press forward with the manufacture of temporary bungalows to the fullest possible extent' until that need is met, because temporary bungalows require fewer man-hours of site labour...

Our London Correspondent

DITHERING

Mr. Sandys's announcement in the Commons to-day of the change of policy on temporary housing had the effect that might have been imagined. If the response of the House could be summed up in a sentence it would be 'When, in the name of goodness, are you going to stop dithering and produce a policy?'. . .

Leader **HOUSING QUESTIONS**

The White Paper on Housing makes a useful basis for the two-day debate in the Commons – not because it adds anything material to what was already known or answers any of the questions that are being asked with growing anxiety, but simply because it clears out of the way most of the facts and figures that are not (or should not be) any longer in dispute. Having put down in black and white all the arguments and explanations which have been reiterated in nearly every official pronouncement on the subject for the last six months and more, Ministers (their critics permitting) can now, if they will, concentrate on those aspects of policy and matters of fact about which the White Paper either says nothing at all or speaks in riddles. It is a minor virtue of that document that it restates the Government's objectives in more logical form. Instead of a 'short term' programme (variously defined as anything from the first two years' production to the million houses required to give each family a separate home of adequate size fit for habitation), to be followed by a 'long term' programme to meet all further needs, we now have three stages. The first, with a target of three-quarters of a million houses is intended to ensure that a separate dwelling of some sort – modern, obsolete, or slum – shall be available 'for every family which desires to have one.' The second will see the replacement of houses already condemned as unfit for habitation and the 'abatement', of overcrowding. The third will be a continuing programme to secure a progressive improvement in housing conditions. It is only the first stage that matters at the moment.

24 March 1945   *p.3*

GOVERNMENT WARNED OF DANGER OF SERIOUS UNREST

Opening the two-day debate on housing in the House of Commons yesterday,

Mr. H. WILLINK (Minister of Health) said the White Paper issued on Tuesday dealt mainly with the Government's primary aim of producing the largest practicable number of separate homes in the first two years after the end of the war in Europe. 'Paper plans and competitive estimates don't put roofs over needy people's heads,' he said: 'they bring only ill-will and disillusionment. A programme beyond the capacity of the building industry might mean, as it meant in 1919, that many houses are started and few are finished and that prices are forced rapidly upwards and 'programmes downwards.'

The Government's estimate of what could be done constituted a huge task, a tremendous commitment, if they were to fulfil it. A programme of 220,000 houses completed in the first two years after the defeat of Germany, plus temporary houses, plus repair of war damage, could only be achieved if the utmost effort was coming from everyone concerned. It was for that reason that the Government proposed to treat those two years as a period of national emergency when emergency measures must be taken and to give the improvement of housing conditions the highest priority among all civil needs. Every effort must be made to use the resources to the best advantage – by extensive use of labour-saving methods of construction, by standardisation, and by the use of labour and industrial capacity normally outside the building industry. The Government would provide subsidies for house-building both by local authorities and by private enterprise and would control the volume of contracts let, building and repair work done on private account, and the price of materials, standard components, and fitments in a way not done after the last war.

Allowing for all those measures and for the utmost drive and resourcefulness in all quarters, the short-term programme set out in the White Paper was the biggest the Government could put before the House as capable of achievement. 'If more houses can be built they will be built,' added Mr. Willink.

TOO MANY PLANS

Mr. SILKIN (Lab – Peckham) said the Government could derive no comfort from the debate and unless they bowed to the House and took immediate action serious consequences would ensue. At the end of two years all we should have at the best was something like 365,000 houses against an admitted need of 1,250,000, although his view was that the need was something like 2,000,000. The Government had no policy beyond the provision of this limited number of houses for the first two years after the war. It was no use having a policy without knowing where the houses were to be built, and that contemplated a land policy for compensation and betterment and the control of land use.

There had been a good deal of indecision about the provision of temporary houses, he continued, and a failure even to carry out what had been promised – namely, that in London there would be provided 250 temporary houses a week from January 1. By now there should have been 3,000 temporary houses provided for London. Up to date they had had less than sixty and probably less than fifty. What had happened to the remainder?

24 March 1945   p.4

Leader   **HOUSING**

Critics of the Government – and every non-Ministerial speaker was a critic – have got little satisfaction or fresh information about its housing policy from the two-day debate concluded yesterday. But they must at least have impressed on Ministers a lively sense of their own anxiety and of the country's readiness for heroic measures to meet a desperately urgent situation. Even crusted Tories demanded a 'war procedure,' with the rights of persons and property subordinated to the national need. Mr. Willink ably defended his refusal to overtax the capacity of the building industry. But means have already been found to raise the prospective labour force to 800,000 in half the time he once thought necessary; and if only about one-seventh of those will be available for new house construction, is it not all the more important that they should be used to get houses built as quickly as possible, at least until each family has a separate dwelling of its own.' The pressed-steel house, which consumes one man-hour of site labour for every three required by other temporary types, cannot be manufactured on a large scale before next spring. Three-quarters of a million of us will then still be homeless; yet Mr. Sandys 'hesitates to start production of this new type . . . at so late a date.' Is that the spirit of war production?

13 April 1945   p.6

GOVERNMENT WILL STICK TO ITS HOUSING PLANS — LORD WOOLTON
Reply to Labour Peer's Attack

A motion 'regretting the failure of the Government to formulate and pursue a co-ordinated policy to meet the grave shortage of housing accommodation' was moved in the House of Lords yesterday by Lord LATHAM.

The Government, he said, had been repeatedly warned of the seriousness of this problem during the past three years, yet they had failed to formulate an effective programme whether for short-term or long-term needs. It was a sorry story of a Government in 'muddle town', which was a congested area of Ministerial departments. It was obvious from the recent debate in the House of Commons that the Government were still without a policy which commanded the nation's confidence. Two years had been lost and it was no good trying to catch up with it by shifts, devices, and expedients. Nothing had been done in regard to the control of land use or compensation and betterment. The delay was one of the principal causes for the absence of a co-ordinated long-term policy.

After quoting the Prime Minister's broadcast on the subject and saying that after that the nation was entitled to expect that something really positive and constructive was being done. Lord Latham stated that the Government's White Paper could more correctly be described as a white sheet. In so far as it recorded any achievement it was mainly achievement by local authorities. It reduced the number of temporary houses to be built from the grandiose figure of half a million in the Prime Minister's broadcast to 145,000. There was no policy in the White Paper as to costs, and the cost of temporary dwellings was becoming terrifying. When did the Government propose to introduce legislation to control the price of building materials?

9

Health
PRE-ELECTION

Discussions about the reform of health service provisions had largely foundered on the rock of professional opposition to the Coalition Government's proposals contained in the White Paper of 1944.

In the early months of 1945 the fears of the medical profession, which would loom large again when the Labour Government took office, were already finding expression in the 'Guardian's' letter columns.

LETTERS TO THE EDITOR

26 January 1945   *p.4*

MEDICAL SERVICE

To the editor of the Manchester Guardian

Sir. – Though we are far away working among those injured in this fight for freedom we are still deeply interested in the affairs at home that concern the medical profession. Many of us have been unable to answer the questionnaire addressed to us by the British Medical Association owing to its non-arrival, but we still have our own views on the White Paper. The impression received from papers sent out from home is that the public are surprised that the profession is suspicious of the whole scheme. Why is the profession suspicious of State machinery? In the past we have had experience of the working of State machinery.

Perhaps we may mention one example of the working of the existing National Health Insurance and draw a comparison with the White Paper. The public generally may not be aware that a complaint against a panel doctor of professional misconduct, excluding criminal offences, may not be taken to a civil court. The doctor is tried by a committee composed of five doctors elected by the local profession, five laymen and an independent chairman.

Evidence is submitted by witnesses in writing. The witness is not sworn and may avoid cross-examination by the simple expedient of non-attendance at the hearing; this, however, does not destroy the written evidence. Neither the doctor nor the complainant may be legally represented, and each must conduct his own case. That injustices are not more frequent is perhaps due to discernment on the part of the committee or to the persuasive powers of the doctors over the independent chairman, who has only a casting vote.

The Minister of Health has power to alter the decision of the committee, and his ruling is final. At present this does not often happen, but there is at least one case known to us where great injustice was done by the Minister exercising this right. It may be asked why the profession puts up with this committee injustice instead of appealing to the law courts. The reason is that any action against a doctor damages him professionally even though the court may decide completely in his favour.

The White Paper proposes that this function be taken over by a local medical board, whose constitution is not stated except that it will include members of the local council, no mention being made of any medical representation whatever. Any doctor would be suspicious of a state of affairs in which he will be tried for professional misconduct by laymen who are primarily politicians and whose knowledge of legal process and professional matters is perforce small.

From the doctors' point of view worse is to follow. The White Paper provides for a Central Medical Board exercising power over the local committee. This board, small in number, is to be composed of doctors appointed by the Minister and not elected by the profession. Throughout the White Paper the Minister insists on vesting power, central and local in the duly elected representatives of the people. Is the profession so incapable of governing itself that it must not be allowed to elect either the Central Medical Board or the medical members of the Central Advisory Council formed to give advice to the Minister on all medical matters? – Yours &c.,

A.D. STOKER, MB, ChB (Ed),
J. ATKINSON, MB, ChB,
G.J. EVANS, MB, BS (Lond) MRCS, LRCP,
SEAC, September 24.

MEDICAL SERVICE

To the Editor of the Manchester Guardian

Sir,   The evils under which medical practitioners labour described by the SEAC medical correspondents are directly traceable to the pernicious system of legislation by delegation, stigmatised by the late Lord Hewart as 'the new despotism' and more recently described in uncompromising terms by Sir Henry Slessor in the 'Spectator'.

The contract of terms and services that the doctor undertaking NHI work completes is, in cases of dispute, construed in a fashion anything but legal. The Minister in the first place takes upon himself the duty of the old grand jury and, if he decides that there is a true bill then acts in the capacities of prosecuting counsel, jury and judge, at the same time denying the doctor any right of appeal to anyone, much less the law courts. What commercial firm would engage in a contract and covenant that the only arbitration of the contract in case of dispute shall be the other party to it?

As one of the essentials of a contract is the intention to create legal obligations, surely the doctor should therefore have at least the right of appeal to a law court if he considers that he is being denied justice. It is this denial to the doctor to have his contract considered by the law of the land that makes many doctors unwilling to accept the idea of the 100 per cent inclusion in the proposed National Health Service, as although at present the doctor labours under this difficulty it is probably only up to 50 per cent of his activities, his present private practice not being included in this disability. But, if all his work is to be so governed, he can see that he is to become a victim of a system similar to the Continental 'droit administratif'.

It is to be hoped that in the new National Health Service the contract of service will contain guarantees that in cases of dispute the doctor shall be enabled to appeal to the law courts if he so desires. This would obviate the kind of case that arose in this division last year whereby a doctor was made legally liable for the welfare of some patients the care of whom he declared himself physically unable to undertake. In other words, he was forced into a contract of service with these patients against his will and judgement. What sort of a 'contract' can that be called?

Yours &c.,

S. WEST, Chairman Lincoln Division BMA,
Ingham, Lincoln, January 26.

15 February 1945   *p.6*

THREAT TO VOLUNTARY HOSPITALS
National Health Service

The familiar voice of Dr. Charles Hill, the 'Radio Doctor' and secretary of the British Medical Association, was heard at Oldham last night strongly criticising certain sections of the Government's proposed national health service. He was speaking to delegates of the Oldham Royal Infirmary contributory scheme.

The voluntary hospital service had, Dr. Hill said, in the main, proved itself efficient, and commanded a loyalty and affection from the people which organs of the State had not yet learnt how to win. Yet the Government proposed to bring the voluntary hospital under a governing board consisting entirely of representatives of local authorities, or, as the price of its separate existence, the voluntary hospital would only receive part of its expenses and would have to get the rest from people who had already paid enforced contributions towards a free State health service. If they wanted the voluntary hospital to survive, Dr. Hill told his audience, they must oppose those two sections of the scheme. He was certain that the Government was already repenting of many of its proposals concerning voluntary hospitals, and he believed that on the basis of the contributory scheme they could have found a way out.

As regards the general practitioner, Dr. Hill said that three things were required in any medical service – efficiency, free choice of doctor by the patient, and the employment of the doctor solely by his patient without the doctor's owing loyalty to any outside employer. But under the proposed scheme the medical profession was apprehensive lest they be transmuted into a branch of central or local government. 'Let the medical services and medical research be extended by all means, let there be no financial barriers to stand between a patient and his needs, but let the medical service remain personal and humane with the interest of the individual patient paramount.'

There were fears that the BMA's opposition to the Coalition White Paper had already produced concessions from the Government which had been concealed from Parliament.

HEALTH SERVICES
Minister and the White Paper

In the House of Commons Yesterday

Mr. Willink (Minister of Health), saying that he welcomed the opportunity of clearing the matter up, answered a number of questions about the White Paper on health services. Proposals in the White Paper were for discussion before the Government decided on the terms of draft legislation, he said.

Before informing the Government of their views on possible alternatives the various organisations – medical, dental, voluntary hospitals and local authorities – were considering, on reports from their representatives, matters which had been discussed. When the views of the different organisations were available the Government would decide on draft legislation and until then the three stages of procedure – White Paper, discussion of White Paper, and preparation of draft legislation – were being adhered to.

The Minister's assurance did not satisfy the Socialist Medical Association.

THE SECRET HEALTH SERVICE PLAN
'B.M.A. Playing Politics'

Opening a national health conference of the Socialist Medical Association in Caxton Hall, London, yesterday, Dr. Somerville Hastings, president, spoke of a document which had been sent to all doctors by the British Medical Association, labelled 'not for publication.' The document contained proposals for a National Health Service which the Minister of Health was willing to put before his colleagues if the doctors agreed.

'But why should the doctors, who are not compelled to join the service, be told about it, while the public, many of whom will be forced to use it, are told nothing?' he asked. 'To extend the "panel," as is proposed, means the continuance of two sorts of patient – the private, who enters by the front door and is seen at once, and the public, which comes in at the back and has to wait long periods;

and two sorts of treatment as well. It also means the sale of practices, paid for by public funds, to the highest bidder, of whom nothing may be known, except that he once passed an examination indicating that he had then a minimum of medical knowledge.'

Mr. Fred Messer, M.P., declaring that any sign of offering less than the White Paper must be resisted, said: 'Both B.M.A., and voluntary hospitals are playing politics and what they are really claiming is freedom of choice of patient by doctor, freedom to exclude women from the profession, freedom to control the hospitals which are dependent on their services, freedom to decide the type of patient admitted to hospital, and freedom to fix charges and to discriminate in treatment between rich and poor.'

27 April 1945   *p.8*

HEALTH SERVICE SCHEME:
'NOTHING YET DROPPED OR ADDED'
Minister's Reply to 'Fantastic' Suggestion

On the motion for the adjournment Dr. Edith Summerskill (Lab.—Fulham W.) in the House of Commons last night drew attention to a document circulated to over 70,000 doctors and marked 'not to be published.' She found it difficult to understand why 70,000 doctors should be given this document and millions of potential patients who would be called upon to finance the White Paper proposals should be left in ignorance. 'It is deplorable to think that negotiations have been conducted by the Minister and interested bodies and the Minister has connived at keeping this secret from the House,' she said. 'In the proposals which the Minister has made to the British Medical Association there is a complete change in the attitude of the Government towards the new health services.'

In the new proposals it was suggested that there should be a few experimental health centres but that the local authority should have no clinical supervision — that doctors would come and work there but their work would not be supervised in any way and that the only contract between the doctor and the local authority would in effect be that of landlord and tenant — that the doctor could conduct his private practice in the health centre exactly as he did outside. 'We had looked forward to the day when doctors would be employed in the health services on a full salaried basis. That has all gone.'

Mr. Willink (Minister of Health): You have referred to some document and given the impression no doubt unintentionally that it is issued by the Government or the Minister. If you are referring to some document which you have received as a member of the B.M.A. it would be better to make that clear.

Dr. Summerskill: The document, as you know full well, was published by the B.M.A.

15

Mr. Willink: You must not say that I know full well it was published by the B.M.A. What I know is that no document has been published by the B.M.A. A document has been sent to members of the B.M.A. and maybe, other doctors marked 'Not for publication.'

'POWER WHITTLED AWAY'

Dr. Summerskill continued: 'At the eleventh hour the time has arrived to reveal this matter, which is of concern to the whole country, to every man, woman and child. I want to prove my case — my assertion that the Minister has made these proposals to the B.M.A. which he has denied time after time. So far as the change in the health service is concerned, this change is not one of detail but a complete change in principle. A great deal of the power of local authorities is to be whittled away. The full-time salaried medical service we all looked forward to and approved last year is to be dropped. There is a suggestion that there will be some part-time service, but otherwise the doctors are to be paid on a capitation basis.

'One can sum up this document by saying that instead of that great reform welcomed last year the Minister is proposing to the B.M.A. that they should have an extension of the panel system. That is all. In spite of this assertion I have made now and before the Minister has deliberately got up in this House and denied it. The time has arrived when I must call the Minister's bluff because on May 3 the doctors are meeting to consider his proposals. The Minister has thrown doubts on my veracity in this House, and the House must know whether it is I or he who is departing from the truth. I go so far as to say that I want to expose a piece of calculated political dishonesty' (Cries of 'Oh').

She read an extract from the document stating: 'Included in this report is an administrative structure put forward by the Minister as a possible alternative to that outlined in the White Paper. They are proposals which the Minister will be willing to put to his colleagues as soon as he knows whether they commend themselves to the medical profession.'

'That is what it says,' Dr Summerskill went on. 'Can Mr. Willink repudiate this? Can he deny again these are not his proposals and that the B.M.A. had no mandate on May 3? Tell the country now!

Mr. Storey (C—Sunderland) thought that Dr. Summerskill had put a most mischievous view of the situation before the House. The alternative proposals, in his opinion, went a long way to improve the White Paper proposals. He hoped no one would try to throw a spanner into the wheel of the negotiations.

Education
PRE-ELECTION

The education debates centred on the shortage of teachers and teaching materials and the future effects of the 1944 Education Act.

3 January 1945   *p.3*

'DILUTION' IN TEACHING PROFESSION
Teachers Fear Danger to Standards and Pay

The staffing position in schools is so desperate that education is being carried on only with the help of old men who are dying at their posts, Mr. W.A. Barron, head master of Brighton Grammar School, told the annual meeting of the Incorporated Association of Headmasters in London yesterday. Mr. Barron is president of the association.

High salaries were urged to attract first-rate teachers and similar suggestions were made at the London conferences of the Association of Assistant Mistresses in Secondary Schools and of the Incorporated Association of Assistant Masters.

Mr. Barron, commenting on the tragic waste in the Services of many of their trained men, added: 'We all know that boys' schools as a whole are being carried on now only by the help of women and old men who would have retired long ago and some of whom are literally dying at their posts. The provision of teachers trained under the emergency scheme is admittedly an emergency attempt to solve a desperate situation. The danger is that in fifteen years we may see the teaching profession with many thousand disgruntled members, 70,000 if the full number is obtained under the scheme, most of them finding themselves in a cul-de-sac with no hope of promotion.'

The Burnham Scale proposals, Mr. Barron added, were good enough to attract the fourth-rate but offered no attraction at all to the first-rate.

The schoolmaster's job could not be confined to teaching. There was no genuine service which they could render to their pupils in or out of school which they should try to avoid.

17

TRAINING THE NEW TEACHERS
Colleges to Open Soon

Mr. R.A. Butler, Minister of Education, announced yesterday that three emergency colleges for training teachers — two for women and one for men – will probably be opened in April.

In his presidential address to the Conference of Education Association at King's College, London he said that in the emergency training scheme provision was made for continuing training after the teacher had started in the school. The ultimate aim was to lengthen the period of training for new recruits. . . .

'Under the new Act,' he continued, 'education will be directed not towards the competitive scramble for what have been regarded as social and financial plums but to the guiding of every child towards his natural right – the forms of life and work in which he is likely to find the greatest measure of happiness for himself and service to his fellows. The Ministry is taking every care and trouble to give the guidance necessary.' . . .

Mr. Butler said that within this variety we must preserve the standards of our old traditional grammar schools and he hoped above all that we should never lose the value of classical education.

THE 'COMMON MAN' IN POWER
Conference of the Association of Assistant Masters in Secondary Schools

Sir Richard Livingstone, Vice-Chancellor of Oxford University, said 'There is no doubt that the common man will far more determine the policy and colour of the country in the next fifty years than he has done in the past. That, I think, is just, but clearly has its dangers. The class to which we have given very little education, no education in most cases beyond the age of 14, is being called into power. That clearly is bound to have a great effect upon the politics and the general civilisation of the nation. One of our problems is to see that the coming into power of the democracy does not mean any fall in the level of the civilisation of the country, but a rise in it.'

EDUCATION PROBLEMS TO BE SOLVED UNDER NEW ACT
Factors Affecting Manchester's Plans

Whatever other social reforms are realised in 1945 it will be memorable as the year in which the first of the National Government's major reconstruction measures was put into operation. The new Education Act – 'the most comprehensive measure in the history of English education' – comes into force on April 1.

Its comprehensiveness, indeed, is too vast to compress into a general small-scale picture; the full results will be revealed only after patient and painstaking preparation; but the immediate and revolutionary effect will be that many thousands of secondary-school pupils throughout the country will no longer pay fees, and within the next few months the voluntary or direct grant secondary schools will have to decide for themselves whether or not they will continue to charge fees or become free like the others.

Although the bulk of the Act becomes law on April 1, a great many of the reforms cannot be effected for a considerable time. Provisional sections provide for the carrying on of the schools in much the same way as they have been carried on in the past until local authorities have submitted to the Minister their 'Development Plans' for primary and secondary education and, in return, have received from the Minister a Local Education Order empowering them to execute their plans. before these plans are prepared, however, a memorandum of guidance on the subject is to be issued by the Minister 'as soon as possible in the new year.'

When the Ministry of Education produced its Primary and Secondary Regulations on 18 March 1945 the 'Manchester Guardian' offered the following comment in its leading article.

Leader **EDUCATION**

Fixing as they do the administrative framework of the educational order whose foundations were laid by the Act of last year, they deserve the most careful scrutiny and a hasty verdict on them would be unwise. One general feature, however, of the design embodied in them – and a highly significant feature – leaps to the eye at once. The substitution of a single set of regulations for the series of separate documents marks the opening of a new era. It means that henceforward education is to be regarded as a continuous process with successive stages and that the old arbitrary divisions with their absurd administrative distinctions between schools serving the same human needs will no longer be allowed to put asunder what nature has joined.

A topic which, since the Education Bill became the Education Act, has been discussed with some warmth is the position of the secondary grammar schools receiving grant direct from the Ministry of Education. Part IV of the regulations and one of the two circulars are devoted to the subject and it is to be hoped that the controversy surrounding it will now subside. Of the 1,398 grant-aided grammar schools 1,166, or roughly four-fifths, will cease next month to charge fees. There remain 232 direct-grant schools, to which the provision requiring that maintained secondary schools shall be free does not apply. The direct-grant list will shortly be revised; and until that revision has been completed it is not possible to say how many schools will in future possess direct-grant status. But whether the number is increased or reduced, the principle to be followed in the matter of fees still requires to be determined.

It would have been preferable that fees should be abolished in direct grant as in maintained secondary schools, but even had that step been taken some system of selection would still have been a necessity. The only system of selection which is either just to individuals or compatible with the best use of the nation's limited educational resources is selection by merit, not by money. It is a matter for satisfaction that the Ministry's regulations should have taken a step in that direction.

On the eve of the implementation of the Act the following leading article appeared.

31 March 1945   *p.4*

Leader   **A STARTING-POINT**

Part II and Part IV of the Education Act come into operation to-morrow. Together they contain the vital core of a measure which will unquestionably remain a high landmark in educational history. It is natural that the conclusion of a twenty years' struggle to secure obvious but obstinately resisted reforms should be followed, among these who strove for them, by a mood of self-congratulation. It was equally to be expected that the Act should be disparaged in some quarters as a piece of paper reconstruction. Both complacent optimism and cynicism masquerading as realism are alike out of place. The former attitude is perhaps the more dangerous of the two. The Education Act is not a terminus; it is a starting-point. It cleared the site of a litter of obsolete rubbish and designed the architecture of the edifice to be erected upon it. The next step is a matter or bricks, mortar, man-power, and hard work. In May,

1940, after eight months of futility, Mr. Morrison said 'Go to it,' and the nation thanked Heaven for a Minister who knew his mind. Mr. Butler's motto should be the same. Parliament has 'done its stuff' and, considering that it is old and tired, has not done it too badly. It is now for us – the public – to see that work starts at once and to insist that it shall proceed without hesitancy or faltering till the job is done.

In that sustained effort the Ministry, of course, must play a leading part. The one fatal course would be another instalment of the timidities and ineptitudes which cause the memory of the last 'Reconstruction' period to stink. The difficulties are familiar. The supply of teachers is deficient. Building workers and materials are short. It must be expected that, as soon as the omens are propitious, the usual economy ramp will be let loose to raise hairs on nervous scalps. The last, which is common form, is to-day generally recognised to be also common nonsense. The second obstacle is genuine, but the parents of a child are under a legal obligation to cause him 'to receive efficient full-time education suitable to his age, ability, and aptitude.' They must not be compelled to break the law by withholding from them the means of complying with it; and, since the means of complying with it consist of schools, schools must be given a high place among building priorities. It is quite true, finally, that, as a result of the planned scarcity of secondary education, which down to last year was the accepted – and fatuous – policy of this country, we possess no large reserve of potential teachers which can be rapidly mobilised. Improvisation, therefore, is inevitable. There is no reason to be ashamed of it, and no reason to suppose that it will not succeed.

It is sometimes suggested that the Act will leave educational realities much what they were, particularly in the sphere of secondary education. Defeatism of the kind has no justification. There is no reason to suppose that the modern secondary schools will necessarily be regarded as inferior to the more specialised grammar and technical secondary schools. On the contrary, the former, if wisely planned, are likely to provide the education best calculated to give the majority of boys and girls a hopeful start in life. And a further point requires emphasis. It is of the first importance that authorities, in making their plans, should take the public into their confidence by regular consultations with parents and with representative organisations, and that those organisations on their side should at once stimulate and assist authorities by educating the public in the possibilities of the Act. A united effort is essential. It must rest on a basis of informed co-operation.

TEACHER SHORTAGE
80,000 More Needed Under the New Act

Eighty thousand additional teachers will be needed when the 1944 Education Act comes into full effect, said Sir Maurice Holmes, Permanent Secretary to the Ministry of Education, giving evidence before the Royal Commission on Equal Pay under the chairmanship of Sir Cyril Asquith in London yesterday.

'Of course, the spread-over will be over a number of years,' he added. 'The minimum figure is 13,000, which will be needed as the result of the raising of the school-leaving age. We hope this will come into effect not later than April, 1947. Taking the figure of 280,000 teachers, it would cost the country £14,500,000 extra per annum for equal pay only under the Burnham scales.'

Sir Maurice said that he did not think women were very 'money minded' when they went into teaching. It was only when they were established as teachers that they began thinking of equal pay.

Equal pay would not introduce a very much different woman into the profession, but it might rather discourage men. The type of man entering the profession might be of a rather lower standard.

There was undoubtedly opinion in favour of equal pay in the profession, including that of the National Union of Teachers, but he thought it had been rather regarded by them as an unattainable ideal, and when it came to the individual teacher he doubted whether the male members of the union were as much in favour of equal pay as their executive.

Social Security and Welfare
PRE-ELECTION

The Coalition Government passed an Act setting up a Ministry of National Insurance in November 1944 and produced White Papers on social insurance and industrial injury insurance. The Labour Party had been critical of the Government for its failure to respond earlier in a positive way to the Beveridge proposals but there was still considerable caution in other quarters, particularly on the question of whether wholescale reform would be practicable in the economic climate likely to prevail in the post-war period.

16 February 1945   *p.6*

PEER'S ATTACK ON SOCIAL INSURANCE PLANS
Sharp Rebuke from Lord Woolton

Calling attention in the House of Lords yesterday to the Government's policy regarding social insurance and industrial injury insurance, Lord NATHAN said he was a whole-hearted supporter of the two White Papers that had been issued. He recognised, however, that the security of income promised by the White Papers could only be real if the necessary goods and services were made available by the entire efforts of the nation. Pointing out that the White Papers were not a programme but only the promise of one, he asked for the necessary legislation with all speed.

The success of a genuine policy of social security was dependent on the Government's ability to keep the cost of living stable after the war by the same methods as during the war. The Minister of National Insurance should be specifically required to review rates of benefits and rates of contribution periodically in relation to the expenditure necessary at ruling prices to maintain health and fitness and to provide for necessities. 'There is an over-riding need for the utmost speed in putting these proposals into practice,' said Lord Nathan. 'The demobilised armies must not find this great scheme still under consideration or in the pigeon-holes when the last shots have been fired.'

23

Lord MANVERS urged on the Government the need for caution. There were many who said that our exports when loaded with Beveridge charges would prove unsaleable in foreign countries. If so it would very likely lead to further unemployment.

'CONFIDENCE TRICK VARIATION'

Lord MONKSWELL declared that it was dishonest and futile to promise the working classes all sorts of good things without making it clear to them that their co-operation in accepting economic rates of wages and conditions of service was the foundation of the whole matter and that without this co-operation the whole scheme must collapse.

All the big political parties, he continued, had united to make to the voters a whole series of reckless promises of a large number of extremely expensive social reforms which for many years at least would add nothing to our material wealth. Obviously, the circumstances required a drastic reduction of taxation, which could only be achieved by the postponement of the social security programme. The Government policy was to ignore the facts, make social security a first charge, and let production look after itself.

'The whole thing is impossible,' he declared. 'The proposals are described by their advocates as a crusade against the ills of life. They would be more correctly described as a political variation of the confidence trick.'

The most immediate product of the new Ministry was the Family Allowances Act passed in June 1945. Family allowances had been the subject of a long campaign of lobbying led by Eleanor Rathbone and were a central feature of the Beveridge proposals. The debate in the months preceding the Act was concerned with the level of benefits but also with the crucial question of whether they should be payable to the mother or to the father.

5 January 1945   *p.3*

SOCIAL SECURITY
Children's Allowances Suggestions

The Charity Organisation Society, in a statement on the Government's White Paper on National Insurance, welcomes the decision to set up a Ministry of National Insurance, but suggests some changes that should be made in the scheme. The society appreciates the reasons given by the Government for the rejection of the subsistence principle, but suggests that a periodical review of rates of benefit should be carried out by an independent board. It urges that children's allowances should be paid out of taxation at the rate of 3s. a week for each child after the first, that the allowance should be paid in the middle of the week, that free milk should be available to all children below the school-leaving age in addition to the children's allowance, that a school meals service should be available to all children, but that the meals should be paid for by the parent out of the children's allowance in order that those children whose parents prefer them to return home for their dinners may not be penalised.

The society is of opinion that training should be separated from unemployment and should not be administered by the Ministry of Labour, that unemployment benefit should not necessarily be dependent upon the acceptance of training and that any training should be given in selected works in preference to a Government training centre.

LETTERS TO THE EDITOR

21 February 1945   *p.4*

FAMILY ALLOWANCES

To the Editor of the Manchester Guardian

Sir, — Last July we warned the public of the danger that the promised Family Allowances Bill might be unsatisfactory in respect of payment to the mother. But the reality exceeds our worst fears. The White Paper, though proposing that the payment order should be made out to the father 'as the normal economic head of the house-hold,' did at least regard it as 'natural and appropriate' that the mother should cash it, and 'it will be drawn in such a way as to entitle her to do so.'

'Entitled' implies a right. But the bill states that 'where man and wife are living together the allowance will belong to the man,' and this apparently will be so even if the children are the wife's by a previous marriage or are her illegitimate or adopted children. Further, if the wife or anyone else (e.g. an Education Committee) considers the man unfit to draw the allowance or has proof that he has misappropriated it, it can only be diverted from him by a court of summary jurisdiction. Clearly a mother, unless she has a case for a separation order, will very seldom dare to appeal to a court.

Those who for years have been working for family allowances did so mainly for the sake of the children and of the nation, which, as Sir William Beveridge and other experts have shown, so badly needs more children to avert race suicide. But a strong additional motive was to raise the status of motherhood. This bill must inevitably have the opposite effect by showing that the State still

25

regards the mother as merely the dependant or appendage of her husband. She may bear children at the risk of her life, and spend her days and nights in caring for them, but they are still considered as belonging to the man because he earns – not the allowance paid for by men and women taxpayers – but the rest of the family income.

Such a proposal disregards all previous experience, such as that of Australia, New Zealand, the USSR – all three having State Acts providing payment to the mother. It further disregards nearly all British expressed opinion – e.g. that of the Liberal party, the Labour party (which at its recent conference recommended it as 'constituting some recognition of motherhood'); also of 160 MPs of all parties who have just presented a memorial to Sir William Jowitt urging payment to the mother 'except in cases where it is shown that for reasons of health, conduct, or any other good reason the mother is unsuitable to draw it.' Of course we have always supported that proviso. But there are also bad fathers, and where 2,000,000 families are concerned a very small minority may be actually many thousands. And it will be the bad fathers who will refuse the right even of good mothers.

Possibly other changes in the bill may be thought more important. But these (for instance, a larger allowance) can be secured later, while payment to the mother, if not secured now, may prove unchangeable administratively, because of the vast numbers affected, and because fathers who would accept the provision now as natural and right might resent a later change as a reflection on their conduct.

There is still time, but very little, to persuade the Government to make a change, or at least to allow the House a free vote on an amendment during committee stage.

The second reading may possibly come on as early as the week beginning February 27; the committee stage possibly one, two or more weeks later, so we urge all men, women and societies who agree with us about this point to act now by writing to the member representing their constituencies asking them to support payment to the mother (subject to precautions against unsuitable mothers) by their speeches and votes. We can supply anyone who desires it with a list of the 160 MPs who signed the above-mentioned memorial urging the change. – Yours, &c.,

ELEANOR F. RATHBONE, Chairman,
EVA M. HUBBACK, Vice-Chairman,
Family Endowment Society,
5 Tufton Court, London SW1, February 17.

Leader   **FAMILY ALLOWANCES**

The case put by Miss Rathbone and Mrs. Hubback in a letter
that we publish to-day for making the payment of family allowances
to the mother rather than to the father seems to us unanswerable.
What are the grounds for giving family allowances? One of them
is the importance of arresting the decline of population and
strengthening the health and physique of children. Another is the
importance of putting an end to a state of things in which children
are the chief cause of poverty. A third is the importance of giving
its proper dignity to the status of the married woman. Nobody will
deny that the chief burden of the production and guardianship of
children and the chief responsibility for their health and upbringing
fall in most cases on the mother. These truths are recognised if the
payment is made normally to the mother; they are obscured if it
is made to the father. We may add that it is easier for the father
to take action if the mother neglects the children than it is for the
mother to take action if the father neglects them.

FAMILY ALLOWANCES
Some Comments on the Government's Bill

Sir Ronald Davison

At last we have the Government's family allowances plan
in legislative form; it is a welcome event. The bill fulfils in principle
the first of Beveridge's 'three assumptions,' this argument was that
before we could attain freedom from want due to interruptions of
wage-earning we must first ensure freedom from want among the
earners themselves. . . . 'Yes,' says the Conservative economist
and critic of this bill, 'but once you start the actual subsidising of
wages you will find yourselves on a very slippery slope. Rates of
wages and real earnings will soon adjust themselves downwards
in some degree corresponding to your state subsidies. Where are
you going to stop?' The straight answer to him is that modern wage-
fixing machinery (note its extension in the new Wages Councils
Bill) means we can safely take the risk of that: nor did it happen
when the subsidy of free education was conferred seventy-five
years ago. . . .

What we are now aiming at is a national minimum for all;
this can never be secured by a wage system based not on the size
of families but on the product of men's labour. No one really
believes that the cost of two or more children has yet become a

determining factor in, say, a cotton spinner's wages. Moreover we are not yet by any means equalising the lot of the single and family wage earner since there are no allowances for a wife or first child and 5s. per week will not suffice to keep a child.

9 March 1945   p.6

FAMILY ALLOWANCES SHOULD BE PAID TO MOTHERS
MPs.' Strong demand in Commons Debate

In the House of Commons yesterday

Sir WILLIAM JOWITT (Minister of National Insurance) moved the second reading of the Family Allowances Bill, which provides for a special allowance of 5s. a week for every child except the first in any family. Their primary object, he said, was to ease the financial burden which oppressed parents with large families and so promote the health and well being of the children. The bill was not intended to be an answer to the complex problem of population, which was being examined by a Commission presided over by the Lord Chancellor.

'In this bill,' said Sir William, 'we do not take over the responsibilities of the parents or filch from parents in the smallest degree the obligation which must remain theirs. All we are doing is to help them to discharge that obligation as they would desire.'

When the Minister was referring to a statement of Sir William Beveridge (L.–Berwick-on-Tweed), the latter interrupted to challenge the accuracy of the quotation.

Sir WILLIAM JOWITT replied: 'The hon. member is such a ready writer that I sometimes think that he forgets what he writes.'

Continuing, he said that the bill had to be read in relation to other social legislation, such as that providing for school meals. When the full scheme of school meals and milk came into operation it would cost some £60,000,000 a year, against an estimated cost of £57,000,000 for family allowances. This fact must be remembered when they compared the proposed 5s. in cash for family allowances with the original proposals of 8s. in cash and kind.

PAYMENT TO FATHER OR MOTHER?

On the controversial question of whether the allowance should be paid to the father or the mother, the Minister said the House would agree that whatever they decided they must be bold. He admitted that there were no insuperable difficulties in making it either one way or the other. The proposal was that the allowance should be the property of the father but that either parent should be able to encash it. In the ordinary happy family it probably did

28

not matter much either way. If they paid the wife there might be a danger that the husband would deduct the allowance from the amount which he ordinarily allowed her. In that sense the husband might be said to have the last word. It must be remembered also that the husband was primarily liable for the maintenance of the child. There were, however, arguments in favour of paying the allowance to the mother. Mothercraft was certainly the most noble and the most exacting.

Sir WILLIAM JOWITT: I don't agree. Every sensible person recognises it, and if they don't they won't recognise it any the more if you pay the mother an extra 5s. a week. In these matters I am neither a feminist nor a masculinist. I am an equalitarian.

BILL'S ONE DEFECT

Miss RATHBONE (Ind–English Universities) urged that it was of great importance that the status of the mother should be raised and to pay her the money would do that. But under the present proposals it made the mother the hanger-on to the father. It was the one defect in the bill which if not changed now would be impossible to change later. It was wrong, she declared, that the allowance should belong to the man, even where the children were children of a former marriage or were illegitimate.

If this bill went through in its present form women's societies were planning to make sure that every politically conscious woman elector knew at the next election how their representatives voted.

A Member: That is blackmail.

Miss RATHBONE: They have a right to do that.

Mr. JAMES GRIFFITHS (Lab–Llanelly), urged that the provisions of the bill should be made available as soon as possible. The Labour party would have liked to see an increased allowance and the first child included. On the question of to whom the allowance should be paid, he was certain that every decent father would say that the allowance should be paid direct to the mother.

Sir WILLIAM BEVERIDGE welcomed the bill and the decision of the Government to leave the question whether the allowance should be paid to the mother to the free vote of the House. 'This allowance,' he said, 'is not wages, nor a prize for fatherhood. It is money given for the purpose of seeing that children as far as possible are properly fed, clothed, and housed. Money for that purpose should be given to the mother.'

Turning to the rate of allowance, Sir William pointed out that in his report he suggested 8s. a week in cash, estimating the existing provisions in kind at 1s. If the provisions in kind were increased, naturally the cash allowance should be reduced.

Drawing attention to the high administrative expenses of allowances in kind, he said that in order to put £40,000,000 in school meals into the stomachs of children £20,000,000 had to be spent on overheads, but the administrative expense of distributing £57,000,000 in cash allowances was only £2,000,000. He imagined that it could be completely agreed that there should be both cash and kind. While he realised that they must divide the total of 9s. between cash and kind he would much prefer to see more of it in cash and less in kind than as proposed by the Government.

He agreed with the principle that the cost of the family should be borne between the community and the family, but that was brought about automatically in the case of every family by the omission of the first child.

With regard to the eligibility only of British children born in this country, Sir William said he thought that if a child was allowed to live in the country it ought to have the benefit of the allowance. He did not want any child to be allowed to live in this country for whom they did not give a guarantee of freedom from want, and if no one else was prepared to move an amendment on the subject he would do so himself. He welcomed the bill and would help it in every possible way. It was not perfect, but they hoped to overcome that.

The war had also promoted the cause of children's welfare in an area other than that of family finances.

12 February 1945   p.4

Leader **SECURITY FOR CHILDREN?**

The decision of M.P.s of all parties to ask the Home Secretary to receive a deputation on the subject of the lack of proper supervision in children's homes and the ill-treatment of some evacuated children will be welcomed. General anxiety about the conditions under which many such children have to live has been increasing for some time; it has been further increased lately by facts which have come to light about the ill-treatment of a young evacuated child and the death, at a farm in Shropshire, of a boy who was said to have been sent there by an Education Committee. The evacuated child, the child boarded out with foster-parents, and the institution child are all part of the same problem, of which evacuation is the least serious and most temporary. It should be made impossible for helpless children with no homes or bad ones to lead unhappy and tormented lives. The Committee of Inquiry to be set up by Mr. Morrison and the Ministers of Health and of Education should make the most wide and searching investigations. There will be found ample room for reform. A country which looks so much to social security for all in the future should not tolerate for its homeless children such conditions as have been recently revealed.

The General Election

*Although the Coalition Government was making steady progress towards reconstruction,
it is not safe to assume a political consensus on social policy. Party conflict became more
apparent as the likelihood of an election became more certain, and even within the Liberal
Party opposition to the ideas of Sir William Beveridge surfaced early in 1945.*

*On 6 January 1945 the 'Manchester Guardian' published a letter from Francis W.
Hirst which attacked Beveridge for abandoning the principles of Gladstonian Liberalism,
notably free trade and the balanced budget. This and other similar attacks drew the following
response from Beveridge speaking at the National Liberal Club.*

18 January 1945   *p.6*

'NO HELP IN BOW-AND-ARROW SCHOOL'
Sir W. Beveridge's Reply to His Critics

. . . 'I have been charged with the strange doctrine that the
historic personal liberties on which our national character had been
founded were no longer worth defending. Strange indeed. But no
relation to anything ever thought or said or written by me.'

Full employment in a Free Society defined essential personal
and political liberties much as Ramsay Muir did. Liberties had their
responsibilities. The evils from which liberty was sought might
change.

The enemies now were not arbitrary power but want, disease,
squalor, ignorance and idleness. The task of Liberalism to-day was
to liberate men from those. That called for a radical programme
of freedoms from social evil.

. . . 'There is no help in the bow-and-arrow school' and 'no
hope from the parrotry of laissez-faire' were among Sir William's
slogans yesterday. He suggested as a practical guide for Liberalism
in the domestic sphere that we should take liberty as our aim,
should oppose any law or any extension of State responsibility
which could not be shown to create more individual liberty than
it destroyed, and that we should accept and promote any law or
state action of which that could be shown.

31

The agenda for the Liberal Party conference (Guardian 23 January 1945), however, contained only one amendment to challenge the official resolution on 'full employment in a free society' to be moved by Beveridge. This was welcomed by the 'Guardian'.

31 January 1945   *p.4*

Leader   **LIBERALS MEET**

. . . no one expects the next election to turn on the organisation of peace. It is far more likely to be affected by the great home questions of housing and social security. Here the official resolution demands the building of 750,000 permanent houses for renting each year in a five-year plan. 'Some middle-class housing must be provided' – under licence. As for social security, the party has the expert. This resolution concentrates on bigger children's allowances and on the subsistence principle of the system as a whole – benefits varying with the cost of living, without which 'security' lacks substance. Throughout the agenda there are encouraging signs of the party's eagerness to apply the newest thought in economics and in industrial and social technique to the complicated problems of our society. It stands out in the employment policy and again in the attitude to social security – and, as another example, American building methods and materials are cited as making the enormous house-building programme possible. There is no disputing the value of this scientific approach – unhampered by the Tory interests in society as it was and by the trade unions' interests in their own sectional concerns. On the other hand, however much it may be regretted, parties of interest have at present a solid basis that a party of ideas has not. That is the Liberal party's great hurdle. Can it now find enough men and women to cry 'a plague o' both your houses' and for a change to support a party that has given itself whole-heartedly to the new knowledge of our time? Perhaps the answer will lie in the response to its public appeal – the first of its kind – for a £200,000 fighting fund.

16 March 1945   *p.4*

Leader   **AN OLD MIXTURE**

. . . Politically Mr. Churchill did not add much to what we know of the approaching sequence of events. . . .

He clearly hopes to continue some form of Coalition, even if he has only a few non-party Ministers to help him. . . .

This Government will go to the country with Labour and Liberals opposing the return of its candidates. . . .

Mr. Churchill in his speech of October 31 admitted the overwhelming case for the election of a new Parliament, but no one has yet suggested a way of having an election without some revival of the party system. A great many of us would have liked to see the Coalition continue until the biggest measures of reconstruction have been put through, until demobilisation has been accomplished, and the economic policy of 'full employment' got under way. Perhaps we may have come to it again. Certainly it is not a course that should be ruled out, nor does one think that the responsible leaders of Liberalism and Labour would wholly reject it in advance. Events must decide.

Increasing hostility between Labour and Conservatives, however, was to make an election on party lines more and more likely.

19 March 1945   *p.3*

LABOUR AND NATIONALISATION
Mr Churchill's Statement 'Misleading and Mischief Making'
— Mr. Greenwood

Mr. Arthur Greenwood, leader of the Parliamentary Labour party, speaking at Oldham yesterday, described Mr. Churchill's statement at Conservative Conference last week about 'Socialists having committed themselves to a programme of nationalisation to the disgust of their leaders' as 'misleading and mischief making'. That, he declared, was an attempt to create dissension in the Labour party.

Speaking at Failsworth on Saturday Mr. Greenwood said: 'Don't think that when the shooting stops in Europe we will suddenly enter into a noonday of peace and prosperity. Mr. Churchill the other day did not promise the people very much. I

33

think he was quite right because I don't think he is going to deliver the goods. Nor do I promise very much in the years immediately following the war. But what the mass of the people strive for with all their might they can get. Nobody can take responsibility for the future of Britain except the people themselves.'

. . . Asked if the Labour party would enter any coalition in the event of no party being strong enough to form a government after the general election Mr. Greenwood said: 'There would be only one thing to do and that is to call a special party conference to decide what action we should take. But there would be great reluctance on the part of the rank and file to go into another coalition.'

26 March 1945   *p.3*

LABOUR'S PART IN COALITION
'Till Our Task is Done' — Mr. Attlee

Mr. C.R. Attlee, Deputy Premier, said last night at Nottingham that Labour's economic differences with the Conservatives would not prevent them from giving their best not only to the task of winning the war but also to 'preparing for the peace.' . . .

On election issues, he said the Conservatives still seemed to hold the optimistic doctrine that if every person put his own interests first the interests of the community would be served. 'Labour takes a view more realistic because it is based on experience. We hold that in peace, no less than war, the national interest must come first.'

. . . 'We hold that when the stage of monopoly has been reached there is danger to the community and that private must be replaced by public ownership.'

9 April 1945   *p.3*

LABOUR PARTY AND THE COMING GENERAL ELECTION
Mr. Ernest Bevin Speaks Bluntly

Mr. Ernest Bevin, Minister of Labour and National Service, threw down the gauntlet for the Labour Party in reply to Mr. Churchill's speech at the Conservative Party Conference when he spoke at a Yorkshire Labour Party Conference in Leeds on Saturday. He said that the political air was charged with the idea of an election in the near future to decide the policy to be followed for the peace and reconstruction after this devastating war.

One would have imagined, he said, that if there was any sense of responsibility among politicians they would have faced the electors not with the old trick of the usual electoral methods, but would place before the electors solemn and brutal facts upon which their judgement was to be asked. This was not the time, he said, to resort to personalities or to repeat the Lloyd George episode after the last war in any form when the country was tired, exhausted and nerve-racked and when the judgement needed to be nursed and not exploited.

9 April 1945   *p.4*

Leader   **A FREE ELECTION**

Mr. Bevin's speech is both timely and refreshing. Already the Conservatives are showing that they do not like it. But if the Prime Minister can go to a party gathering and abuse other parties why should the other parties not also have their fling? We have got to have an election soon. There is no way of escaping it, although to read some Conservative speeches lately one might suppose that it is the wicked Liberals and Labour who are putting the country to all the trouble of voting.

A few months ago we could have hoped that even a free election would be an election in which the parties would be putting forward largely the same programmes. The Conservatives, it was thought, would stand by the great series of Coalition White Papers and the other parties would be offering advances on them. It is not sure now that this will happen. The Conservative party's reactionaries have become more powerful. We may fairly doubt the party's sincerity about social security, about housing, about town and country planning, about a national health service, and about full employment. By its 'easy and fickle froth and chatter' (to borrow a Churchillian phrase) about the ending of 'controls' and the restoration of 'free enterprise' it is preparing the same kind of economic mess into which it landed the country in the years after the last war. With one breath it demands the uncontrolled 'free enterprise' that will lead us into inflation and a profiteers' paradise; with the next it insists on no interference with the monopolistic practices that have made free enterprise a mockery over large tracts of British industry. The Conservative party has to be criticised for this; if the Prime Minister lends himself to these reactionary forces the choice was his.

Nor can the Conservative party shelter behind Mr. Churchill in order to escape all probings into the miserable years before the war. Mr. Churchill was then an exile, contemptuously rebuffed by the very party now hanging on to his coat-tails. But many 'men of Munich' survive, and the public memory is not short. Should the other parties refresh it, as Mr. Bevin did, the Conservatives have no right to object. If we are to have a free election let it be one on the merits of the parties past and present.

21 April 1945   *p.4*

Leader   **LABOUR'S POLICY**

The Labour party offers to-day considerable hostage to fortune by publishing its election programme so far in advance. It was necessary, presumably, to give the party conference at Whitsuntide something to excite itself about and to prepare the candidates for all to say the same things. But with the election now pushed off a little farther early publication has its disadvantages. Considered as an election document and not as a mere exercise in doctrinal piety the policy declaration is not likely to lift up Labour hearts. It contains some good and well-put points, but it is also stuffed with a great deal of cotton wool. One can only think that the Labour Ministers felt embarrassed at the thought of publishing anything which might seem to criticise the Coalition even by implication. The result is uninspiring. The Labour party will certainly have to improve on this if it is to strike the public imagination. . . . On agriculture, housing, the land, the health services, and social insurance there are fine-sounding phrases but not much for the aspiring candidate to get hold of. The Beveridge scheme for instance is dismissed in one sentence: 'A Labour Government will press on rapidly with legislation extending social insurance over the necessary wide field to all.' The Conservatives will not say less! . . .

It may be contended that Labour is working under difficulties and that so long as it is part of the Coalition it cannot go much beyond Coalition White Papers. But if this were valid could it not have been pointed out with the assurance that a Labour Government with a clear majority, which is what is sought, would not be content merely with Coalition compromises?

It was the opening shot in an election campaign which was to prove both long and increasingly bitter, culminating in Churchill's final election broadcast reported as follows.

FINAL ELECTION BROADCAST
Mr. Churchill to the Forces:
'I could not serve in Labour Government'

Broadcasting from Chequers on Saturday night the final speech in the series of political addresses, Mr. Churchill gave a message to the forces overseas in which he declared, 'It would be impossible for me to serve in a Labour Government when that party is wedded to policies which I regard as ruinous to the future of the country.'

'Beware that you are not deceived,' he said. 'There is no truth in stories now being put about that you can vote for my political opponents without at the same time voting for my dismissal from power. I gravely deplore the unfair tactics adopted by those who have kept on trying to deceive you on this point.'

And here I must make a digression into what may be called the Laski episode. It was a revelation to me when I, in all goodwill, invited Mr. Attlee to come with me to Berlin in July in order to keep the flag of unity flying, that this hitherto almost unknown person Professor Laski, who has never sought to face the electors yet sits at the head of what is called the National Executive committee, of which the larger part are not even members of Parliament, that he – I cannot call it presumption – should have the right to lay down the law to the publicly proclaimed leader of the Labour Party and tell him that he could only go to the conference in the capacity of an observer and that no continuity in our foreign policy could be undertaken.

Many days have passed since that happened. Mr. Laski has in no way withdrawn his instructions to the Labour Party Leader. On the contrary he has shown himself the master of forces too strong for Mr. Attlee to challenge by any effective counter-action. Mr. Laski still remains the chairman of the Socialist executive. No vote of suspension, censure or even depreciation has been passed upon him. It appears that this Socialist executive committee possesses power over Socialist Ministers of a most far-reaching character: that it would decide the action a Socialist Government could take in particular questions and that it could require the submission of Ministers to do its will.

This means, for instance, that in foreign affairs when there had to be discussion of some difficult question secrets might have to be divulged to this committee of 27 members, very few of whom are Privy Counsellors, and though I am sure very great care would be taken difficulties might arise. It also means that the Socialist Ministers filling all the high offices of State would not be primarily responsible to the Crown and to Parliament but would have to refer back to an utterly unconstitutional undemocratic body, however well meaning, lying in the background whose names until the recent trouble have not been known to the public. Such arrangements, my friends, are abhorrent to the methods hitherto pursued in British public life. They strike at the root of our Parliamentary institutions and, if they continue unabated, will be one of the gravest changes in the constitutional history of England and of Britain.

The leading article of the same day commented on the broadcast.

2 July 1945   *p.4*

Leader   **LAST BROADCAST**

The political broadcasts are over at last. The Prime Minister had the final word and he was at his most persuasive, even at the expense of precise accuracy. Much of the broadcast must have stirred all of us. A man cannot return from such a tour as Mr. Churchill has made without being intensely moved, and it is in keeping with the finer part of his genius that he should transfer the plaudits from himself to the mass of the British people from whom they came. Some sentences, it is true, came perilously near bathos, but we can be sure none the less that Mr. Churchill spoke from the heart. His emotion, like that of the crowds along the road sides, was genuine. But what Mr. Churchill did not do, though millions of his countrymen (and admirers) will, is to distinguish between the great war Prime Minister whom the people delighted to honour and the party leader seeking votes for himself and his friends. It is a fundamental distinction. And after Saturday's broadcast many must be wondering whether we are not witnessing a rather dangerous innovation in English political method, the deliberate fostering of the 'leadership principle.'

On the 'Laski episode' the article continues:

. . . What Mr. Churchill chooses to ignore or to distort is that the Labour party is a democratic organisation with the faults and virtues of a democratic body. One fault (or virtue) is fear of the excessive personal ascendancy of any one man, and its experience with Mr. MacDonald in 1931 has bred an undue suspicion of leaders among a few of its 'chairborne' (and 'airborne') troopers like Mr. Laski. There is not much more to it, or to them, than that. There is little fear of those terrible constitutional changes that Mr. Churchill, the greatest constitutional innovator of our times, professes to fear. It is, however, lamentable that in these closing

days of the campaign Mr. Churchill and so many other
Conservative speakers should have become so arrogant in their
assumptions and be giving no credit to their opponents for sincerity,
constitutional propriety, or even political honour.

The theme is continued in the next day's leading article.

3 July 1945   *p.4*

Leader   **THE RED LETTER**

Mr. Churchill's efforts to dominate Parliament and the country
have reached a point that can only be called indecent. He has given
four out of the eight broadcasts allotted to the Government; the
Government orchestra became almost a one-man band. He has
toured the country and exploited for his party political ends the
genuine affection of the people for him as a war leader. Not content
with all this he carefully times two days before the election his last
'bombshell, – another Zinoviev letter, or, as it will be known, 'the
Laski letter'. Probably never in our political history has a party
leader exhibited such a shameless determination to subvert the
constitutional processes of an election to his own ends. This is a
serious charge and one that must be made with regret against a
leader to whom the country owes as much as it does to Mr.
Churchill. But no one who tries objectively to review his actions
since the election can feel anything but serious disquiet.

Similar disquiet was expressed about social policy.

The elector who wants to know what Mr. Churchill's social
policy is, and to judge whether a Conservative Government would
let him carry it out, must seek the answers in the contents and
omissions of White Papers and in the sayings and doings of
Conservative Ministers. What will he find? First, that there is indeed
to be an 'amalgamation and extension' of our national insurance
system, but nothing more radical than that. The cardinal purpose
of the Beveridge Plan – to abolish want in adversity by linking
benefit rates to a minimum subsistence standard – has been
expressly repudiated; the conception of social security was
jettisoned along with the name. Secondly, and as a necessary
condition of a comprehensive insurance scheme, there is to be a
national health service; but in what form nobody knows.

4 July 1945   *p.4*

Leader   **THE LIBERALS**

That there will be a big Liberal vote to-morrow is pretty plain. How far this will be reflected in the return of a large number of Liberal members we shall see. Under our grotesquely unfair electoral system the handicaps are many. But, even if Liberals cannot set as their highest hope to-morrow the achievement of a Liberal Government, a compact, strengthened Liberal party in the House can exercise an influence far in excess of its numbers. It will be the greatest possible asset on the side of steady progressive government and Radical measures. There is no reason to be other than frank about these matters. The chances of Labour sweeping the country and obtaining a clear majority over all other parties are pretty remote. To do that it would have to capture scores of seats where Conservatism is strongly entrenched and where, in view of their traditions, the nature of Mr. Churchill's personal appeal may be supposed to carry special influence. This is not the election that is going to shake Tory England. None the less Labour should win seats. If the tide flows strongly enough there might be at least the possibility of a combined Liberal and Labour majority sufficient to form a Government of the Left. That, however, is a contingency to be met when it arises. The first need is to secure as large a Liberal party as possible in the House. Whether a Progressive majority can be secured or not there is no question of the importance to healthy government of a strong third party. This to the Conservatives is a terrible thought and Cabinet Ministers are stumping the country, denouncing it. For they know that the Liberals can win seats that Labour could never win and that the Conservative majority would thereby be so much reduced. Liberal successes are an essential means of averting the great danger that faces us, the danger of an overwhelming Conservative majority like that of 1918, of 1922, of 1924, of 1931, of 1935.

5 July 1945   *p.4*

Leader   **THE POLL**

This election is the most hateful in recent memory because this great leader has now dismantled the splendid figure that dominated the imagination of the world. He has turned himself into a party leader who catches at any device for winning votes. Mr. Churchill is not satisfied with the gratitude and admiration of the British people. He asks of them that they should be ready to sacrifice their independence. A man or a woman must either vote against a man they admire or else agree to saddle the country with a Tory Government for another five years – five of the most crucial and critical years in its history. He talks of their dismissing him, turning him out to grass, hinting that unless they give him a tremendous majority he cannot serve them.

and offered the following advice:

5 July 1945   *p.4*

Leader   **THE CHOICE**

. . . We should remember that the scales are heavily weighted in favour of a Conservative majority. This is inherent in our unfair electoral system. In every election the Conservatives are represented far in excess of their backing at the polls. The chances (or danger) of a clear Labour majority able to carry out a Socialist programme are slender, almost remote. But if the votes are cast wisely there is at least the chance of a Liberal–Labour majority, the most fruitful kind of Coalition in these times. The policies of Liberals and Labour for the reconstruction period are close enough to form a sound basis of working agreement, and the men to carry this out will not be lacking.

This was also the theme of a report 'From Our Political Correspondent'.

5 July 1945   *p.5*

BRITAIN POLLS TO-DAY
After a Ruthlessly Fought Campaign

TORIES NEGLECT REAL ISSUES
Scaremongering and Misrepresentation Given First Place

The election has been a depressing and disillusioning experience, and the disillusionment is mostly with Mr. Churchill. When he has not been developing the scares – the 'Gestapo,' the threatened savings, and the Labour Executive dictatorship – he has been fighting the election on his personality.

What were his thoughts at Walthamstow last night when he heard the booing? The significance of the booing could be exaggerated, but this was the man who had London at his feet in May. Who could have imagined even a single individual booing Mr Churchill then? What will the people of Europe make of it – the people who have nearly divinised him? And this Walthamstow meeting. For a week the Tory press had been trumpeting it about that this was to be the biggest political gathering ever held in this country. There were to be 45,000 people at it and it was to be open to all comers, no tickets. In the result there was an audience of 10,000.

It was Mr. Churchill who knocked the election right out of focus as well as heating it up with his first broadcast. The nonsense about a Labour 'Gestapo' and the mischief about the threatened savings went with an attempt to present the election as the final battle between light and darkness, between free enterprise and Socialism, between the British way of life and a sinister foreign political philosophy.

The election results were not declared for three weeks in order to allow the services to vote. The overwhelming Labour victory brought the following response from the 'Guardian'.

27 July 1945   *p.4*

Leader   ## SILENT REVOLUTION

Britain has undergone a silent revolution. Few suspected it. Hardly a politician from one end of the country to another had ventured to forecast what has happened at the polls. The people kept their secret. Yet throughout the country, in country no less than in town, they swung to the Left. And when they voted Left they meant it. They had no use for the middle-of-the-road Liberals; they voted Labour and they knew what they were voting for. The Conservative press had seen that they should know the worst; the Prime Minister had tried to scare them in broadcast after broadcast. But their marrows were not frozen; they took the risk. And so here we are for the first time in British history with a clear Labour majority in the House of Commons and the crushing defeat of Conservatism after over twenty-five years of dominance. We enter into a new political world, and though we (and the Labour leaders too) may shiver just a little at the thought of what lies ahead, we enter it with confidence.

A Labour Government will have the responsibility of carrying us through and we must give it all the support and loyalty we can. No Government has ever had a harder task before it in time of peace, but none has ever had a greater opportunity.

The Conservative record has been enough to wipe out the sentiment for a National Coalition, which again was evidently not as deep as many thought. Reactionary in social and international policy before the war, the Conservative party held out no hope for the future. Its reconstruction was to be bold, if the high hopes of full employment and social security were to be fulfilled, it was not the Conservatives who could be entrusted with the task. The soldiers' vote, in particular, went against them, but it was only the reflection of the way the mass of the people at home were taking.

Reflecting on the first appointments to the new Government the 'Guardian' said:

28 July 1945   *p.4*

Leader   **THE DAY AFTER**

To put Mr. Aneurin Bevan at the Ministry of Health is Mr. Attlee's most unconventional stroke. It reminds one of MacDonald's putting Mr. Wheatley in the same post in 1924. Mr. Bevan has certainly ability, hitherto mostly shown in the arts of Opposition. It remains to be seen whether he has the assiduity and sticking power to be a humdrum Minister of the Crown, one of whose main functions will be to get smooth running with touchy local authorities and sensitive and not unassertive medical men. . . .

It is an interesting experiment to put Miss Wilkinson at the Ministry of Education; she has drive and courage.

Leader   **PARLIAMENT OPEN**

The most interesting British political experiment of our lifetime begins to-day. We shall hear the King's Speech of the first Socialist Government to have a clear majority and the power to carry its measures through. Some of our American friends are shivering with apprehension, and the good Mr. Hoover (he of the Great Depression) has been warning his country of a terrifying world sweep – outside the happy United States – towards Socialism and Communism. Britain has almost been given up for lost because the country has taken the change in its fortunes so quietly. Yet there was good reason for this lack of excitement, as we shall probably see to-day. It is quite certain that the bulk of the programme which any British Government, called to power at this moment, would present would be common ground. So much the War Coalition did for us.

But while the heads of our New Deal for a Britain at peace would be for the most part the same whatever party had come back, much more is expected of a Labour Government. In some ways this this is its misfortune, for the early months of a new Parliament, always the most favourable for the boldest measures of a Government's programme are this time overshadowed by pressing emergency problems. We know that had the Conservative Government come back it would have devoted itself first to some of the White Paper measures, especially to social security. The Labour Government must do that too, but it must also, if it is to fulfil its promises, do much more. How far can it start on the way towards its announced 'Socialism'?

The question must have given the Cabinet anxious thought. Most of the innumerable Socialist 'blue-prints' of the last twenty years have been based on the assumption of 'normal' conditions – fairly good trade at home, fairly quiet conditions abroad. Instead, this Government has been born in an atmosphere of crisis. Peace is just breaking out; our internal economy is distorted and has to be run into new moulds; the external world is in chaos and vast tracts of it on the edge of famine, while we, with the rest of the nations, are only just starting painfully to rebuild the shattered fabric of international life and international peace.

16 August 1945 p.4

Leader   **THE KING'S SPEECH**

The King's Speech is an excellent reflection of the manner in which the British people at least face their part of the task. It puts first international co-operation; the healing of the wounds of war, and the securing of full employment and a higher standard of living. Its heads present an adequate and satisfying opening programme for Government and Parliament. May they both live up to it! Most of it, of course, has been taken for granted – social security, workmen's compensation, national health service, land use, housing, continued controls, civil aviation, and so on. The specifically Labour measures are the transfer of the Bank of England to public ownership, the nationalisation of the coal-mining industry, and the repeal of the Trade Unions Act of 1927. It is on these that the main controversy will turn, for, although there will be much to offend Conservative interests in Labour's handling of things like the health service and land-use, these three represent the biggest break with tradition. Yet it will be surprising if, when the fight comes, they can be made out to be desperately revolutionary acts. . . .

Housing
POST-ELECTION

Once the election was over the 'Guardian' began to focus on the priorities in social policy, and once again housing policy came to the top of the list.

2 August 1945   p.4

Leader   **HOUSING QUESTIONS**

The suspense of waiting for the declaration of the poll has given place to a still more tantalising hiatus. Having learned after three long weeks the result of our ballots, we must now exercise what patience we possess while the Big Three confer and Parliament adjourns before we can be sure what that result implies. Some crumbs of enlightenment have come our way. We know who will occupy the highest offices of State and have heard vague talk about the 'priorities' in nationalisation. But what the vast majority of us chiefly want to know is exactly how the Labour Government will tackle the housing problem and – since these questions are inseparable – what it proposes to do about the planning of land use and the readjustment of local government areas. This curiosity implies no lack of confidence: it was, indeed, as much as anything else, confidence in Labour's superior ability to get houses built that decided the electoral issue. By the same token it is Labour's success or failure in this field that will largely determine its future strength.

Will there be a Minister of Housing? The Coalition Government resisted that suggestion on the ground that a Minister of Works to co-ordinate the supply of materials, a Minister of Health to co-ordinate local housing demands, and a Minister of Labour to provide the man-power represented the most efficient division of functions. So it does – if these are the only functions for which the Government assumes responsibility. The Labour party decided after all that it would not nationalise the major building concerns during its first term of power, but it presumably will organise the bulk purchase and general use of standardised housing components, establish a system of priorities as between large houses and small, control the placing of contracts in accordance with the industry's capacity, and see to it that the industry makes full use of modern equipment, techniques and methods of site management. These positive functions will be better discharged by an independent department (working, perhaps through an executive housing corporation) than by a liaison committee. But in the sphere of physical reconstruction and especially of physical planning, much more depends on the calibre of Ministers and their advisers than on the machinery through which they work. It would be fatal if the Minister of Town and Country Planning were to continue to be treated as the least important member of the Government or if the Minister of Housing regarded the interests of building workers – as conceived by themselves – as his primary concern.

On the question of a Minister for Housing the reply came quickly from the Lord Privy Seal, Mr. A. Greenwood.

18 August 1945   *p.3*

MR GREENWOOD'S REPLY
Public Ownership Policy

The Minister of Health and the Secretary for Scotland would be the authoritative people for dealing with the building of houses. The Minister of Works would not concern himself with housing policy, but he would be the Ministry of Supply to the building industry. It would be his job to see that the production of all the materials needed for housing was pursued on an organised plan. Housing policy, subject to the Cabinet, rested with the Minister of Health and the Secretary for Scotland. The Minister of Works would be responsible for the programme of prefabricated houses and for houses of temporary construction. He would continue also to be the builder for Government departments.

18 August 1945   *p.4*

Leader   **HOUSING LAYOUT**

The outlines of a housing policy were no more than dimly discernible in Mr. Greenwood's speech yesterday. There is nothing seriously wrong with the shape they seemed to be taking, but beyond that judgment must for the present be reserved. Evidently the Cabinet had no cut-and-dried plan ready to be put into immediate effect. It is still feeling its way through the somewhat tangled situation it inherited. The promised Ministry of Housing and

Planning is 'in cold storage.' That is all to the good: the functional relationship beween housing and the planning of land use is a matter for more deliberate thought than can be given to it in the present emergency. For the time being the Government has adopted a layout which concentrates authority – and responsibility – for policy-making in one Minister, and that is an improvement; but otherwise no radical change has been made. For the rest, we now know that first needs will come first, and therefore that the speculative building of middle-class houses for sale must wait; that the prefabrication of components by former munition workers will be further developed; and that rural housing is to be dealt with as an integral part of the general programme. We have yet to learn how that programme is to be financed, how the building industry will be 'organised' how material costs will be reduced, what density standards will be set, and by what means the Government intends to ensure, that houses are built in the right places.

20 August 1945   *p.6*

CALL FOR HOUSING SPEED-UP
Mr. Bevan's Message to Local Authorities

Mr. Aneurin Bevan, Minister of Health, in a message to all local authorities in England and Wales, urges that they should aim at having the first instalment of their permanent houses under construction before the autumn. If any authority is not likely to be in a position to apply for authority to let contracts for the first batch of post-war houses by September 30, he asks that he should be informed at once of the reasons.

The earlier condition that tenders should not be invited until roads and sewers are complete is now cancelled. Where progress can be speeded up by contracting for the construction of roads and sewers at the same time as the building of the houses, this should be done. As soon as satisfactory prices have been obtained for the first part of the post-war programme, the Minister will consider proposals for a further instalment.

Each authority is urged to make arrangements for a continued flow of houses on the basis of a programme expanding with the expansion of the builidng industry. Steps, it is stated, should be taken now to acquire land for this programme in advance. The previous condition that only land required for the first two years' programme should be bought is cancelled. It is particularly important says Mr. Bevin (sic) that large sites should be in hand well in advance of the time when building can begin so that lay-out can be planned with proper regard for the essential community services.

HOUSING CAMPAIGN
Mr. Bevan to Have the Last Word

From our Industrial Correspondent

London, Thursday.

We are to wait until after the Parliamentary recess for the full statement by the Minister of Health on the Government's housing programme, but the resignation of the Director General of the Ministry of Works at the same time as that of the Controller General, which may be of less significance, suggests that the new responsibilities of the Ministries concerned are already more closely defined than has been announced.

On the face of it there was no reason to suppose that the duties exercised by Sir Frederick Pile are to be taken from the Ministry of Works. Mr. Greenwood said clearly in the House that it would continue to be responsible for prefabricated and temporary houses and would act as a supply department for the building industry as a whole, and those matters would appear to cover Sir Frederick's main responsibilities. Yet the Minister agreed that the status and scope of his post would be completely altered.

POLICY AND DESIGN

In taking over the direction of the housing campaign the most important functions being assumed – or resumed – by the Ministry of Health are those of policy and perhaps also design. The Ministry of Works entered into these realms in the same way that most housing responsibilities have been assumed – by force of circumstances. Responsibility for Government building naturally extended during the war as Government responsibility extended until it included most building and in an equally natural way it spread to prefabrication. To build prefabricated houses meant designing them. The Ministry showed enterprise in this direction with its experimental houses. Moreover, decisions on the subject of prefabrication or of component parts for ordinary houses or of allocation of labour between repair and new building brought the Ministry into the realms of policy.

Now the Ministry of Works becomes merely a supplier of whole factory-made houses, of component parts, of materials, to the demands of the Ministry of Health, and the decision to limit the programme of temporary houses to the 150,000 already planned is a further restriction.

The Ministry of Town and Country Planning does not appear to be much affected by the new scheme. Its powers have already been limited and where it has objected to a site approved by the Ministry of Health it has found itself overruled. The danger now is that unless planning powers are reinforced the effort to get houses built anywhere and everywhere will seriously affect the future amenities of the people.

And, of course, the Ministry of Labour will continue to be in a sense the key Ministry, for while a number of building materials are scarce it is on the finding of labour that the success of the building campaign depends.

In the past the co-ordination of the ministries concerned was mainly carried out on the Civil Service level. In the future we are promised that the Ministers themselves will be constantly getting their heads together. And Mr. Aneurin Bevan will have indisputably the last word.

21 September 1945   *p.4*

Leader   **NEW TOWNS**

The paralysis that gripped the Coalition in all matters relating to the control of land use has left the Labour Government with a great deal of leeway to make up. It is three years now since the Uthwatt Committee completed its masterly analysis of the legislative defects that prevent the proper planning of physical reconstruction. A White Paper on the control of land use was produced, but it proposed to shelve the crucial compensation issue for another five years, and it remains to this day undebated. As far as the short-term housing programme is concerned it is no longer possible to escape the consequences of this waste of time. The sites have been bought and for the most part developed, and building must go forward with all speed however badly those sites may be located. The question now is whether the Labour Government can retrieve the situation in respect of long-term redevelopment; for several authorities, despairing of the powers they need, have already compromised or abandoned their prospects of securing a decent living standard for their future citizens.

In this perspective the steps announced by Mr. Lewis Silkin, welcome as they are, appear rather inadequate. As Minister of Town and Country Planning his main and most immediate task is to make possible the establishment of new satellite towns to accommodate the people who will be displaced if the congested districts of existing cities are redeveloped at densities compatible with healthy and agreeable living conditions for the people who remain.

These new towns must be 'self-contained and balanced communities for work and living,' situated beyond the green belts that should surround their parent cities. The Minister could hardly have made a better choice for the chairmanship of the committee that is to consider the implications of this task, for it was Lord Reith who in 1941, as Minister of Works and Planning, urged the major local authorities to plan boldly without regard for deficiencies in the law as it stood, and who since then has striven to secure the redemption of the pledges his exhortations implied. Meanwhile Mr. Silkin will himself discuss with the local authorities' organisations what he mildly describes as the difficult problem of fitting the new urban growth into the existing structure of local government. This will be the crucial test of his skill and resolution. There would be no such problem if planning and local finance were in the hands of regional authorities.

25 September 1945   *p.4*

Leader   **HOUSING TECHNICIANS**

Of the many bottle-necks to be broken before the housing drive can get into its stride the first in order of priority is the shortage of technicians. The actual erection of houses will raise problems enough in due course, but up to the present local authorities have been prevented from getting to grips with them by lack of officers qualified to work out detailed lay-out plans, to survey sites, to engineer service installations, to draw up contracts, and to prepare designs. Until these preliminary tasks could be completed it was of little use for the Minister of Health to cut red-tape and urge local authorities to press on with their permanent housing programmes. Now, however, Mr. Bevan has secured 'general authority' for the release under Class B of local government officers certified as necessary for urgent housing work.

10 October 1945   *p.3*

LAND FOR HOUSING
New Powers for Local Authorities

Mr. Aneurin Bevan, Minister of Health, told the Association of Municipal Corporations at a housing and rent control conference at the Central Hall, Westminster, yesterday, that local authorities were to be given new powers to obtain housing sites. 'I cannot tell you what our proposals are this afternoon,' he said, 'but I can tell you we are going to furnish you with additional powers of land acquisition.' The Government were setting up a central department with liaison officers as a first step.

He believed that the main housing problem could be solved by the local authorities, and, urging them to overhaul and speed up their procedure, suggested that emergency committees with executive powers should be set up as in war-time. There would be criticism, he said, but 'start as you mean to go on.'

Mr. Bevan said he had refused a number of housing tenders which he considered too high, and would continue to do so. The housing programme was going to be ruined by high costs unless they introduced some discipline in the early stages.

11 October 1945   *p.3*

SELECTING TENANTS FOR NEW HOUSES
Advice to Local Authorities: Lodgers and Garden Sheds

A report giving advice on the management of housing estates under post-war conditions has been sent to every local authority in England and Wales by the Minister of Health, Mr. Aneurin Bevan. It was prepared by the Housing Management Sub-committee of the Central Housing Advisory Committee, of which Lord Balfour of Burleigh is chairman.

Pointing out that temporary houses are small, that they are of less stout construction than permanent houses, and that there will be more frequent changes amongst their tenants, the report says:

Unless the families selected for tenancies are those which may be expected to maintain a satisfactory standard of care and cleanliness there will be grave danger of conditions arising which will bring the temporary houses into disrepute. For these reasons any automatic or mechanical method of selection is peculiarly inappropriate and we recommend that normally a visit by a trained officer to the applicants in their present accommodation should be an essential part of the process of selection.

We concur in the suggestion made to us in evidence that in the case of temporary houses local authorities should impose and carefully maintain restrictions against sub-letting, the taking in of lodgers, and the erection of garages, sheds, and other structures by the tenants.

So far as permanent houses are concerned the committee recommend that a broad view should be taken of the class of person to whom they are let. They think that during the present emergency the term 'working class' should be more widely interpreted than has been customary. 'As between two applicants the choice should basically be governed by their relative need, not by the nature of their respective callings,' the report states.

Points schemes for selecting tenants should be used as a sieve for sorting applications into priority groups, not for determining the final order in which applicants should be offered tenancies.

The committee consider that it should be made clear to all applicants that there is no favouritism in choosing tenants. They think this would be helped if in considering applications the appropriate committee of the local authority dealt with them under code numbers rather than names.

Residential qualification in some schemes might prove a hardship and strictly adhered to, would not be in the public interest. A long qualification would be out of keeping with the extensive movements of the civil population during the war and with the need for increased mobility of Labour.

In any scheme, it is stressed, a proportion of the tenancies should be allotted to recently married couples without children.

In order to avoid any waste of accommodation, as a temporary measure permission should be given freely for the taking of lodgers or the sub-letting of rooms in permanent houses where it is possible.

18 October 1945 *p.5*

GOVERNMENT'S HOUSING PLANS
No Figures, but Promise of 'Progress' Reports

A BILLETING APPEAL — AND A WARNING

From our Parliamentary Correspondent

Westminster, Wednesday.

Mr. Aneurin Bevan rose in a full and expectant House to make his speech on the Government's housing policy. he rose from beside Mr. Attlee and Mr. Morrison. Not so long ago the Prime Minister and the Lord President of the Council used to sit cheek by jowl on the Treasury Bench, just as they did to-day, but then they were deep in a communion of resentment against Mr. Aneurin Bevan, the able if sometimes splenetic critic of Mr. Churchill and the Coalition.

To-day, while Mr. Bevan was speaking, they now and again exchanged large smiles of approbation at sallies and gibes very much like the old ones, but now launched by Mr. Bevan in the reverse direction and at the Tories. Not only is the prodigal son home, but those smiles of Mr. Attlee's and Mr. Morrison's announced that in their opinion he is going to be well worth his keep. He has originality, imagination, Celtic fluency, and touches of audacity that remind one of Lloyd George. He made his speech with contemptuous disregard of a full manuscript which he had. He has a more extensive vocabulary than anybody in the House except Mr. Churchill. There is even danger in this ready speech of his.

53

TORIES MOCKED

The rebel is not dead in him. Office is not repressing him. He was the Socialist polemist in his first sentences, when he mocked the Tories for their impudence in putting down their motion after their neglect of the housing of the people during the last 25 years.

How the Labour benches enjoyed this change to the offensive! They had seen very little up to to-day of a Labour Minister on the attack. And Mr. Bevan furnished them with more instances. They in turn rewarded him with great cheers or cheers and shouts of laughter mixed.

18 October 1945   *p.4*

Leader   **HOUSING DRIVE**

Mr. Bevan has made a confident start as Minister in charge of housing. There was no hint of the defensive in his first full exposition of the Government's policy on this most critical of issues. He might excusably have dwelt on the indecision of his predecessors and blamed them in advance for any failure on his own part to produce quick results. Instead he began by shouldering full personal responsibility for any future shortcomings. He expressed himself entirely satisfied with his powers and with the functional efficiency of the administrative machinery at his disposal. Thereby he made it clear that the promised Ministry of Housing will stay 'in cold storage' indefinitely, and on this point few will dispute that Labour's second thoughts are the wiser. So long as the Government does not intend to build houses on a large scale itself, but only to organise the demand (public or private) on the one hand and the supply of materials and equipment on the other, a division of labour will undoubtedly produce the best results.

Before the war, as the Minister pointed out, private enterprise had largely solved the housing problem of the higher income groups. For them, the present difficulty is purely one of war-damage and war-time arrears of repairs and replacements. But the much-advertised inter-war output of the private builder did little or nothing for the weekly tenants of poorer homes. For them the ravages of time and enemy action during the last six years merely aggravate the results of a half-century of neglect. Four million of their dwellings are over eighty years old; most of these are already uninhabitable by any modern standard, and the rest will be as bad before their turn comes to be demolished and replaced. This is the heart and core of the housing problem. It inevitably follows that our limited resources of house-building labour and materials must be put at the disposal of agencies capable of building houses to let at low rents until the back of this most important task has been broken.

54

This early period of Labour's plans for housing also offers an interesting portent of much later developments:

5 November 1945   p.3

HIGH BUILDINGS IN THE COUNTRYSIDE
Mr. Bevan Plans an Experiment

Mr. Aneurin Bevan, Minister of Health, addressing a conference of the Association of Building Technicians in London on Saturday expressed himself in favour of high buildings in the countryside and said an attempt was being made to persuade one or two great cities to make the experiment of high buildings with countryside around them. It would be far more healthy.

'It is much better,' he said, 'for a man to step out into the countryside from a high building than to buy a small car and poison the atmosphere on a Sunday morning. I would prefer to see a cow strolling round the house than see a man get a car to look for a cow.'

In his first 'Progress Report' (November 13 1945) Bevan made it clear that standards would not be compromised in the housing drive. The 'Guardian's' leading article on 15 November reflected on this and on the Building Materials and Housing Bill.

15 November 1945   p.4

Leader   **HOUSING PROGRESS**

He has however, given a straigtforward pledge that he will not sanction the building of houses with less than 900 square feet of floor space. That is a gratifying step and one which bespeaks confidence, for a hard-pressed Minister would find the temptation to revert to pre-war standards hard to resist. Further, he has introduced a Bill giving the Ministry of Works powers to erect traditional as well as prefabricated houses for local authorities to produce, distribute, and buy in bulk all housing materials and components. Coupled with the 'virtual monopoly' of house fittings exercised by the Ministry of Supply through control of raw materials and the placing of blanket orders, this measure should suffice to combat any organised attempt to restrict the output or to keep up the price of any commodity essential to housebuilding. But whether enough has been done to ensure that such commodities will be forthcoming in ample quantity is uncertain.

Health
POST-ELECTION

The BMA obviously had mixed feelings about the outcome of the election.

27 July 1945   *p.10*

DOCTORS AND A 'NEW SITUATION'

There was loud applause from members of the British Medical Association, meeting yesterday in London, when the secretary, Dr. Charles Hill, announced that Sir William Beveridge was among the defeated candidates.

After it was clear that Labour would have a majority and when a discussion was taking place on differences which have arisen during the debates on the question of a national health service Dr. R.W. Cockshut, of Hendon, said: 'We are all in the same boat now. From now on an entirely new situation faces us. We should forget our differences now that the whole question is probably to be reopened and we are probably facing a Government which is pledged to bring in a State medical service.'

Mr. A. Dickson Wright, Harley Street surgeon, said: 'We see the profession drifting towards the Civil Service. We all feel anxious and agitated about it, and we shall need every opportunity to express ourselves.'

The leading article of 29 August expressed reservations on somewhat different grounds.

29 August 1945   *p.4*

Leader   **LABOUR AND HEALTH**

During the Commons debate on the Address Mr. Greenwood announced that the Government's health plan would follow its social insurance scheme on the legislative agenda and that the

Social Insurance Bill would not be introduced until early next year. This means that there is still plenty of time for further consideration of the administrative structure that will best serve the generally agreed purposes of a national health service. It also means that adequate temporary arrangements will have to be made for the employment of demobilised doctors. Further, it means that the health plan, when it is introduced must be no interim measure but as complete as is consistent with the flexibility required to leave scope for further development in the light of experience. For that reason Mr. Greenwood's proposal to 'go back to the White Paper' was somewhat disquieting. If, as the context suggests, this statement referred only to Labour's repudiation of the further concessions to professional interests which Mr. Willink seemed ready to commend to his colleagues, all is well. But if 'back to the White Paper' represents the full extent of the progress contemplated by the Labour Government in this field the electors who voted for it on its programme will be grievously disappointed.

The White Paper was essentially a compromise between what is needed and what was possible in war-time circumstances under a Tory-dominated Coalition Government. The Labour party accepted it as such at the time, in the hope of getting something accomplished before the end of the war, because the plan it outlined, for all its deficiencies, 'would provide a basic service capable of extension and improvement so that, in the end, a unified and complete health service might be developed from it.' The party expressly recognised, however, that such spontaneous development would become 'difficult or even impossible' if vested interests were permitted strongly to entrench themselves. The first great weakness of the White Paper was the excessive looseness of the structure it proposed: it commanded support, in default of anything better, because it would have opened the way to evolutionary progress, but by the same token it offered ample opportunity for reactionary forces to obstruct the advances it made possible.

The Autumn saw the opening moves in a battle between the Minister and the BMA which would continue almost unabated up to the inauguration of the NHS in July 1948.

6 September 1945   p.5

MR. BEVAN AND MEDICAL SERVICE
'A Few Experiments'

Mr. Aneurin Bevan, Minister of Health, believes that, in a year, he will be able to lay before the people a medical service which will be the envy of other countries, and that in five years the housing problem will have been solved.

In a speech to the Royal Medico-Psychological Association in London last night, he said 'I do not believe that, when we get down to details, I shall find there is very much that separates me from the medical profession. We are all anxious to provide the best kind of medical service and it is the duty of the Minister of Health to provide the profession with the best apparatus. I hope we shall be able to organise a medical service which will give the general practitioner a relief from his loneliness and the isolation in which so many live to-day.

CO-OPERATION, NOT ANTAGONISM

'I want from the medical profession co-operation and not suspicion and antagonism. We are going to do some unorthodox things. Whatever reputation I have achieved it is not one of orthodoxy. I shall be making a few experiments, and I hope to get enthusiastic co-operation from the medical profession. We shall have to pull together in every way, including attracting more nurses.

'Unless we are prepared to plan our social lives intelligently we shall find increasing neurosis and no amount of clinical treatment will solve it. We have emerged from a great war a matured people, and therefore we face these difficult problems with confidence.'

'I am not going to achieve my tasks by any bull-in-the-china-shop methods, but I am satisfied that, in another year, we shall be able to lay before the people of Great Britain a medical service which will be the envy of every other country.'

22 October 1945   *p.3*

HEALTH SERVICE
Bill to be Presented Early Next Year

Mr. Aneurin Bevan (Minister of Health), presiding at a meeting of the Society of Physiotherapists in London on Saturday, promised that by the early months of 1946 he would be presenting a bill for a comprehensive health service.

'I think I shall find a great deal more readiness to co-operate in the medical profession than has been suggested,' he said. 'I do not anticipate the difficulties that some people are gleefully mentioning. I believe doctors and people associated with suffering are good craftsmen and women, and their professional pride takes first place in their thoughts; it is to that professional pride I hope to make my appeal.'

Leader ## A NATIONAL HOSPITAL SERVICE

Some progress appears to have been made towards the drafting of a Government plan for the future organisation of our hospital system. Accounts differ as to the extent of the progress, and still more as to the character of the plan. It seems clear, however, that the proposal now holding the field aims at a unified national service which would embrace all existing hospitals, voluntary and municipal. That, of course, was to be expected, for nothing less could achieve the objectives set out in the Coalition White Paper or remedy the shortcomings revealed in the regional surveys initiated by the Ministry of Health. It remains to be disclosed, however, what decisions (if any) have been taken (or are being considered) on the vitally important administrative issues involved in the creation and running of a unified hospital service. In this context the White Paper merely registered the irreconcilability of opposing views in a deliberately indefinite form of words. Labour's election manifesto was equally vague, but the party's official policy was set out in its pamphlet 'National Service for Health.' Here it is proposed that in each region a series of large general hospitals with specialised departments should be organised by the health committee of an elected regional authority. Voluntary and public hospitals alike would be 'brought into the national scheme on terms which will satisfy the nation's sense of equity.' But nothing is said about the internal management of the hospital unit. It is on this point that public authorities have most to learn from the voluntary institutions.

Leader ## CONSULTATION FIRST

The prospects of co-operative harmony between the Minister of Health and the medical profession over the forthcoming Bill to establish a national health service appear to be improving. A realistic temper was displayed by many speakers at the recent annual conference of insurance practitioners, some, indeed, in view of the Government's electoral mandate were in favour of dropping policy discussions and concentrating on a largely unexceptionable series of safeguards for the future State practitioner's professional status. Mr. Bevan, it was recalled, had looked forward to cordial negotiations on terms and conditions of service, and this was interpreted in some quarters as implying that he contemplated no further discussions before the Bill is introduced. But an anxious inquiry by the BMA has elicited from the Minister an undertaking to give the profession, through its 'negotiating committee,' an opportunity to express its views on other questions before the Government finally decides what proposals it will submit to Parliament. At the same time he made clear his opinion that to go over again all the ground covered by the Willink negotiations would be a waste of time. This is as it should be, and the doctors' spokesmen have expressed their satisfaction with it. In effect the Government is applying to the medical profession the Labour doctrine that the workers' representatives are entitled not only to negotiate with their employers on the terms and conditions of their service but also to be consulted about its form and management.

1 December 1945   *p.4*

Leader   **THE TRAFFIC IN PRACTICES**

The prospects of harmonious negotiation between the Ministry of Health and the British Medical Association were dimmed yesterday by the publication in the BMA's official journal of two articles on the sale and purchase of medical practices. One asserted that the abolition of this traffic would mean, in effect, 'civil direction in peace-time.' The other began with the astonishing suggestion that Labour members of the Coalition Government had 'presumably' supported a policy of not interfering with the practice market. It went on to claim as a matter of fundamental professional principle that the doctor should be free to choose his successor and even questioned whether the Government, in buying up practices, might not be 'depriving the public of the right to choose its own doctor.' In fact, of course, the very existence of the trade in practices is proof that this right is not effectively exercised in present circumstances for the goodwill of a practice would have no market value if the seller's patients were not transferable to the buyer. Moreover, there was no reform that commanded a more consistent majority in the polls of the profession recently conducted by the British Institute of Public Opinion than the proposed abandonment (with adequate compensation) of the buying and selling of practices. Yet this is the issue on which it is suggested that doctors should judge the direction of the Government's policy 'and whether they want to follow it.' The BMA could hardly have chosen a less tenable rallying-ground.

FUTURE OF OUR HOSPITALS
Lord Woolton's Fear That State May Destroy the 'Spirit of Service'

Lord Woolton yesterday formally presented prizes and badges to nurses at the Manchester Royal Infirmary who this year passed the final examination.

Speaking of the future of British hospitals, he said he did not know what the present Government was going to do, but he would beg them to be very careful before they took any action that would destroy the voluntary spirit in the management of the hospitals. The State was inclined to think itself very wealthy when spending our money, and by expenditure it could do many things.

'But,' he continued, 'there is one thing that money cannot buy, and that is the spirit of service. The whole of the hospital tradition of this country has been built on the humanising spirit of service which made people feel it to be an honour to help the suffering. It seems to me that the introduction of the State as the controlling factor in hospital work means death to initiative and probably to progress. I do hope the Government, with all the power that it has got – power let me add, that it has properly got because the country elected them, – I do hope they will hesitate before they take steps to create a national health service which will close the door to all those people who want to give their services as volunteers to the hospitals.'

STATE TO 'DISTRIBUTE' DOCTORS?
'Highly Improbable that I Will Permit Sale and Purchase of Practices' — Mr. Bevan

In reply to a question in the House of Commons yesterday by Dr. Hastings (Lab.–Barking), who asked whether he could offer advice to doctors demobilised from the forces as to the purchase of practices, the Minister of Health (Mr. Aneurin Bevan) said the Government had not yet finally decided upon the proposals for a National Health Service.

They believed, however, that it would be incompatible with the provision of an efficient service that the future exchange of medical practices – and the creation of new ones – within the National Service should be left entirely unregulated and no effective steps taken to secure a proper distribution of doctors to fit the public need.

They appreciated that intervention in whatever form, will probably have the effect of preventing the sale and purchase of practices of doctors taking part in the new service, and the Government therefore thought it right to give warning of this probability at once and in advance of the formulation of their full proposals.

'VAGUE AND MENACING'

Mr. Willink (C. Croydon N.): 'Are you aware that this vague and menacing statement will cause the greatest possible anxiety and distress among a section of the population to whom the goodwill they have built up is their major asset? Is he further aware that many of his present colleagues in the Government agreed that this matter of great complication was not essential to the introduction of a National Health Service, and can he explain what he means by the method of regulating the distribution of doctors?'

Mr. Bevan: 'I have every reason to believe that the announcement I have just made will be received with great satisfaction by most of the profession, and most of the best elements of the profession regarding the sale and purchase of practices as extremely undesirable, and they will be very glad indeed I am about to discuss with them the conditions under which this is to cease.' . . .

14 December 1945   *p.3*

SEVEN POINTS FOR HEALTH SERVICE
Doctors Want 'Freedom'

Freedom of choice for the doctor and patient is stressed in a statement issued yesterday by the Negotiating Committee of the Medical Profession, which puts forward seven principles regarded as essential in any form of national health service. The principles are:

1.   The profession is in the public interest, opposed to any form of service which leads directly or indirectly to the profession as a whole becoming full-time salaried servants of the State or local authorities.
2.   The profession should remain free to exercise the art and science of medicine according to its traditions, standards, and knowledge, the individual doctor retaining full responsibility for the care of the patient, freedom of judgment, action, speech, and publication, without interference in his professional work.
3.   The citizen should be free to choose or change his or her family doctor, to choose, in consultation with his family doctor, the hospital at which he should be treated, and free to decide whether he avails himself of the public service or obtains the medical service he needs independently.

4. Doctors should, like any other workers, be free to choose the form, place, and type of work they prefer without Governmental or other direction.

5. Every registered medical practitioner should have a right to participate in the public service.

6. The hospital service should be planned over natural hospital areas centred on universities in order that these centres of education and research may influence the whole service.

7. There should be adequate representation of the medical profession in all administrative bodies associated with the new service in order that doctors may make their contribution to its efficiency.

Education
POST-ELECTION

In the sphere of education early doubts were expressed about the efficiency and justice of the 11 plus examination used as a means of determining eligibility for grammar schools. The 11 plus was not a requirement of the 1944 Education Act but rapidly became standard practice in the majority of local authorities. The following letter is typical of many.

30 July 1945   *p.4*

To the Editor of the Manchester Guardian

Sir, – As a father of three children and a head master of many years' experience I am in complete sympathy and agreement with the hundreds of parents whose children are suffering from the administration of the Education Act. I regret particularly the cases of children already attending a grammar school and turned out at the age of eleven because of their failure to satisfy the standards of an examination which in very many cases is no fair criterion of a child's 'aptitude and abilities.' Such tests take no account of a child's temperament or of those qualities of character such as drive, determination, loyalty, and team spirit so necessary if a boy is to benefit from a grammar-school education. Moreover, they ignore the late developer, putting a premium on the early maturity that is not necessarily a sign of intelligence. – Yours &etc.

PARENT-CUM-TEACHER.

24 September 1945 *p.4*

Leader ## A CASE FOR DRIVE

It is common for the enactment of important legislation to be
followed by an interlude in which, by contrast with the stir and
animation accompanying its passage, the issues that evoked it
seem temporarily quiescent. A measure so comprehensive as the
Education Act of last year has naturally not proved an exception
to that rule, but the inevitable pause has, on the whole, been a
creative one. In the last thirteen months the majority of authorities
– though there are still some laggards – have taken stock of their
tasks and prepared plans to meet them. The Ministry has translated
the provision of the Act into terms of regulations. Committees
appointed before it became law, like that on the recruitment and
training of teachers and youth leaders, have offered valuable
guidance on the consequential changes required in order to enable
its full fruits to be reaped. Lay opinion, which welcomed
educational reconstruction when it was still a project in the future,
has as yet seen no reason to modify its verdict. It would be idle
to pretend that it views the present situation without anxiety. Its
disquietude arises, however, not from disillusionment with the
scheme of reform presented to it by Parliament, but from the fear
lest reform, having got on to the Statute book, may fail to get farther.
It expresses a wholesome determination on the part of the public
to secure the benefits promised it and to secure them for its children,
not merely for its grandchildren.

*The future of the direct-grant schools proved to be an area in which the aims of the 1944
Act were open to interpretation.*

17 October 1945 p.8

FUTURE OF DIRECT-GRANT SCHOOLS
Report of Vote on the Supplementary Estimate for Education

MR. BUTLER 'SHOCKED' BY MINISTER'S STATEMENT
OF POLICY

Miss WILKINSON, replying, said: 'I am very anxious to retain
variety in education. But on the other hand, when this Parliament has
decided that there should be as far as possible complete free secondary education it is my duty to carry that out as far as possible.'

65

Because of the democratisation of the direct-grant schools she felt that a certain number of them should be retained to provide that variety of education which was desired. In the case of schools of very old tradition which had reached a very high standard in teaching technique and schools which had various other claims for special consideration she had been prepared to give direct-grant payments. 'But I see no reason why many of these should not become free secondary schools under the local education authority,' she added.

Mr. BUTLER, who said the Opposition took great exception to the policy Miss Wilkinson had outlined, added: 'I cannot say what a shock her statement gave me to-night: and what a very adverse impression it will make throughout the whole world of education. Can the Minister tell me what are the conditions she has laid down for these direct-grant schools to fulfil?'

'It seems to me,' Mr. Butler went on, 'that the Minister is obsessed with the idea of the free nature of education. She should, in my view, adhere to what she has already said in her speech, that variety of schools, provided that children of parents however poor may go to them, is in the interest of education. The direct-grant school has a great tradition. It is not a school designed to keep out children of the poor, and if she thinks that is the object of these schools she is obsessed by an entirely wrong idea.

'These schools form a general link as between the free and independent schools and the big boarding schools and the State system. If her policy is to result, as it is clearly starting to result, in some of these schools going independent, does she believe she is going to achieve the linking up of all types of education which has always been the ideal on this side of the House?'

10 November 1945   p.5

DIRECT-GRANT POLICY
Forceful Critics

MISS WILKINSON FIGHTS BACK

From our Parliamentary Correspondent

The question of the direct-grant schools was discussed on the adjournment in the House of Commons to-day, and speakers on both sides of the House – Mr. Anthony Eden and Mr. R.A. Butler among them – begged Miss Wilkinson to reconsider her action. The short debate reached a high level, demonstrating once again how much the debating power of the House has been raised by the new Labour members.

Perhaps the best speech of all was made by Colonel E.M. King, the Labour member for Penryn and Falmouth and a former head master, who obviously turned his guns reluctantly on the Minister of Education, but none the less effectively on that account. The speech was persuasive and closely argued, ending in the rejection of the notion that Socialism necessarily involves uniformity. At all events, the one sphere in which uniformity was both undesirable and impracticable was education. In the light of that conclusion Colonel King begged Miss Wilkinson not to treat the English educational system as though it were a chain of Marks and Spencer stores.

The arguments against Miss Wilkinson's decisions are well enough known by now, and little that was novel remained to be said, but Mr. Hugh Linstead, the Tory member for Putney, put the old arguments more brightly than anyone else. He could not discover any principle of selection on which Miss Wilkinson had acted. Indeed, he pictured her as having behaved like the Red Queen, sweeping through the Ministry of Education and calling out 'Off with its head' in respect of any school she did not like. The House, both sides, dissolved in laughter.

SCOLDING FROM 'RED QUEEN'

The Red Queen, at that moment, was absent, but she appeared during the later stages of the debate, all composed, as it seemed, and ready for anything.

Colonel F.C. Byers, from the Liberal benches, spoke vigorously and well for the preservation of direct-grant schools, and Mr. Eden made the threatened Warwick Grammar School, in his own constituency, the text for another forceful speech against the Minister's decision.

Miss Wilkinson sailed into action with every colour flying. She gave a Red Queen scolding to Colonel King, who, like Alice, wanted to answer. However, it was too late, it was time to adjourn. She blazed a little at Mr. Butler for having reproached her with levity, and she read the whole Tory party a lecture on its failure to realise what happened to it in July. There is some justification for that, because the Tory party is rather inclined to behave as though it were still sharing the government of the country with the Labour party in a new Coalition and to affect surprise at the absence of the will to compromise on the Treasury bench.

Thus Miss Wilkinson came to the direct-grant schools, and with a what-is-all-this-fuss-about manner she began to slay her critics – at least that was her ambition. What had she done? She had only told her officials to apply to the selection of the direct-grant schools the principles which the Fleming Report had recommended. The selection, said the report, should be made according to four considerations: (1) the financial stability of the school, (2) its non-local or special characteristics, (3) the nature of the education given by the school, (4) the views of the local education authority — et voilà! the application of the principles had produced the present list.

The possibility of a variety of practice in the provision of secondary education also received early official recognition.

14 December 1945   p.8

THE MULTI-LATERAL SCHOOL
Ministry's Guidance

A Ministry of Education circular issued yesterday states that, where the needs of localities can best be met by continuing two or more types of secondary education in one school, the Minister was prepared to consider proposals from education authorities for bi-lateral or multi-lateral schools.

A reversal of the policy favouring schools of not more than 500 to 600 students is not considered justified. Where a multi-lateral school is planned it should include provision for all modern school pupils in the locality, and large schools must be capable of being separated later into small units if necessary.

Generally, the proportion of accommodation allocated to the different types of secondary education would be 70 to 75 per cent to modern schools, and 25 to 30 per cent to grammar and technical schools.

It was not proposed to increase the annual intake to the grammar schools, nor was any drastic reduction advised. The grammar schools of the future would provide a normal course of education up to the age of eighteen for most pupils.

But it was the shortage of teachers which continued to cause most concern, particularly with the impending raising of the school-leaving age, scheduled for April 1946.

22 December 1945   p.3

THE SHORTAGE OF TEACHERS
Minister's Assurance

The Minister of Education (Miss Ellen Wilkinson), has this week received a deputation from the Council for Educational Advance, representing the Trades Union Congress, the Co-operative Union, the National Union of Teachers, and the Workers' Educational Association.

Introducing the deputation, Professor R.H. Tawney, chairman of the council, said that much concern was felt lest the raising of the school-leaving age should be prejudiced by insufficiently rapid progress with the emergency training of teachers. He knew cases of applications who had been kept waiting for weeks or even months before interview and between interview and placing in an emergency college. He urged the need for the emergency scheme to be both stepped up, to provide places for all approved candidates without delay; and speeded up, because there was a real danger that good candidates would be lost because they were being demobilised and would take up other employment. He hoped the scheme would be made the responsibility of a special section of the Ministry.

He had noticed suggestions in some quarters that local education authorities might not be ready to raise the school age by April, 1947. He sincerely hoped there would be no question of any further postponement. He also urged that the raising of the school-leaving age to 15 and then to 16 should not be regarded as two separate problems but as one reform in two stages, and that both the plans of local education authorities and the whole scheme of emergency training should be made accordingly.

Miss Wilkinson, replying, said there would be no going back on the date for raising the school-leaving age to 15. As to the next stage, there could be no doubt that the Ministry's ultimate target was 16. The date and priority of this move would have to be considered in due course.

Social Security and Welfare
POST-ELECTION

In October 1945 the Government introduced the first stage of its Social Security programme.

11 October 1945   p.5

COMPENSATION FOR DISABLED IN INDUSTRY
New Measure's Big Reforms

CONCESSIONS TO APPEASE LABOUR CRITICS

From our Parliamentary Correspondent

Westminster, Wednesday.

The House of Commons began yesterday a two-day second reading debate on the Industrial Injuries Insurance Bill. They will not be rollicking days, but they will speed on the way to the Statute-book a great reforming measure and the first part of the social insurance plan.

The present bill is a modified version of the bill drafted under Mr. Herbert Morrison's direction when he was at the Home Office in the Coalition Government and makes compensation for industrial injuries part of the country's social services. It also relates benefits to the degree of disability and not to loss of earning power. This is one of the big changes the measure makes.

In introducing the bill Mr. James Griffiths, the Minister of National Insurance, did admirably. He has been known for his Celtic eloquence and his great heart. To-day he showed himself complete master of the details and intricacies of workmen's compensation, and they are not trifling. Once, when commending the rehabilitation proposals of the measure (without which he would have had nothing to do with the bill, cash benefits not being enough) he let us see just a little of the Welsh orator moved by the tragedy of the forgotten 'compo' men. He sat down to a generous cheer from all parts of the house. Mr. Griffiths is not going to be among the failures of the Government: he may, if he keeps this up, prove one of its chief successes.

The Government also gave indications as to its future plans.

12 October 1945   *p.5*

HIGHER OLD-AGE PENSIONS
New Bill Soon

'SUBSTANTIAL' RISE IN BASIC RATE

The intention of the Government to increase substantially the basic rate of old-age pensions and pensions for widows over sixty was announced by Mr James Griffiths, Minister of National Insurance, in the House of Commons yesterday.

Replying to a series of questions, he said that old-age pensions and pensions for widows over sixty and children were being supplemented by the Assistance Board under regulations approved in December, 1943. About 1,000,000 out of a total of 4,000,000 pensioners were at present receiving supplementary pensions at a cost of £80,000,000 annually.

'The Government,' he continued, 'intends substantially to improve the basic rate of pension payable on retirement so as to reduce the need for supplementation. Proposals to this end, which will also include improvements in the rate of other National Insurance benefits, will be included in a bill which will be introduced early next year and which it is hoped to pass into law this session. A considerable time will be needed to bring these far-reaching changes. A bill dealing separately with pensions would be unsatisfactory. It could only be partial in its application and would not accelerate the improvement of pensions by any considerable period.'

But it was the role of the Friendly Societies in the planned insurance scheme which fuelled most debate.

FRIENDLY SOCIETIES EXCLUDED FROM STATE SOCIAL INSURANCE
'Cold-Blooded Violation of Pledge'

The Government decision, announced in the House of Commons yesterday, not to include the approved friendly societies in the national insurance scheme was condemned at the National Conference of Friendly Societies in London as 'cold-blooded violation of the Government's election pledge.'

'This conference is staggered,' said Mr. T.S. Newman, the president, who afterwards told a reporter: 'We regard it as another deliberate breach of faith on the part of the Government, and we are certainly not going to take it lying down.' It was stated that the Labour party had, of its own volition, issued a declaration of policy favourable to the societies forming part of the scheme.

The announcement of the Government's decision was made at question-time by Mr. J. Griffiths (Minister of National Insurance), in reply to Mr. Tom Smith (Lab.–Normanton). He said that the Government had reluctantly come to the same conclusion as its predecessors, that it would be impracticable to use the approved societies as organised bodies in the administration of the comprehensive social insurance scheme. . . .

Mr. Tom Smith asked whether, in view of the fact that this was a departure from a promise made, the Minister had acquainted the approved societies of this decision.

Mr. Griffiths replied that it was his duty to report the decision of the Government to Parliament. Promises had been made to look further into the question of the best way of using friendly and trade union societies, and non profit societies, and the decision was that to work a scheme covering the whole of the population it would be essential for the Government to have its own administrative machinery everywhere throughout the country. To have other machinery covering a section of the benefits and a section of the people would be a duplication which they believed in the long run could not be justified.

Mr. Logan (Lab.–Liverpool, Scotland): Am I to understand that the approved societies as such are now about to disappear and the State itself is going to run the whole service independently of any other association?

Mr. Griffiths: The meaning of my statement is clear. The Government have decided we must have one comprehensive machinery to work this. (Labour cheers).

FATE OF FRIENDLY SOCIETIES
Labour M.P.s' Concern

From Our Political Correspondent

The Labour Parliamentary party had before it to-day the statement which Mr. James Griffiths, Minister of National Insurance, made in the House on November 22, that the Government found it impracticable to use the friendly societies as an organised body in the administration of the national insurance scheme now being drafted.

'You have already reported the anxiety which the friendly societies feel about the future and their claim that Labour has broken a pledge. Many Labour members share the distress of the friendly societies, and said at to-day's meeting that they had pledged themselves during the election to preserve the friendly societies. It was also claimed by some speakers, I understand, that this pledge had been given as a result of a directive from headquarters.'

Mr. Griffiths, however, made it quite clear that his recent statement represented fixed Government policy and he would not be budged from this position. He explained that he had not only put the Government's case to representatives of the friendly societies but had met the Labour party's social group and talked to them about it.

'NO NEW DECISION'

Moreover Mr. Griffiths reminded the meeting that this was no new decision of policy.

LETTERS TO THE EDITOR

4 December 1945   *p.4*

FATE OF FRIENDLY SOCIETIES

To the Editor of the Manchester Guardian

Sir, – Your Political Correspondent understands that the Labour party candidates' pledge in relation to friendly societies was given as a result of a directive from headquarters. This is quite correct, the material wording was:

The Labour party is of the view that in our future social insurance scheme the system of approved societies shall be abolished with the exception of bona-fide friendly societies and trade unions, which have a long and honourable record of work both in public and voluntary health insurance and should be free to come in if they so wish . . . There is no place in the new scheme for any society which is connected with profit-making insurance companies or other private interests.

There is, however, a grave risk that in the party turmoil the real issue may be submerged, and your readers may like to be reminded of the original proposals in this matter as contained in Sir William Beveridge's report. His plan provided for retaining on a new basis the association of friendly societies with national health insurance (paragraph 31 and Change 3).

When the Coalition Government's White Paper was issued it was found that these agency proposals of Sir William's had been rejected and three main reasons were given why friendly societies could not be used as agents. During the Commons debate in November, 1944, Sir William said:

These three reasons against the proposed society agency are about the three weakest reasons in defence of an indefensible position that I have ever seen put forward. . . .

We can and should keep the friendly societies as responsible agents. If voluntary insurance is to continue as well as compulsory insurance we must make it easy for people to insure, we must avoid that duplication and overlapping which otherwise would take place in the home of every person who joins friendly societies. – Yours &c,

H.A. Andrew, Secretary of the Independent Order of Oddfellows Manchester Unity Friendly Society, 97 Grosvenor Street,
Manchester 1,
November 29.

This was one of the few areas of dissent within the parliamentary Labour Party and one unlikely to disturb what the 'Guardian' referred to as Labour's new self-confidence.

LABOUR'S NEW SELF-CONFIDENCE
First Lap of Parliament

By our Parliamentary Correspondent

The Government must be moderately well pleased with itself at the end of the first lap of the first session of the new Parliament. True, its positive achievements so far do not amount to a great deal. Up to the present it has not got beyond taking its coat off to the tremendous tasks of reconversion and housing, but it has managed, after what seemed a rather shaky beginning, to get its eye in, to use cricketing language, and to spread a feeling of confidence that it is in for a full innings.

For a week or two at the beginning one had twinges of doubt, a suspicion that the timidity and touchiness (partly the product of Ramsay MacDonald's inferiority complex) which had afflicted the two previous Labour Administrations was at work again. These misgivings were not diminished by the earlier handling of demobilisation, but Mr. George Isaacs quickly atoned by his response to criticism and his acceptance of a greatly accelerated programme of releases. This rapid readjustment of the programme was, in fact, the first hint that we might be mistaken in suspecting the new Government to be in danger of repeating the blunders of the earlier Labour Governments. Here was a proof of resilience. From that time the Government's confidence in itself and its capacity has been steadily mounting and, as is the way of things, the government's confidence and assurance have communicated themselves to the back benchers. Let there be no mistake about it. The Labour party in the House of Commons is a very happy family at the moment. Indeed, it has never before in its history known the unity and cohesion it enjoys to-day. This state of things may not endure. Centrifugal pulls of one kind or another are always working in some section of the Labour party. But there are no signs of fissures anywhere. Moreover, there was never before such a strong counteracting centripetal pull as there is in the five-year nationalising programme. That goal in Labour eyes must surely plead irresistibly against any threat to unity before its achievement.

The censure debate on the nationalisation programme had furthermore:

demonstrated that the Opposition is without a policy and divided in its outlook between a negative anti-Socialist Right, including Mr. Churchill, and a progressive Left prepared for an empirical approach to nationalisation.

(1946)

Housing

Housing was perhaps the area of social policy in which the Opposition sustained the most vigorous criticism of the Government. The debate began, in 1946, with the following attack on housing policy.

29 January 1946   *p.6*

TORIES' CASE AGAINST THE GOVERNMENT
Mr. Eden Opens the Attack

Mr. Anthony Eden, speaking in support of the Conservative candidate in the Preston by-election last night, complained that the government, instead of mobilising the national effort, was obsessed by its ideological prejudices and that the nation's needs were being subordinated to a party's dogmas. . . .

Of housing, he said, speaking for himself, the progress he saw was miserably disappointing. The duty of any Government after the general election was to give all possible encouragement to every agency that could increase the number of homes. Judged by this criterion, the Government was not doing its duty by those to whom it promised so much.

'For my part I do not believe that we shall get either the number of houses or the reduction in costs that we need until we have the competition of private enterprise, and what is more, the local authorities themselves are becoming increasingly impatient with the delays and difficulties which are put in their way by the Government.'

In this, as in so many other subjects, the Government was not grappling with the jobs that most needed doing. Last week the Minister of Works admitted the most serious shortage in the industries that made building materials. At the end of the year less than 4,000 men had been released under Class B to these industries instead of 10,000 that had been planned. The Minister of Health showed no understanding of the building industry; he did not realise its character or its variety.

'GENEROUS' HOUSING SUBSIDIES
Mr. Bevan to Introduce a Bill Next Week

Mr. Aneurin Bevan, Minister of Health, told the National Federation of Building Trades Employers last night that he hopes to introduce into the House next week a bill for the provision of housing subsidies.

'They will be found to be generous to local authorities,' he added, 'so that every financial inhibition that stands in the way of the housing problems will be removed.'

'I am exceedingly anxious,' Mr. Bevan continued, 'that we shall not try to solve the housing problem by lowering the building standards or by driving down prices. It would be lamentable if we allowed ourselves in this emergency to be driven into building cheap, squalid houses that would haunt us for the rest of our lives.

'Building houses, or deciding to build houses immediately at the end of a great war, is the most colossal task to which the nation can set its hand. That is why I think in years to come I shall be canonized by the building industry because I am trying to avoid the harvest of bankruptcies that overtook the building industry at the end of the last war.

'What matters is not the number of houses we have succeeded in building in the last six or seven months, but the number we shall succeed in building in the next six or seven years. I would much rather be judged on long-term results. Houses will be going up this year in very great numbers, not as fast as we want them to, but nevertheless they will be going up.'

Leader ## HOUSING PROGRESS

Mr. Bevan, having refused to comfort us with 'crystal-gazing' estimates of future house construction, now atones with a profusion of hard facts about actual performance up to January 31. These figures call for careful study. The first to catch the eye – a total of 3,469 new permanent houses for the whole country – seems pitifully small; but that is the measure of the scale on which building had started within the first two months after the end of the war in Europe. The most important figure – 116,229 families rehoused – puts the position on a different light. The key to a fair judgement of the report as a whole lies in the distribution of the labour force. Of 404,100 building workers nearly half were engaged on war damage repairs, which have added 70,223 to the number of dwellings available, besides making 411,000 occupied houses tolerably comfortable. Another 70,000 workers were making up war-time arrears of normal repair and maintenance work to prevent more thousands of decrepit houses from becoming uninhabitable. Conversion and adaptation of existing large houses, yielding extra accommodation for 9,945 families, employed 60,850 workers, while 32,400 engaged in erecting temporary bungalows account for over 12,000 more new dwellings completed. Only 28,000 workers were actually building new permanent houses. This division of labour is a proper reflection of the need to concentrate first on those jobs that will increase house-room at the highest speed and at the lowest cost, but it cannot be taken as a basis for estimates of what may or may not be achieved when the summer building season is under way.

28 February 1946 p.4

Leader **LABOUR FOR HOUSES**

It is now clear that the building labour force is increasing far more rapidly than the first condensed accounts of Mr. Bevan's voluminous report had suggested. . . .
. . . the number of permanent houses built before the summer's fine weather ends should reach quite a creditable level – provided always that the labour made available does not continue to 'leak away' into unnecessary repair work.

7 March 1946 p.5

SUBSIDIES FOR HOUSES
Must Come Down — and So Must Cost of Building — Ministry of Health

From our Parliamentary Correspondent

Westminster, Wednesday

Mr. Aneurin Bevan left it to his Parliamentary Secretary, Mr. C.W. Key, to move the second reading of the Housing Subsidies Bill in the House of Commons to-day. That was generous of him. Mr. Key discharged the task, as he put it, with great 'pride and pleasure.' The pleasure was there all right. He might have been introducing the bill at the Albert Hall. His manner was that of the Labour platform at its most emphatic. There were also occasional burning proclamations of the obvious, such as 'There is no greater social problem facing this country than housing,' or 'The need for houses is acute and urgent.'

In spite of this the speech contrived to be a clear and effective exposition of the bill. That was because Mr. Key's deep knowledge of the housing problem much more than made up for any such blemishes as have been mentioned – that, and his plain sincerity. While he commended the subsidies as the most generous ever submitted to the House of Commons and as having exceeded the highest hopes of the local authorities Mr. Key conceded that they were only justified by the necessity of keeping rents down in the presence of present high building costs. Both high costs and high subsidies must come down, but Mr. Key argued that that must be done by improved output of houses and building materials. The bill actually provides, as Mr. Key explained, for future revision of the subsidies by order.

Mr. Key managed to give some satisfaction to Mr. Willink, the former Minister of Health, by announcing that the subsidies are to extend to two types of non-traditional houses – a house of steel construction, designed by the British Iron and Steel Federation, and the 'Airey' house, a house of precast concrete.

Anticipating Conservative criticism, Mr. Key argued that so far from being cold-shouldered the private builder would have every encouragement to build for the local authorities, who alone in the Government's view, could produce the great bulk of the new houses for letting.

MR. WILLINK'S AMMUNITION

Mr. Willink is solemn but able. His criticisms almost entirely centred on the Tory allegation that the private builder is being neglected, largely out of political prejudice, coupled, of course, with the argument that the local authorities cannot of themselves produce the required number of houses. Mr. Willink naturally went to the White Paper for most of his ammunition and he did not fail to make play with the fact that on January 31 this year more than 25 per cent of the local authorities had not then obtained authority to tender for a single house. 'Where is your housing drive?' scornfully demanded Mr. Willink of the Government Front Bench.

Mr. Aneurin Bevan, who was holding himself for the winding-up speech, kept his peace, but only by the severest self-repression. You do not get twenty years spent in the Labour 'maquis' out of your system very easily.

The Government's policy for housing depended not only on building more permanent dwellings but also on overhauling the machinery for planning and land-use. The New Towns initiative was a central plank in this policy but one which brought a cautious response from the 'Guardian'.

Leader   **NEW TOWNS**

It is now clear that the Government intends to resolve the conflict between counties and county boroughs over the rehousing of the latter's 'over-spill' populations by itself assuming responsibility for the building of new towns. That was to be expected. Mr. Silkin indicated yesterday that his forthcoming New Towns Bill would also facilitate the enlargement of existing towns. What remains to be seen, however, is whether the means proposed in either case will meet the urgency of the need. It is, of course, common ground that satellite towns must, when completed, be their own corporate masters. The fear of losing rateable value has discouraged many authorities (including the L.C.C.) from planning realistically for dispersal on a drastic scale, but a general reorganisation of local finance cannot in any case be long delayed. Even the slum-dweller's sentimental regard for his home is of less importance than the crying need to get the slums rebuilt without delay.

The housing debate continued to revolve around the issues of progress in house building and planning policies.

THE HOUSING PROGRAMME
Minister's Candour

DEARTH OF LABOUR AND MATERIALS
From our Parliamentary Correspondent

Westminster, Monday.

Mr. George Tomlinson, the Minister of Works and Buildings, used no soft soap when speaking in the House of Commons to-day on the supply of building materials. Mr. A.S. Bossom, the Conservative member for Maidstone and an architect, said it was one of the frankest speeches he had heard from the Treasury Bench.

Certainly the speech, to say the least of it, discourages all optimism about the immediate future of housing. In his closing passage the Ministry even talked about the possibility of disaster if everybody concerned does not co-operate to the full in producing the necessary materials.

Mr Tomlinson frankly confessed that the present supply of labour and materials is quite inadequate for the housing programme. He actually quoted and endorsed a statement by an authority that the present supply of labour and materials could be absorbed in maintenance work without building a single house. As for the supply of bricks, a 'famine' can only be avoided by exceptional efforts.

The following extract is a typical example of the progress reports on house building which were published each month.

27 March 1946   *p.5*

SECOND PROGRESS REPORT ON HOUSING
Accommodation for 122,911 Families

NEARLY 20,000 HOUSES COMPLETED OR STARTED IN FEBRUARY

From our Political Correspondent

Westminster, Tuesday.

The housing figures for February were published to-day and the detailed tables showing the position in each local authority will be out later this week. The February figures for England and Wales show the total number of permanent houses completed during the month as 735, which with temporary houses makes a total of 4,264 completed in February.

The total under construction at February 28, as compared with January 31, had increased by 15,323, which includes 14,432 permanent (including 8,000 estimated under construction by private enterprise) and 891 temporary.

A comparison of these figures with those at January 31 is shown by the table.

The general picture is that in the past eleven months 18,198 houses have been completed (new permanent houses, destroyed house rebuilt, and temporary houses) and 53,414 houses of all kinds are under construction. In the same period 122,911 families have been rehoused, 104,713 of them in houses other than new. This total figure compares with 113,057 at January 31.

TENDERS AND LICENCES

Tenders approved in February for new permanent houses by local authorities amounted to 11,843, and 5,652 licences were issued to private builders for permanent houses. Tenders approved in the past year now cover the erection of 57,137 permanent houses,

84

and licences issued to private builders cover 32,912 permanent houses.

The comparable figures for February in Scotland are—

Houses completed.................................. 496
Under construction.............................1,232
Tenders approved..............................5,208
Licences issued 123
Families rehoused 3,930

LABOUR FORCE

The toal labour force engaged on the building or repair of houses in England and Wales at the end of February was 410,000, compared with 404,100 at the end of January. In addition 23,000 German prisoners of war were preparing housing sites in this country. The distribution of the labour force (with the January totals given in brackets) is as follows:—

War-damage repairs................................... 184,200 (197,100)
Preparation of sites..................................... 14,900 (15,700)
Erection of temporary houses 30,400 (32,400)
Erection of permanent houses..................... 44,100 (28,050)
Repair and maintenance............................ 70,000 (70,000)
Conversion and adaptation 66,400 (60,850)

The progress of individual housing authorities shows a slight improvement over the figures for January. Of 1,469 housing authorities 118 had obtained possession of no sites at the end of February, compared with 148 at the end of January: 268 authorities had not obtained authority to go on tender on a specific scheme at the end of February, compared with 393 at the end of January.

THE INCREASE SINCE JANUARY 31

	Up to January 31.		February.		Total to February 28.
HOUSES COMPLETED					
Permanent Houses on New Sites					
Local authorities	352	...	93	...	445
Private enterprise	1,116	...	484	...	599
Total	1,909	...	735	...	2,644
Temporary Houses	12,025	...	3,529	...	15,554
Total completed	13,934	...	4,264	...	18,193
UNDER CONSTRUCTION					
Permanent Houses					
Local authorities	16,765	...	6,090	...	22,855
Private enterprise (estimated)	5,000	...	8,000	...	13,000
Destroyed houses rebuilding (all sources)	2,726	...	342	...	3,068

Total	24,491	...	14,432	...	38,923
Temporary Houses	13,600	...	851	...	14,491
Total under construction (excluding those completed)	38,091	...	15,323	...	53,414

29 March 1946 *p.4*

Leader # NEW TOWNS

Whatever may be the ultimate fate of Manchester's request for compulsory powers to buy land for the creation of satellite communities it has already served the useful purpose of precipitating decisions by the Ministry of Town and Country Planning – decisions which should have been taken a long time ago if they were to save us from a repetition of the planless misdevelopment of pre-war years. The first fruit of this Parliamentary pressure is the release of the Reith Committee's interim report on new towns. This is a document of first-class importance, admirable in its grasp and uncompromising advocacy of the ideal pattern for civic dispersal. Whether it affords the most promising approach at this late stage to the practical problems that beset us is another matter. If the agencies it describes were already at work they would unquestionably be the best instruments of a clearly defined policy for relieving urban congestion – if any such policy had been adopted. If the Government had taken powers to divert industrial development from crowded cities to smaller towns within each region as well as from one region to another and had entrusted those powers to the Ministry of Town and Country Planning instead of to the Board of Trade, then the committee's insistence on self-contained (as distinct from 'satellite') communities might have merited unqualified support. But the large county boroughs are to-day the only bodies able and willing to meet the immediate need for large-scale rehousing and the satellite town is often the only available alternative to an immediate resumption of suburban fringe development. There is grave risk here of letting an attainable good be lost through belated perfectionism.

18 April 1946 *p.3*

PLANNING NEW TOWNS
Mixed Population Not Exceeding 20,000 the Aim

Variety of employment in new towns with the avoidance of 'one-class' neighbourhoods is recommended in the second interim report of Lord Reith's New Towns Committee, published as a White Paper yesterday.

The bill to provide for the creation of new towns by means of development corporation was also formally presented. The committee recommends that compulsory powers of purchase should be available and the population limit decided upon at the outset should be adhered to. There should be expedited procedure for the compulsory purchase of undeveloped land. A balance of income groups and of varied interest was desirable.

Movement of population must be co-ordinated with that of industry and, where necessary, temporary transport provided. The corporation should be financed by the State and there should be relief from payment of interest during the early years of development. The corporation should have powers to borrow, make advances, and establish subsidiaries, and should not be at a financial disadvantage compared with other housing agencies as to subsidies.

The committee considers that the speed at which individual new towns or town extensions can be built ought not to be estimated above an average of 1,000 to 1,250 houses a year. This corresponds to a growth of population at the rate of something like 3,500 to 4,250 persons a year.

20,000 MAXIMUM

The committee says it prefers to regard 20,000 as the maximum population to be absorbed in an entirely new town and 10,000 as the maximum to be added to an existing small town.

25 April 1946   *p.5*

CREATING THE NEW TOWNS
Development Corporations Financed by the Government

A REBUFF TO LOCAL AUTHORITIES

From our Political Correspondent

Westminster, Wednesday.

The New Towns Bill 'to provide for the creation of new towns through the agency of development corporations established and financed by the Government' was published to-day. It follows on the publication of the two interim reports of the Reith Committee and is regarded by the Government as an emergency measure taking precedence over the Compensation and Betterment Bill, which is not likely to appear for some time.

The New Towns Bill will be given a second reading in the House of Commons quite soon, possibly in the second week after the Easter recess.

The proposals in the bill are not new in principle; somewhat similar provisions have been made in various Acts since the Housing and Town Planning Act of 1909. This time, however, it is hoped that a machine has been designed which will produce, quickly and efficiently, the new towns that are needed.

CHOOSING SITES

Broadly, the plan is that the Minister of Town and Country Planning, after consulting local authorities, will make an order designating an area as the site of a new town. He will then appoint a corporation consisting of a chairman, deputy chairman, and up to seven other members. He will consult the local authorities before making these appointments.

The corporation will itself make a plan for the development of the area and will have power to carry out development, though the intention is that the corporation should undertake no more development by itself than is necessary.

The Government supposes that in general the provision of houses and services will be undertaken by existing authorities whether local or statutory, and that these bodies will lease the land they require from the corporation. Ninety-nine-year leases are suggested as normal. If, however, it is found that outside interests are not prepared to put up shops and so on – this happened at Welwyn – the powers in the bill would enable the corporation to make good the deficiency.

It will be noted that the Government's decision in favour of a Government-sponsored development corporation is a departure from the recommendations of the Reith Committee. This committee, in its first interim report (Cmd. 6579), proposed that the agency for building new towns should be a public corporation sponsored either by the Government or by local authorities or an 'authorised association.' The Government thinks it simpler to have one type of corporation only.

BALANCED COMMUNITIES

It is a cardinal feature of the new towns project that the new communities should be balanced, economically and socially. In the case of Stevenage, it is reported that there will be sufficient industry for the town. The bill includes no powers of direction for industry, however, and at present all that can be done by the Minister of Town and Country Planning is to find out what the Board of Trade has on its books.

Leader **STORM OVER STEVENAGE**

Mr. Silkin has measured for himself the strength and spontaneity of local opposition to the proposed development of a community of 50,000 people around the small town of Stevenage. Since no possible site for the industrial area so necessary in any new town is now entirely free from housing, some residents will either have to move or find themselves hemmed in by factories – an alternative which few would sincerely prefer. Beyond that Mr. Silkin heard no objection which has not been met by his New Towns Bill, whose second reading he will doubtless move to-day with a renewed confidence that it is the best solution to the overspill problem. So, maybe it is for Stevenage. So also it might have been for Mobberley and a hundred other projected satellites if it had been passed two years ago and accompanied (or preceded) by a solution of the compensation problem. But in their natural preoccupation with the needs of London both the Reith Committee and the Ministry of Town and Country Planning appear to have overlooked the unique experience of Manchester in satellite development and the peculiar urgency of slum clearance in the industrial North. If Manchester must wait for Government-sponsored corporations to come into being, collect staffs and do the two years' preliminary work which the city started six months ago its rehousing programme will be seriously delayed. And if Manchester remains helplessly slum-ridden while Stevenage becomes world famous the blame as well as the praise will be at Mr. Silkin's door.

TWENTY NEW TOWNS TO HOUSE A MILLION PEOPLE
– Mr. Silkin's First Target

From our Industrial Correspondent

Westminster, Wednesday.

To-day Mr. Silkin introduced his New Towns Bill to the House of Commons and to Lord Reith sitting in the Peers Gallery. A perspicuous exposition of his bill is what you would expect from Mr. Silkin, but he also brought a quiet ardour to the task. Once when he was trying to picture the new towns, with their balanced and self-contained communities, the admixture of all social classes and income limits, bright and gay, and furnished with theatres and concert halls and golf courses, his eyes brightened, and Mr. Silkin is no visionary.

It was good to see the congratulatory nods on the Tory benches when Mr. Silkin sat down. His sincerity and ability always commanded their respect in past Parliaments. While Mr. Silkin was speaking Lord Reith spent some time with his head buried in his hands as though he were praying, but perhaps he was only hiding his blushes at the compliments paid to him by the Minister for the work of his committee.

Mr. Silkin began at the beginning. According to him the first man to get agitated about 'suburban sprawl' was Sir Thomas More, but, said the hero of Stevenage, Sir Thomas More was beheaded and that must not be regarded as a precedent. Queen Elizabeth, Cobbett, and Ebenezer Howard all found a place in Mr. Silkin's roll of the anti-sprawlers and that brought us to the Reith Committee and its interim recommendations.

'GALLANT SPIRIT' OF SLUMS

Much, of course, of what Mr. Silkin had to say has been anticipated in the bill and the White Papers. Some of his obiter dicta made an interesting part of his speech. He wants the slum spirit transferred to the new towns. It sounded awful until Mr. Silkin explained that he meant that gallant spirit of mutual helpfulness that animates the poor, but which for some reason is completely dissipated once they are put into new housing estates. . . .

While explaining the function of the corporations which are to be entrusted with the creation of the new towns Mr. Silkin said with an emphasis that was quickly remarked by the Tories that private enterprise would be invited to participate in the building of houses and to take leases of land. The small builder would not be left out, nor would the builder of the single house. The sprightly minded Captain Crookshank broke in to remark 'I hope the Minister of Health agrees with this.' Mr. Silkin's answer was that Mr. Bevan is one of the backers of his bill.

4 July 1946   *p.4*

Leader   **HOUSING DELAYED**

Food and foreign affairs have for the time being distracted public attention from the housing shortage. It will not be long, however, before Mr. Bevan's performance in this sphere will again be subjected to critical scrutiny – and this time to better purpose. The first of his monthly returns, which aroused so much unfavourable comment, had little significance except as a basis for later comparisons. The May figures, however, indicate how much use has been made of the spring to get construction started after the winter's work on site preparation and the planning of

90

material production. By the end of this month we should be seeing in the total of new houses completed the effects of the Minister's activities, and in the total under construction we should have a rough idea of the number of new dwellings that can be finished while this year's building weather lasts. So far the record is no more than hopeful. About fifty thousand new permanent houses reached the 'under construction' stage during the three spring months, but only 20,000 temporary bungalows had begun to be erected on the 82,000 sites already developed for them by May 31. The Labour force engaged on housing work of all kinds rose by barely 80,000 in the same period: about 80 per cent of this increase, however, was accounted for by recruits to new permanent house erection. Manchester's own experience suggests that materials rather than labour now form the bottleneck, and that a high proportion of unfinished houses are held up in their last stages by the lack of a few components. It is at this point by his own admission, that Mr. Bevan's winter labours in the organisation of supplies must prove their worth.

6 July 1946

Leader   **NEW TOWNS**

Yesterday the New Towns Bill was given both its third reading in the Commons and its first reading in the Lords. Evidently Mr. Silkin appreciates that he will not much longer be able to resist such disastrous proposals as the L.C.C. scheme to build an 800-acre housing estate in the Chessington sector of London's green belt unless he can offer alternative accommodation in Stevenage. He is also conscious of the need to staff his new town corporations with men 'big enough to try things out and make mistakes' chosen for their ability and character without regard for their previous associations. The more is the pity that he steadfastly refuses to make use of the organisation and experience already in being in this field and that he fails to appreciate the different and still more urgent needs of blighted industrial cities at a distance from London.

A FINAL REPORT ON NEW TOWNS
Truly Balanced Communities of from 30,000 to 50,000

From our Political Correspondent

Westminster, Tuesday.

The final report of the New Towns Committee set up to advise the Minister of Town and Country Planning and the Secretary for Scotland on the principles on which new towns should be established and developed as self-contained and balanced communities has been published to-night (Cmd. 6876, price 1s. 3d.). It is to be read with two interim reports of the committee, one published on January 21, 1946 (Cmd. 6759), and the other on April 9, 1946 (Cmd. 6794).

The first interim report dealt mainly with the form of agency for building new towns, and the second was produced when it was decided to introduce the New Towns Bill and dealt with factors that had to be considered in advance of legislation. In the final report 'we deal not only with the physical tasks involved and with the devising of machinery for them, but also with the more complex and delicate problem of founding the social structure of a new town and fostering its corporate life.'

NEW COMMUNITIES

Since the committee first began publishing its reports there has been some development of the proposed new town at Stevenage, where the Minister of Town and Country Planning, Mr. Lewis Silkin, found rather more criticism from the residents than he had expected. The final report pays special attention to the choice between expanding an existing community or founding a new one when developing a new town.

'We have had in mind,' states the report, 'the desirability of the widest general interest in this project (that is, building new towns), especially among those who, in one way or another – possibly as residents – will be directly concerned. The task is essentially a social enterprise which demands, if it is to be well done, the close and continuous scrutiny and support of a really well-informed public opinion.'

In the late summer and autumn the housing problems were dramatically highlighted by a new phenomenon, 'squatting'.

SHROPSHIRE 'SQUATTERS' MOVE INTO A VICARAGE
Invasion of Army Camps Still Growing

30 FAMILIES TAKE OVER CONDEMNED TENEMENT IN EDINBURGH

With the authorities still turning a blind eye to the squatters' movements increasing numbers of the homeless and overcrowded were yesterday setting up house in disused military camps all over the country – there are now five such settlements in Bristol. At the same time, about thirty families have moved into a condemned tenement in Edinburgh.

An original move has been made by five families who are now settled in Bayston Hill Vicarage, Shropshire, which was occupied by the Rev. W.G. Branch until he left at the end of last year to take up a living at Bletsoe, Bedford.

The new vicar requires a considerable portion of the vicarage, but of the 17 rooms only a large dining-room, study, and bedroom are not occupied by the families. The 'tenants' have so far received no notice to quit, and the whole situation is being considered by the Bishop of Lichfield.

THIRTY 'SETTLEMENTS'

A Ministry of Works official, disclosing that there are 850 Service camps declared redundant, said last night that very few of them were suitable for use as homes. 'Up to now about 30 have been grabbed by homeless families, who have chosen camps of good quality construction such as that at Chalfont St. Giles (Bucks).'

Apparently none of the local authorities intends to act against the squatters until they have discussed the legal aspect with the Ministry of Health and the War Office. Most of them are willing to help the squatters in the way of essential services, but the Bristol Housing Committee last night warned twelve families who yesterday claimed empty huts on Shirehampton golf course that they were trespassing and that the committee refused responsibility for their comfort or convenience.

THE SQUATTERS' REPLY TO MR. BEVAN
Not Prepared to Move Until Something Better is Provided

The first reactions of the squatters to the Minister of Health statement that camps which are unfit for housing must be cleared before winter and that others for which 'the Government has an urgent alternative need' should also be vacated came from Buckinghamshire, where a spokesman of the residents at Beech Barn (Chesham Bois) last night declared, 'We can assure the Minister he would find it very difficult to remove us. We are not prepared to move until we are given something very much better.

'The Government may have promised homes to the Poles, but they also promised them to the British, and we consider our ex-Service men and their wives and children to have first claim. We were promised that housing would be treated as a military operation, but so far the only military operation has been carried out by squatters all over the country.'

The previous night squatters at Chalfont St. Giles had endorsed a declaration by their chairman, Mr. Glasstonville. 'We will not stand for anyone being turned out. We are here and we will stand by one another.'

Midlands squatters, however, have taken their first step towards organising themselves on a large scale. Delegations from commandeered camps all over the area met in Birmingham, and a committee of Midlands squatters was formed.

'MOONLIGHT INVASIONS'

Meanwhile the invasion of Service camps is still growing. Although in a few cases the military and caretakers have successfully defended their preserves, they have no answer to the tactics of squatters who have crept up by night and established a strong 'colony' by daybreak.

19 August 1946   *p.4*

Leader   **SQUATTERS' RIGHTS**

In telling local authorities to provide at once proper sanitation, water and lighting services in the camps invaded by homeless squatters Mr. Bevan has clearly taken the right course. But what he says about the situation is a good deal less than what he has done about it. Legally of course the squatters are completely at fault but the grounds on which the Minister prefers to base his criticism of their action – and to justify his own previous inaction – are not so strong. It is true that some camps will have to be cleared before winter turns them into slums and death-traps and that to adapt the rest and provide other accommodation for their intended uses will delay the building of permanent houses. But few will agree that the purposes for which they were being reserved are more urgent than housing.

The Minister of Health has laid no claim to service camps as they fell vacant becuase he does not want to delay permanent

94

housing by spending labour and materials in making them decently habitable. The present mess, as his statement makes plain, is the outcome of his violent prejudice against temporary sub-standard housing in any shape or form.

21 August 1946   *p.6*

GOVERNMENT PONDERS HOW TO REMOVE
THE SQUATTERS
Problem May be Thrown Back to Local Council

From our Political Correspondent

London, Tuesday.

The Cabinet is understood to have discussed squatting almost as soon as the movement of families into empty camps began, and it seems that Ministers have largely thrown the problem back to the departments, who are anxious that the regions and the local authorities should not escape their responsibilities.

But the Ministers directly concerned about squatting – the Ministers of Health and Works and the Service Ministers – have been grouped into some sort of a committee, with the Home Secretary, Mr. Chuter Ede, in charge. (Mr. Bevan is in Switzerland. Mr. Alexander is involved with the Peace Conference, Mr. Lawson is convalescing after an operation, Lord Stansgate is in Cairo, and Mr. Ede is shortly going to the Channel Islands with a Privy Council commission).

The Home Secretary is indirectly concerned with prisoners of war. He has told the House of Commons that he was looking for camps for Borstal boys (as a substitute for Dartmoor among other places), and he is, of course, responsible for law and order.

MINISTRIES' ERROR

The Government realises that it was trying for homeless families to see camps standing empty, and that it was an error for one department to take so long in occupying a place that had been evacuated by another department. Mr. Ede's committee is intended to be a guarantee that the same kind of thing does not happen again, and, in fact, the departments are likely to hang on to camps much longer than necessary in order to maintain occupation until the departments which are to take over are quite ready to move.

For, of course, there are many plans for the continued use of the camps in Government service: as resettlement centres, teachers' emergency training centres, quarters for the Poles coming to this country from General Anders's Army, and for prisoners of war.

95

The Government has given a general direction that camps intended to be used for resettlement and the training of teachers must be cleared of squatters, but that the same treatment cannot prudently be applied to squatters in camps originally intended for the Poles or prisoners of war.

It is not clear how the Government proposes to remove squatters. The procedure is now being thought about, but it is clear that Whitehall is expecting a splendid display of initiative from the local authorities.

29 August 1946   *p.4*

Leader   **SQUATTING MADE ORDERLY**

The Minister of Health's instructions to the regional committees set up to review and classify Service camps are a good deal more sensible than his statement of ten days ago. There is no talk now of asking squatters to 'return to the homes from which they have come, so that the camp can in due course be cleared' for the followers of General Anders. Nor is it any longer suggested that where camps are taken over by local authorities the squatters in possession should be expected to withdraw in favour of house-hunters higher on the official lists. It is admitted by implication that some of the camps already invaded, far from being urgently required by the Services, were held in reserve for contingencies that are unlikely to arise for at least eighteen months, and it is provided that in future the Services shall give the Ministry of Works three or six months' notice of the possibility of a camp's being vacated. Squatters now in occupation are not likely to be evicted except in 'extreme cases;' in general, they will be disturbed only if they are called upon to move from those which 'are or could be made redundant to Service requirements.' All this is a great deal better than either an anarchic scramble or sporadic and half-hearted attempts to enforce inappropriate laws. What it amounts to is that the Minister of Health has been jolted into doing what he should have done of his own accord a long time ago.

9 September 1946   *p.3*

MR. BEVAN'S SYMPATHY FOR SQUATTERS
Building Programme Hampered by Black-Market Repair Work

Mr. Aneurin Bevan, Minister of Health, told a meeting at Bristol on Saturday that he had 'much sympathy' with the situation in which many of the squatters found themselves. 'But if I had myself advised people to go into some of the camps they would

96

then have attacked me for giving substandard accommodation, he added.

Many of the camps were quite unfit for homes, he continued, and 'it would be impossible to bring the accommodation up to normal standards without sacrificing labour and materials required for the completion of permanent houses.

Later he told a reporter that some of the camps were specially needed and squatters would have to be removed.

Mr. Bevan said the total number of houses of all types either built, building, or projected was 325,000. Since the Government took office 60,000 permanent and temporary houses had been built, and the total built or building by the end of July was 223,000. The Government had taken every possible action and what was now required was for industry to build the houses. 'I am quite certain in a few years' time we will have broken the back of the housing programme,' he added.

9 September 1946   *p.5*

1,500 IN SQUATTERS' INVASION OF WEST-END FLATS
Main Body in Seven-Storey Block

ARMY LORRIES BRING THEM TEA FROM KENSINGTON BARRACKS

The West End of London yesterday afternoon was the scene of the biggest squatters' 'invasion' so far. More than 1,500 people took part in an organised operation which began with the commandeering of a seven-storey block of four-roomed flats, the Duchess of Bedford House, Duchess of Bedford's Walk, West Kensington.

In heavy rain groups of people carrying bedding converged on High Street, Kensington, from all over London at two o'clock, some coming from as far as Stepney. As if at a signal, they had streamed through the streets towards their destination.

Within ten minutes 1,000 people were through the doors of the Duchess of Bedford House and were being directed to individual flats. Altogether 500 families appeared to stake their claims, and unlucky people waited in the vestibule while efforts were made to fit them in. Outside the flats a number of loaded furniture vans were drawn up besides more than a score of taxis.

Those who could not find accommodation stood patiently in the rain while scouting parties were sent out to inspect neighbouring property with a view to further 'requisitioning.' Councils of war were held under lamp-posts in the rain, and there appeared to be an elaborate system of communications by messenger-runners.

STRAINED SYMPATHY

The squatters' invasion of private houses and blocks of flats in the West End of London organised by the Communist Party has met with a comparatively calm and good humoured reception. Its prospects for success however are comparatively slight, for the circumstances are radically different from those in which the precedent has been set. The squatters who occupied Army camps reserved for 'contingencies' were asserting – in an unorthodox fashion – the legitimate claims of homeless civilians to accommodation of a kind which the Government had neglected to use for this purpose. . . .

But the Government has not by any means neglected to requisition empty private dwellings where the owner cannot prove that they will be occupied as soon as they are made habitable. . . .

The Communists in fact, having missed the chance to lead a movement deserving of Mr. Bevan's sympathy, have forced him to set a limit to his indulgence – and their sponsorship will not dispose him to err on the side of sympathy.

SEIZURE OF LONDON FLATS
Government's Serious View of New Organised Squatting

NORMAL LETTING FORESTALLED

From our London Staff

Fleet Street, Monday.

The Government takes a serious view of the invasion, by squatters, of houses and flats in Kensington and Marylebone. The matter is believed to have been discussed by the Cabinet today, and a statement of policy is expected very shortly from the Ministry of Works.

The sympathy which Mr. Aneurin Bevan has expressed with the position of the squatters in empty military camps is not extended to the London squatters. There is an essential difference. The former have occupied hutments which were standing vacant, with no obvious prospective tenant; they were perhaps destined for some useful purpose, but not for the important function of housing the people, to which they are now being put. But the houses in London would in the near future have reverted to their normal purpose as homes. All that has happened is that one set of tenants has forestalled another.

This, rather than the distinction between occupying public and private property, is the main reason why the Government is hostile to the London squatters. A subsidiary reason is that the movement is obviously and avowedly not spontaneous like that of the camp squatters. It is being openly run by the Communist party, whose London district committee announced today that it would 'take whatever steps are necessary for the legal defence of these squatters should the property owners attempt to take action for their eviction.'

19 September 1946   *p.5*

THE SQUATTERS IN RETREAT
Two Buildings Evacuated

From our London Staff

Fleet Street, Wednesday.

The retreat of the squatters has begun. The Ivanhoe Hotel, in Bloomsbury, and Abbey Lodge, in Regent's Park, have both been completely evacuated, and workmen from the Ministry of Works are back on the job of preparing the rooms for their lawful users.

Late last night the families in the Duchess of Bedford house, bowing to the High Court's ruling in four test cases, decided to evacuate their new quarters. Some have already gone, and all will be out by Friday.

Those who have nowhere to go – whose vacated quarters have been snapped up by others, or are in such poor condition that they cannot bring themselves to return – will be accommodated for the time being at Bromley House, Bow. This building, formerly an L.C.C. rest centre, has been used recently to house building workers brought in from the surrounding country to carry out bomb-damage repairs in London. It will take about 300 people.

The Government has no wish to try to make the retreat a rout. It is not intended to bring any cases for damages against the squatters who are leaving, and it is not yet certain what will become of the orders outstanding against the few squatters selected as test cases. The charges of conspiracy against some of the alleged organisers are, of course, still to be heard. There has been no decision to drop them.

PLANNING AREAS

The Government's Bill to deal with the twin problems of compensation and betterment, expected early in the next session, will come too late to prevent much avoidable repetition of past mistakes. It promises, however, to make up for its tardiness by the breadth of its scope. It will tackle the difficulties created by the inflated cost of densely developed urban land. It will also, apparently, revoke all existing operative planning schemes. This does not mean, of course, that the work of those responsible for the great city plans of the last two or three years will be wasted; these are still in the provisional stage and for the most part have been based on the assumption that such legislation would be passed. It does mean, however, that a fresh start can be made wherever it is desirable in the new circumstances. Mr. Silkin has strongly hinted that the opportunity may be taken to transfer executive planning authority from local to wider regional bodies and this possibility evoked enthusiasm from his audience of planning technicians. Thus once again experience of practical necessities has forced the Government to anticipate the long-postponed reform of the structure of local government. Will the projected agencies be ad hoc bodies unrelated to other instruments of regional administration and exempt from direct responsibility to the people for whose benefit they are intended to work? Or will they form part of a new pattern soon to be given democratic strength and substance by the election of regional councils?

ROOFING TAKES FIRST PRIORITY IN BUILDING PROGRAMME
Mr. Bevan Announces a New Drive

From our Labour Correspondent

London, Sunday.

If the housing problem could be considered dispassionately as an exercise in logistics there would be comfort enough in 'plans' and 'targets' and in estimates of the number of people who may expect to find homes by the end of 1947. But although housing is essentially a logistical task, it is also – and far more urgently – a desperate human problem.

It was this frank recognition of the human side of housing that gave Mr. Bevan's press conference yesterday its main importance. Mr. Bevan was concerned to do two things – to set an immediate 'housing target,' not in figures but, as it were, in hope, which people can visibly see and comprehend, and to spur the building industry to new efforts in transforming plans and contracts into homes.

Mr. Bevan's immediate target is 'a roof by Christmas for every unfinished house whose walls have reached eaves level.' There are about 30,000 at this stage of construction in building under local authorities and about another 30,000 – the figure is not so easy to compute – in the hands of private builders. Mr. Bevan has given all 'eaves level' houses what he calls a 'super priority' for materials, as high as that 'given to aircraft on the ground during the Battle of Britain.' This drive for 'roofs by Christmas' should mean that something like 60,000 new houses will be ready for people to live in by about the end of the year, and it means also – what is psychologically important – that everyone who sees a house with walls roof-high can know that something is being done urgently to 'finish the job.'

THE INDUSTRY'S PROBLEM

Mr. Bevan was emphatic that the main responsibility for getting houses built now lies with the building industry. The State machine, in which the local authorities are essential working parts, he declared, has not in any sense 'broken down.' Contracts have actually been placed for rather more than 435,000 houses, and what is needed now is not more 'stimulation' of the local authorities to multiply contracts, but stimulation of the building industry to get the houses already under contract built more quickly.

One difficulty in checking black market building is the structure of the building industry, with its enormous number of small units. Mr. Bevan said that since the war 50,000 building workers had taken out licences as 'builders.' 'This is a tendency,' he said, 'that we do not contend we have the right to prevent. In our society, if a man wants to become self-employed, we have no wish to prevent him from doing so. But it does add enormously to the ''atomisation'' of the industry, and it adds to the units who are able to undertake building operations themselves.'

PREVENTING 'BLACK MARKETING'

But in spite of the difficulties, Mr. Bevan is determined that black market building shall be reduced. This will be done in two ways; in part directly, by reducing the number of licences granted for work and by more rigid inspections and more prosecutions of offenders, with, Mr. Bevan hoped, 'penalties which fit the crime'; and partly indirectly, by urging the public to understand that 'any householder who uses building labour and materials unnecessarily is simply pushing back the day when a family now suffering great hardship can get a home.'

Discussing the proportion of houses built to let and houses for sale, Mr. Bevan said that of the 60,000 permanent and temporary houses completed already 48,000 had been let at reasonable rents to those who needed homes most badly and 12,000 had been built by private builders for sale. That was a ratio of four houses to let for every one for sale, and he intended to see that that four to one ratio was maintained.

'It is worth noting,' he remarked 'that the squatters were hardly in a position to buy houses. These incidents are simply nothing to the trouble there would have been if we had had in power a Government which handed the housing programme over to the speculative builder to produce houses to sell. Accommodation has so far been provided for 200,000 families – 120,000 of them in London – and the great bulk of this has been made available for letting and fairly allocated to those in greatest need.'

24 September 1946   *p.7*

HOUSING SPEED-UP
10 New Non-Traditional Types

As part of his plan to speed up housing Mr. Aneurin Bevan, Minister of Health, has arranged for the production of ten types of houses of non-traditional construction. In a circular to local authorities he states:

Sufficient experience has been gained of the building of non-traditional houses for it to be evident that they have considerable advantages at the present time. Not only do they make less demand than traditional houses on scarce building materials and on bricklayers, but they can be erected more quickly.

Two types of non-traditional houses of permanent structure already in large-scale production under the direction of the Government are the B.I.S.F. steel-framed house and the Airey concrete house. The ten additional types now going into production are British Steel Construction, Cussins, Dyke clothed concrete construction, Easiform, Orlit, Scottswood, Steane Unity, Wates, and Wimpey 'no-fines.'

Plans are being made as simple as possible both for the producer and for the local authority, and Mr. Bevan has asked local authorities with a view to accelerating and expanding their housing programme to accept the particular type of house which is being produced within specially designated areas.

'BAMBOOZLING' THE PUBLIC
Mr. Bevan Denounces Press Campaign Against Government's
Housing Policy

Denouncing certain newspapers for trying to bamboozle the public about housing Mr. Aneurin Bevan, Minister of Health, at a public meeting in Barking last night gave the figures of the progress of the Government's housing campaign. Since March 1945, he said, accommodation had been provided for a total of 222,564 families, including 126,742 in the London area. One family in thirty in the London area was living in a requisitioned house. . . .

'The Government has been criticised for giving no housing target. I have now given the only target which is worth anything in practice and one which every building worker can understand – namely to concentrate on finishing those houses now in course of construction which we can reasonably hope to see completed this year. You would have thought that the Tory press, if it were sincere in the sympathy which it expresses for the people now suffering great hardship, would have welcomed this drive and called upon all concerned to concentrate their efforts on this clear objective – to provide new homes before the end of the year for 30,000 more families. Instead, the millionaire press has either made no comment or poured out words of discouragement.

'The only contribution these newspapers make to the housing problem is to abuse me for refusing to hand over the whole programme to the speculative builder to produce houses for the people with the money to buy them. The Labour Government's policy is quite different: it is to give preference to the families in greatest need who want houses at reasonable rents.'

NEW ATTACK ON PRIVATE FIRMS

From our Parliamentary Correspondent

Westminster, Monday.

Dialectically Mr. Aneurin Bevan hit the Opposition for six in to-day's housing debate, and yet the speech was not altogether satisfying. These polemical forays come so easy to him and they give no end of delight to the Government's supporters. There seemed to be a good deal of the offensive–defensive about to-day's. In substance the speech came to this. In the case of permanent houses the Government and the local authorities have done their job. If there is any lag in building now it is owing to the failure of the private contractor who builds for the local authorities, there being as Mr. Bevan pointed out to an 'ignorant Opposition,' only negligible direct building by local authorities.

The attack on private enterprise from this unexpected angle caused much diversion on the Labour benches and a good deal of surprise on the Conservative. There followed a defence of the principle of building to let in preference to sale on familiar lines, interrupted by some spirited interchanges between Mr. Bevan and Mr. Hugh Molson as the Minister tried to ensnare the Opposition into committing itself to the view that the housing shortage can be solved by building houses for sale. . . .

WHY NO HELP?

Finally Mr. Bevan referred to the campaign that he had started to complete all houses 'now up to the eaves' before the winter, a result which the building industry advises him is quite capable of achievement. It was here that Mr. Bevan carried his offensive against the Opposition to its extreme point. He complained that neither the Opposition nor the Conservative press had done anything to help this campaign. Why had they not helped? Mr. Bevan's answer was delivered with a hiss of scorn. The Conservatives, he alleged, did not want houses but only the opportunity to exploit the anxiety of the people. Also they were angry because 'they and their friends' had been prevented from making large fortunes out of the country's housing needs. Of course Mr. Bevan had salvos of Labour cheers to endorse these charges.

Nothing else in the speech achieved quite this fury, but the discourse frequently developed a hot temper. According to Mr. Bevan the Conservatives had been guilty of frivolity in raising the debate at all. They had shown both levity and ignorance in their discussion of the problem at Blackpool and elsewhere. There was derision for Lord Woolton, who had failed to prepare plans for housing when he was Minister of Reconstruction, and there were acid allusions to Mr. Churchill and Mr. Eden who presumed to speak on housing outside Parliament but not inside.

Mr. Bevan threw himself down on the Treasury bench at the end of his speech and passed a hand through his hair. He had certainly purged his feelings.

UNEXHILARATING

The debate had been opened from the Opposition front bench by Mr. Manningham-Buller, a barrister who got an Under-Secretaryship in the 'Caretaker' Government. He speaks with a funereal monotony that is rather depressing, so that, though he put his case clearly, he was not exactly exhilarating. The conclusion of his argument was that housing was in its present sorry plight, as he described it, for two reasons: one, a shortage of material which was entirely the responsibility of the Government, and, two, the Government's reliance on the local authorities as their chosen instrument.

22 October 1946   *p.4*

Leader   **THE PACE OF HOUSING**

Once again the Opposition, by devoting its speeches to the claims of the speculative builder, has failed in its public duty to focus attention on the real weaknesses of the housing drive. Mr. Bevan is on firm ground in claiming that the country is satisfied with the ethics of putting need before ability to buy at least until the immediate shortage of houseroom is met. Moreover, since few houses are being built by direct labour, the local authorities have done all they can by acquiring and developing sites, preparing plans and placing contracts faster than the building industry can cope with them. The issue of public versus private is dead in this connection: the important question now is why all houses are taking so long to complete and, in particular, why private builders under contract to local authorities are taking so much longer than private builders (sometimes the same firms) working under licence.

11 November 1946   *p.4*

Leader   **STEVENAGE**

Mr. Silkin has now made an order under the New Towns Act designating Stevenage as the site for a future community for some fifty thousand people. In doing so he has also answered the various general and particular objections raised at the recent public enquiry which has proved a useful check on detailed planning though little more than a formality as far as policy is concerned.

21 November 1946   *p.4*

Leader   **LIBERTY AND LICENCES**

Mr. Bevan and Lord Henderson, surveying the general housing picture yesterday, both professed to find it 'satisfactory.' Both, as the Americans would say, were whistling in the dark. Unless something can be done to curb the mounting cost of house-building even the modest progress already made may be severely checked. The main reason for the gross disparity in numbers between houses built and houses building is, as Mr. Bevan said, that the building labour force is spread too thinly over the contracts placed. Yet the labour force is now about as large, if not so well-balanced, as before the war. The trouble is that too much of it is 'hiding itself.' The Government, in the sacred name of liberty, has permitted fifty thousand more building workers to set up as builders on their own account in the last ten months.

21 November 1946   *p.6*

LORD ADDISON REPLIES TO HOUSING CRITICS
Coalition's 'Fairy-Like' Estimates

Opening a debate on housing in the House of Lords yesterday, Lord Llewellin said there was probably no one who was really satisfied with the present situation. We did not see housing queues, but if every applicant on the local authorities' lists were to fall in line there would be a queue that would appal the conscience of the country. A member of the L.C.C. had stated that at the present rate of house-building the L.C.C. could not clear their waiting-list for a quarter of a century.

Temporary houses, said Lord Llewellin, were a necessary stopgap, although he hated the look of them. The original plan was to have 150,000 of those completed within two years of the defeat of Germany, but at the end of September only 57,000 had been completed. Why had the programme fallen so much behind?

In the White Paper issued by the Coalition Government in March 1945, there was a plan for the erection of 220,000 new permanent houses within two years of the defeat of Germany. That was mocked at as totally inadequate by Labour candidates during the general election, and yet only about 28,000 permanent houses had been completed in the last 17 months.

Lord Addison (Leader of the House), replying on the debate, said that the Coalition Government's estimate of the houses to be provided within two years after the end of the war with Germnay was, in view of the shortages that were bound to prevail, a fairy-like idea.

Up to September 30 the number of permanent houses built or building was 198,000 and of temporary houses 83,000. The two together totalled 282,324. Of these completed there were 31,000 permanent houses and 57,000 temporary ones. The numbers under construction were 166,000 permanent and 26,000 temporary houses. For this to have been done fifteen months after the end of the war was an exceedingly creditable performance.

Referring to houses built or building in rural councils for agricultural workers he said the total number of tenders approved by local authorities was 29,478. The number to be built by private builders was 15,917, making a total up to September 30 of 45,395. It was a long way from what they hoped to achieve but it was an encouraging start.

21 November 1946   *p.8*

HOUSING SITUATION ANALYSED
Bigger Labour Force Required and Better Co-ordination
– Select Committee

From our Political Correspondent

Westminster, Wednesday.

While Mr. Aneurin Bevan, the Minister of Health, was telling the Building Industries' Congress in London to-day that 'the rate of building in the building industry is not as satisfactory as it should be,' the Select Committee on Estimates of the House of Commons has published a much wider analysis of the housing situation (House of Commons Paper No 191, price 6d.).

The committee finds a danger of overlap in functions between Government departments, a need for firm contracts to be placed earlier, a need to reduce the number of forms in the system of licensing and to simplify them, a case for better co-ordination between departments, particularly in the regions, and for a larger labour force in building and in the making of building materials.

21 November 1946   *p.8*

MR. BEVAN'S PROMISE TO BUILDERS
Full Details of Government's Programme

Mr. Aneurin Bevan, the Minister of Health, addressing the Building Industries' Congress at the Central Hall, Westminster, yesterday, said on the whole the housing picture was satisfactory, though the number of houses completed showed a tendency to fall behind the number under construction. The available building force was spread too thinly over the contracts placed.

'It is clear,' he said, 'that the rate of building is not as satisfactory as it should be. The industry in 1947 will have to give closer attention to this aspect.'

Only in one or two instances were local authorities lagging, and, said Mr. Bevan, 'I am preparing a few quick kicks for them in the immediate future.' One of the most gratifying features of the year's development was that the rural authorities had marched ahead of other authorities in housing progress.

The Minister promised that he would tell the leaders of the building industry what the Government's programme was likely to be and would provide them with detailed and concise information so that they could form an estimate of the situation.

BLACK-MARKET REPAIRS

Speaking of black-market repairs, Mr. Bevan said, 'In 1947 all our plans will be nugatory unless we get some better measure of discipline in the industry.

'There is something really obscene about the large number of people who are having all kinds of unnecessary decorations done at the expense of people who could get new houses if they did not do it.'

30 November 1946   *p.4*

Leader   **THE HOUSING FIGURES**

Detailed analysis of the latest housing figures shows that there is ground for a slight abatement of dissatisfaction. By far their most gratifying feature is the rapid and sustained advance over the last three months in the rate at which temporary houses are being completed.

24 December 1946   *p.4*

Leader   **EIGHTEEN MONTHS' HOUSES**

The November housing returns have not fulfilled the hopes held out by the rate of improvement in the three preceding months. The only gain is that for the first time the number of permanent houses completed under local authority contract in Great Britain as a whole exceeds the number finished by private builders under licence. It also exceeds the corresponding figure for October but the margin of improvement is still getting smaller. Evidently the impetus of Mr. Bevan's drive for 'roofs on by Christmas' has barely sufficed to neutralise the seasonal downward trend.

Health

If the Minister of Health's considerable difficulties in his housing policy had to some extent been shared by those of the Ministry of Planning there was to be no such joint shouldering of the burden in his other main area of responsibility, health services. 1946 opened with a thinly veiled statement of intent by the BMA which became more explicit as the year progressed.

3 January 1946   *p.6*

B.M.A. APPEAL
Parliamentary Fund to be Replenished

From our Political Correspondent

Fleet Street, Wednesday.

An appeal just issued by the British Medical Association to its members to contribute to a 'medical representation in Parliament fund' has aroused some curiosity since it appears just as the doctors are deeply concerned about the Government's plans for a national health service. 'Money subscribed to this fund,' states the circular, 'can be used to strengthen the position of the profession in relation to Parliament in ways for which association funds cannot be employed. We need a substantial fund and we need it soon.'

Dr. Charles Hill, secretary of the association, states that this is a 'routine appeal.' The fund has been in existence for many years, but no subscriptions were invited during the war years. Now it has been decided to replenish the fund. Dr. Hill adds that the fund, though Parliamentary, is non-political, and that doctors of various parties have been helped with their election expenses to a modest extent in the past.

One must assume, therefore, that the sentence 'We need a substantial fund and we need it soon' is, so to speak, a flourish. Certainly there is no lack of doctors in the present Parliament. On the Government side they include Lord Addison and Dr. Edith

Summerskill, who are both Ministers; Mr. Somerville Hastings, who is president of the Socialist Medical Association, and Dr. L. Haden Guest. Doctors in Opposition include Sir Ernest Graham-Little and Lieutenant Colonel M. Stoddart-Scott, who was an Assistant Director of Medical Services during the war and is a persistent questioner in the Commons.

18 February 1946   *p.6*

DOCTORS AND STATE MEDICAL SERVICE
Demand for 'Maximum Freedom of Choice'

A conference of general medical practitioners, specialists, pharmacists, and other health workers was held in Manchester yesterday to discuss some of the problems which must arise from a State medical service.

Although the meeting was sponsored by the Socialist Medical Association a large proportion of those who attended are not members of the organisation, and there appeared to be some foundation for the view expressed by Dr. S.A. Winstanley, a member of the B.M.A. council, that opinion is 'gradually sliding a little' towards acceptance of a salaried service. If, however, there was support for a State scheme some anxiety was also felt regarding the dangers of bureaucratic interference.

Dr. Richard Doil, who led the discussion, outlined the arguments in support of a system of 'centralism' which, by ensuring subordinate initiative, would contain the necessary safeguards against bureaucracy. He wished to see the delegation of authority for running health centres right down to the smallest unit, so as to ensure that the administration would be in the closest touch with the 'consumers.' For the service to be humane and efficient there would have to be maximum freedom of choice.

Dr. Winstanley addressed a word of warning to the Socialist Medical Association. 'I believe most of its members are relatively young,' he said, 'but I hope they are not so young that they have not yet learned to appreciate the value of freedom. I am very much afraid we shall lose our freedom entirely. If the system comes in and every practitioner becomes a civil servant, then freedom has gone for all time. It will not be possible to unscramble the egg.'

DOCTORS' FIGHTING FUND
Campaign if Cabinet is 'Obdurate'

Every doctor in the country is being asked to guarantee at least £25 towards a 'fighting' fund which is being established to 'further the cause of the medical profession in any major dispute which may occur between the Government and the medical profession in connection with the proposals for the National Health Service.'

It is sponsored by the Council of the British Medical Association, which, with a membership of over 50,000, has guaranteed £100,000, and every doctor is urged to guarantee as much as he can – at least £25 is suggested. The National Insurance Defence Trust is to consider what its contribution will be.

Details are given in the 'British Medical Journal.' The fund will be in two parts, one from which administrative, propaganda, and allied expenditure will be met and the other to compensate practitioners who, because of their adherence to the cause of the profession, suffer exceptional financial hardship.

A leading article in the Journal states: 'Should Parliament prove obdurate and refuse to modify proposals in the bill which the profession might consider to strike at the essential freedoms of medicine, the doctors might have to decide not to work in the new service.' Patients would have to be served outside the service.

'It is to be hoped that the bill will be so framed as to make the willing co-operation of doctors possible and so avert a costly and bitter struggle which, whatever the outcome, will leave behind it a sense of frustration and discontent.'

'PURE BLUFF'

Dr. D. Stark Murray, vice-president of the Socialist Medical Association, commenting last night on the B.M.A. statement, said: 'This is pure bluff. The B.M.A. Council knows it has just completed very satisfactory negotiations on compensation, and the terms doctors will be offered will make any strike impossible.

'In any case, the B.M.A. represents not more than 65 per cent of the profession and, as its own questionnaire showed, 60 per cent of its members are in favour of a complete health service and 62 per cent voted in favour of salaries or basic salaries as a method of payment.'

Leader   **STRIKE FUND**

The Council of the British Medical Association is asking for a minimum guarantee of £25 from every doctor to create a fund which will be used at the Council's discretion 'to further the cause of the medical profession' in any dispute it may have with the Government over the forthcoming National Health Service Bill. It is, of course, quite right and proper that the B.M.A., as a trade union, should try to bring pressure on Parliament to secure favourable terms and conditions of work from a prospective employer. But the cost of such a campaign, we are told, will be borne from existing resources; the main purpose of the new fund will be to compensate doctors who suffer financial hardship through boycotting the public service 'should Parliament prove obdurate' and refuse to modify certain proposals in the Bill. The guarantees are to be called in if and when the Council deem it expedient. But the Council already knows the worst of Mr. Bevan's intentions. Moreover, reports indicate that his Bill will by no means exceed the Government's electoral mandate, and that it will not deal with the doctor's scale of pay. The Council's announcement must therefore be interpreted as a threat to raise a strike fund and call a strike unless members of Parliament betray their constituents' trust in matters of general public policy. As such it is to be deplored, whether meant as a bluff or in earnest, for it can only cause the medical profession to forfeit public confidence at a time when its disinterested counsel is most needed.

On 21 March 1946 Aneurin Bevan introduced the National Health Service Bill to Parliament A White Paper was also published explaining the main provision. The 'Guardian' expressed general approval in its leading article but felt that the Minister had:

Leader   **THE HEALTH BILL**

. . . retained the worst feature of the original plan for a general practitioner service. Not only will doctors be free to stay out and practise privately (as, indeed, they should be); they will also be allowed to take private fees from patients who have already paid in taxes and insurance contributions for treatment by them as participants in the public service. The dangers of this provision were recognised in the Coalition White Paper – which could suggest no means of guarding against them – as well as in the

Labour party's critical commentary. The plain fact is that no safeguard is possible. Any patient seeking the attention of a doctor in the public service will have to declare whether or not he proposes to pay extra for it. Doubtless all doctors will explain that he will get the same treatment in either case and many doctors will mean it but the patient will not believe it. Poor patients will claim their rights and be convinced that they are getting an inferior service, rich patients – and many others who cannot really afford it – will insist on paying fees in the expectation of preferential treatment, and will go elsewhere if they do not get what they are paying for. This, in short, is a false freedom that can only survive to the extent that it is abused. It must inevitably poison the doctor–patient relationship. It is the reef on which this splendid venture with all its prospects for developments might founder at the outset. Whatever else the Parliamentary Labour party may decide to let pass in the way of provisions that conflict with its declared policy it must draw the line at this.

23 March 1946   *p.3*

BMA STATEMENT ON THE HEALTH BILL
Members May be Advised Not to Participate

From Our London Staff

Dr. H. Guy Dain, Chairman of the B.M.A. Council, said yesterday after giving an interpretation of his council's report that it remained for the members to decide whether or not to participate in the Government's scheme. Unless it were modified considerably the association would advise its members not to participate, but Dr. Dain emphasised that until the members had made their views known there was no way of assessing the collective opinion of the profession.

25 March 1946   *p.5*

DOCTORS WILL NOT STRIKE — B.M.A. SECRETARY
'Much Good' in Bill

Although doctors may disagree with legislation, the question of depriving the public of their services will never arise. Dr. C. Hill, secretary of the British Medical Association, made this clear yesterday during a factual analysis of the National Health Service proposals at a meeting attended by some 700 doctors at Wimbledon Town Hall.

While there was much good in the National Health Service Bill, the Minister's proposals, he said, would break up existing partnerships and destroy what was good in group practice before even the first health centre was built.

The good in the bill included the regional organisation of hospitals. 'But the public must ask itself whether it wants the family doctor to be paid by the State, to work in State premises, to be responsible to the State, whether it wants the consultants and specialists to work in State hospitals. These things would inevitably destroy the freedom, the responsibility, the initiative, the independence of judgment and speech which are essential to British medicine.'

26 March 1946   p.4

Leader   **MEDICAL REACTIONS**

Mr. Bevan's Bill is not designed to secure the best form of national health service that is possible in present circumstances. Rather has he sought to win the maximum degree of professional co-operation short of making his scheme unworkable or precluding its later evolution into something nearer to ideal. In that aim he seems assured of success. There will of course be Conservative opposition to some of his proposals on ideological grounds but the main demands arising from the professional anxieties, interests, and prejudices of medical men have largely been met – often it may be argued to an extent that seriously compromises the principles of public responsibility. The Socialist Medical Association, though conscious of substantial defects, appears disposed to overlook them for the sake of a speedy enactment of the major reforms. The 'Lancet,' representing a middle standpoint, recognises in the course of a broadly favourable leading article that a great deal has been conceded to professional opinion. At the other extreme the Council of the British Medical Association is hard put to it to find material points of conflict between the Bill and its own basic principles except on two issues. It is driven to seek cause for battle in hypothetical dangers or in something dangerously near misrepresentation.

These two objectives, however, deserve careful attention. One is that industrial medicine remains the preserve of the Ministry of Labour, as also, it might be added, does non-medical rehabilitation. . . .

The other is that regional bodies should be responsible for all treatment as distinct from environmental services in order to secure their 'effective functional integration.'

. . . The difficulty is that as yet we have no elective public authority at the regional level which could answer to the people

114

or the discharge of such comprehensive duties. Joint boards of local government representatives advised by professional councils, such as the Coalition White paper suggested, might have served at a pinch but the doctors would have none of them. If responsibility is now divided it is because Mr. Bevan had deferred in respect of the hospital and specialist services to medical abhorrence of local government control.

. . . Political opposition will presumably concentrate on the nationalisation of hospitals. It is generally agreed that an economical, efficient and comprehensive hospital service must be organised on a regional basis, but spokesmen of both voluntary and municipal hospital authorities have joined in pleading that the regional body need only plan and advise, leaving them as hospital owners to execute and administer. That plea, however, has been put out of court by the revelations of the regional hospital surveys sponsored by the Ministry of Health. The overlappings, gaps and deficiencies in the present service are far too grave to be put right by 'co-ordination' of this half-hearted order.

. . . In fact, however, Mr. Bevan's provision for the enlistment of local initiative, voluntary service and charitable impulse are so liberal that the voluntary hospitals will lose no freedom which they would keep under their own scheme except their freedom to neglect or to defy the behests of the regional boards.

28 March 1946   *p.6*

DR. HILL'S 'OFFER' ON HEALTH BILL
'Clear Up Differences'

Dr. Charles Hill, secretary of the British Medical Association, speaking at Bristol yesterday on the National Health Service Bill, said: 'If the Government is going to steam-roller the bill through we are in for a most unholy disturbance. But if they will clear up differences then the medical profession will whole-heartedly co-operate.

'What has the voluntary hospital done to deserve the fate of complete annihilation, for that is what it is? The new proposals will provide an inhuman, aloof, remote hospital service in a country where local and voluntary hospitals alike have a reputation for performing a vital, personal and human service.'

B.M.A. QUESTIONS
Doctors and National Health Service

'The freedom of the doctors, as of the public, is at stake,' said
Dr. Charles Hill, secretary of the British Medical Association, at
a meeting in the Albert Hall, Manchester, on Saturday, attended
by about 1,500 Lancashire and Cheshire doctors. Yesterday he
addressed an equally large meeting in Liverpool.

Dr. Hill answered many questions on the National Health
Service Bill, but before the Manchester meeting began he indicated
to reporters that it was really a private conference and that they
should adhere to a summary which he supplied. This was largely
rhetorical.

'Are you satisfied,' asked Dr. Hill, 'that you can give the best
personal service if you are salaried servants of the State or of any
other authority?' Doctors would look at this question from the point
of view of the individual patient. Did it matter that the citizen should
have the right to choose and to reject his family doctor? If so, could
that right be maintained if doctors were paid in any other way than
according to the work they did and the responsibility they
undertook? Sooner or later choice would go if doctors were salaried
officers of the State.

'Will it be good for your patients that your progress in your
profession should depend upon the judgment of any higher body
rather than on that of the patient?' A warning followed this
question: 'The certificates which you will sign will be in effect,
blank cheques on the Treasury.' Should they be influenced in their
professional judgment by any thoughts of the solvency of this or
any other fund or by the reaction of the Treasury, which also paid
them? Doctors should be free to serve what they believed to be
right; they should not be in a position to be influenced by the State
in the interests of its funds.

SOCIALIST DOCTORS' REPLY TO B.M.A. CRITICISM OF HEALTH BILL
'Ignorant of Contents'

A spirited reply to critics of the National Health Service Bill
was made at a Socialist Medical Association meeting at the
Midland Hotel, Manchester, yesterday by Captain W.D. Griffiths,
M.P. for Moss Side Division and chairman of the Manchester branch
of the association, and Dr. D. Stark Murray, vice-president of the

association. Captain Griffiths described the bill as a great step forward and spoke of how it would overcome the shortcomings of the present medical service as applied to his own constituents, who were typical of a broad section of the British public.

Dr. Stark Murray said that he had met no considerable body of opinion either amongst his colleagues or his patients opposed to the bill. Nor had he yet met any doctor who had yet subscribed to the British Medical Association 'strike fund.' Displaying a large sheaf of cuttings, he said they were just some of the statements made this week on behalf of the B.M.A., and he was prepared to find in any one inaccuracies as to how the British system of government worked, ignorance of how the medical profession conducted its business, and ignorance of what was contained in the proposed bill.

9 April 1946 *p.5*

TORIES AND THE HEALTH BILL
Rejection Motion

LOCAL LOYALTY TO HOSPITALS

From our Political Correspondent

Westminster, Monday.

The Opposition's specialists on health matters who have been considering the National Health Service Bill since March 21 tonight produced an amendment for the rejection of the second reading which should come before the House of Commons soon after the Easter recess. The amendment is in the following terms—

That this House while wishing to establish a comprehensive health service declines to give a second reading to a bill which prejudices the patient's right to an independent family doctor, which retards the development of the hospital services by destroying local ownership and gravely menaces all charitable foundations by diverting, to purposes other than those intended by the donors, the trust funds of voluntary hospitals and which weakens the responsibility of local authorities without planning the health services as a whole.

STATE HOSPITALS
'Purpose Will be Purely Material'

A 'grave' picture of the implications of a State hospital service was drawn yesterday by Mr. J.W.A. Earle, Chairman, at the annual meeting of the committee of management of the Manchester Northern Hospital. The inevitable purpose of such a hospital, he said, must be to restore people to health in order to take part in the world's affairs – a merely material purpose.

He trembled to think what might be the result. A hospital might consider whether a person was worth the trouble of curing; was he the kind of person who ought to live, grow up, and have children? Referring to a sterilisation ward in a Frankfort hospital, which a member of the board had seen, Mr. Earle asked: 'What is the logical halting-place between that and using people for experiments?'

Speaking of the proposed 'pooling' of hospital endowments, he said the Northern Hospital had over £95,000 given by people to that hospital and for no other purpose. 'Why that should be taken and used to pay off the bank overdraft of another hospital at the other end of England is beyond my understanding. As a lawyer I call that a gross breach of trust and in the highest degree immoral.'

Leader **MEDICAL PRACTICES**

Politicians and doctors alike have now had time to digest Mr. Bevan's proposals for a national health service. Criticism is increasingly addressed to the terms of the Bill itself (or at least to the hypothetical consequences of the enactment) rather than to the principles which it was expected to embody. The force of this reactionary opposition has been much reduced in the process – so much, indeed, that Mr. Bevan may well have more trouble with complaints from his own party that he has needlessly and dangerously compromised the policy to which it undertook to give effect. As expressed in their motion for the rejection of the Bill the strategy of Opposition leaders is purely defensive. It advocates no alternative and maintains no consistent principle but impartially voices the negative reactions of the several interests that consider themselves adversely affected. The doctor's view has yet to be formulated but the success of the British Medical Association's fund will, as the secretary has observed, afford a fairly good indication of the professional attitude. Meanwhile the B.M.A. council is endeavouring to mobilise opposition to four features of the Bill –

the prohibition of the traffic in publicly remunerated practices, the arrangements for controlling the distribution of practitioners, the form of remuneration, and the health centre provisions – not so much on their merits as on the ground that they would lead 'sooner or later; directly or indirectly' to a whole time State medical service.

26 April 1946 p.5

LIBERAL CRITICS OF HEALTH BILL
'Far Too Much Left to Regulation'

From our Political Correspondent

Westminster, Thursday.

The House of Commons will start the second-reading debate of the National Health Service Bill when it reassembles on Tuesday. The Opposition has tabled a motion for the rejection of the second reading. The Liberals, who appointed a special committee to examine the bill in great detail, have finished their work, and to-night Lieutenant Colonel Frank Byers, the Liberal Chief Whip, has issued a statement on their behalf.

The Liberals welcome 'the proposal to set up a National Health Service which will be available to all irrespective of their means,' and it is pointed out that the bill in many respects follows clearly the Liberal party's report, 'Health for the people,' published in 1942. Nevertheless, the Liberals claim that the bill deals only with cure and ignores the prevention of disease and the maintenance of health. To that extent it is not comprehensive.

INADEQUATE CONTROL

'The primary and overriding criticism,' continues the statement, 'is that far too much is left to regulation, with the result that the Minister can make vital alterations to the service and can modify initial arrangements drastically. Parliament has then inadequate control over the development of the health service and will be unable adequately to supervise the actual provisions of the bill.'

Another criticism is of the omission from the scheme of the industrial medical service – a most retrogressive factor.' The statement adds, 'Great developments have been made in the industrial medical service during the war, and it is felt that these will largely be lost if nothing is done to place the industrial medical service on a permanent footing in the Ministry of Health.'

It is also claimed that the nursing and midwifery professions hae not been treated adequately in the bill. They should at least be represented on the general council, regional hospital boards, hospital management committees, and boards of governors of teaching hospitals.

Other points made in the statement are that while all hospitals should have their basic needs met from state funds, they should also be allowed to raise money locally for the provision of special amenities, research, and experiment; that the remuneration of doctors should be 'largely obtained from capitation fees rather than from a high basic salary' to avoid 'the danger of the doctor being reduced to the rank of a salaried civil servant'; and that the public should have access to some such official as a public relations officer at regional boards and management committees so that grievances could be ventilated and redressed.

30 April 1946   *p.4*

Leader   **MEDICINE'S DEBATE**

During the next three days the general framework of Mr. Bevan's scheme for a national health service will be discussed at length by representatives of the patient (in the House of Commons) and of the doctor (in the Panel Conference and the special representative meeting of the British Medical Association). The major debate on the second reading will be exceptional in that the broad purpose, scope and character of the proposals in question have long since been exhaustively canvassed and approved by all parties. Attention will therefore be concentrated on the particular innovations for which the Government alone is responsible. . . . The focus of criticism has tended to shift from the provisions for hospital reorganisation to the arrangements for a general practitioner service. By excepting the teaching hospitals from transfer to State ownership and substituting regional boards for joint authorities Mr. Bevan seems to have won at least the acquiescence of specialist opinion; now it is becoming evident that the local authorities also are prepared to consent. The attitude of the B.M.A. remains to be determined.

MR. BEVAN'S CASE FOR HEALTH SERVICE BILL
Doctors 'Not to be Minister's Slaves'

Moving the second reading of the National Health Service Bill in the House of Commons yesterday,

Mr. ANEURAN BEVAN (Minister of Health) said the first reason why a health scheme was necessary was because it had been the firm conclusion of all parties that money ought not to stand in the way of obtaining an efficient health service. It was cardinal to a proper health organisation that a person ought not to be financially deterred from seeking medical assistance at the earliest possible stage.

Dealing with hospital facilities, the Minister said that the hospital organisation had grown up with no plan and no system and was unevenly distributed over the country. In the older industrial districts hospital facilities were inadequate and many hospitals were too small to provide general hospital facilities. 'Although I am not a devotee of bigness for bigness's sake, I would rather be kept alive in the efficient, cold altruism of a large hospital,' Mr. Bevan declared, 'than expire in a gush of warm sympathy in a small one.' (Laughter and cheers.)

Declaring that the scheme would universalise the best of advice and treatment, he said, they were short of many things – dentists, nurses, and hospital accommodation – so that it would be some time before the bill could fructify fully in effective universal service, but it was the object to provide it as soon as possible. Specialists would be available not only at institutions but for domicilary visits when needed. The practical difficulties of carrying out these services were very great. 'When I approached this problem I made up my mind that I was not going to permit any sectional or vested interests to stand in the way of providing this very valuable service.' . . .

Concluding, the Minister said that the scheme would place this country in the forefront of all countries in the world in medical services. 'It will lift the shadow from millions of homes. It will keep many people alive who would otherwise have died. It will relieve suffering. It will produce a higher standard for the medical profession and will be a great contribution to the wellbeing of our common people.'

Prolonged cheers greeted the end of Mr. Bevan's speech.

M.P. CHALLENGED

Mr. RICHARD LAW (C.–Kensington, S.), opening the debate for the Opposition, said it was an extraordinary thing that a Minister who had absolutely no administrative experience of a Government department and no great knowledge of the subject matter of the bill should set his own intuition and his own judgment against all that was most informed in the medical profession and those connected with the hospital services. The British Hospitals' Association, the British Medical Association, and the British Dental Association were opposed. The three royal colleges had criticised it with varying emphasis.

Here Mr. BEVAN jumped to his feet and asked: 'Have the royal colleges gone on record against the bill?'

Mr. LAW repeated that they had criticised the bill for various reasons. 'I think I am right in saying that the Royal College of Surgeons passed a resolution which condemned aspects of the Minister's proposals in the most categorical terms. The Royal College of Obstetricians did the same. They said, if my memory serves me, that the Minister's proposals would lead to a great increase in maternal mortality.'

This statement was greeted by cries of dissent from the Government benches. There were loud counter-cheers from the Opposition.

Mr. BEVAN: I must ask Mr. Law to amplify his statement, which might cause a great deal of alarm. Does he say that the Royal College of Obstetricians have gone on record that the bill will increase the maternal mortality rate?

There were shouts of 'Quote the document.'

Mr. LAW: Unfortunately, I haven't the document and therefore I am unable to quote it.

Government supporters set up a shout of 'Withdraw'.

1 May 1946   *p.4*

A BIG 'HOUSE' FOR MR. BEVAN
Masterful presentation of Health Bill

The legislative machine is whirring again. Mr. Aneurin Bevan was 'up' at 3 00 to-day in the House of Commons/presenting the great National Health Bill at the same time, if one is not too irreverent, as the conveyor belt was carrying the Trade Disputes Bill into the Lords.

But let us stick to Mr. Bevan. This was his day. He had a big House and a most flattering reception from the Government benches and an hour and a quarter later he sat down to salvo after salvo of cheers from the same quarter. And he deserved it. He had moved the second reading of his bill in a speech that was masterful yet conciliatory, cogent and persuasive and brightened by some amusing dialectics at the close when he came to answer the Opposition and the Liberal National amendments. . . .

Here was a real Parliamentarian acting on the House through living speech and not the meticulous reading of a manuscript.

Leader   **MEDICAL FEES**

    The first professional practitioner to speak in yesterday's debate on the Health Bill concentrated his criticism on its weakest point. By permitting patients who could claim free treatment to pay private fees, Dr. Comyns argued, it permitted doctors to give two standards of treatment. It might be contended that the advantages of leaving doctors free to choose between public and private practice outweigh the evils of a dual standard, but when the same doctor works in both fields and his patients must choose whether to pay him extra fees or not the evils are magnified without any compensating gain. These evils are in no way diminished because the patient, having chosen to claim his rights without extra payment, cannot change his mind without changing his doctor. Nor is it any justification to point out that if all patients claim their rights this provision will be a dead letter. Mr. Bevan, to do him justice, used no such argument. He apologised for the offending clause and acknowledged that if the amount of fee-paying proved great the whole system would have broken down. He offered only pragmatic and rather weak excuses for taking such a risk. In the first place he was confident that there would in fact be little fee-paying, and in the second he thought it could not be prohibited without creating a black market. We must hope that his optimism will be vindicated: but is a black market any less black because the Government tolerates it?

HEALTH BILL CLASH
Greenwood–Willink

359-172 FOR SECOND READING

From our Political Correspondent

Westminster, Thursday.

    The National Health Service Bill passed its second reading in the House of Commons to-night by 359 votes to 172. A great attendance of members had been heating up during the closing stages of the debate. There was a jubilant Labour cheer when the figures were announced, but less important bills have stirred as much enthusiasm.

DOCTORS' OPPOSITION TO HEALTH BILL
Hecklers at B.M.A. Meetings

Some opposition was reported yesterday at two public meetings organised by members of the British Medical Association to put forward their views on the National Health Bill. At Golder's Green, a statement by Sir Alfred Webb-Johnson, president of the Royal College of Surgeons, that the Minister of Health had the power to create a State monopoly, was greeted with the cry, 'About time too.'

Dr. Charles Hill, secretary of the B.M.A., who described the Health Minister's speech in the Commons as 'both statesmanlike and conciliatory,' said they agreed with Mr. Bevan that hospital development must not be at the caprice of charity, but to make a monopoly of hospital ownership to relieve it of the necessity of competing by virtue of the quality of its service with non-State establishments was contrary to public interest. . . . he said, 'We welcome the Minister's attitude on the debate. We hope it means that during the committee stages he will make such changes in his bill as will secure within the general framework the essential freedom of the individual patient, the essential freedom of the individual doctor and locally owned and locally responsible hospitals.'

There were indications, he thought, that Mr. Bevan did not desire to pursue the extreme course some of his supporters desired.

On 9 May 1946 the Spens Report on the remuneration of general practitioners was published.

Leader ## THE DOCTOR'S PAY

It is unfortunate that the Spens Report on the remuneration of doctors taking part in a comprehensive national health service was not published at an earlier stage for much of the less reasonable opposition to Mr. Bevan's Bill within the profession may well be attributable to the fear that a public service could not be expected to yield such high rewards as private practice. In fact, the Spens Committee proposes a substantial degree of levelling up and though the Government is not yet committed there is every likelihood that the terms it offers will, by and large, be no less generous. To the followers of humbler callings a service which will bring over £1,000 a year to three-quarters of its practitioners between the ages of forty and fifty, with more above than below the £1,300 mark and some earning up to £2,500, will indeed seem enviable. But before voicing any protest they should reflect first on the long preliminary training which few sons of middle-class families can take without getting into debt; secondly, on the urgent need to attract the abler doctors into the public service and the abler students into the medical profession; and, thirdly, on the fact that the health scheme aims at relieving doctors as well as patients from any financial anxiety that might interfere with its effectiveness. It should also be realised that the professional class as a whole, on whose expanding numbers and rising calibre our society increasingly relies, has suffered a reduction in its standard of living so disproportionately large that it can hardly compete with business and trade for suitable recruits.

20 May 1946   *p.6*

DOCTORS AT HEALTH CENTRES
Salary Provision Urged

A proposal that doctors who work in the new health centres of the National Health service may be paid by salary if they choose was approved by the Socialist Medical Association at its annual meeting at the Conway Hall, London, yesterday. The suggestion was part of a resolution warmly welcoming the National Health Service Bill.

'The association urges that the administrative provisions should be an interim measure pending the reform of local government as a whole,' the resolution stated. It recommended a single administrative body 'at a regional level' under democratic control, and responsible for all the services of the region.

22 May 1946   *p.8*

SPECIALIST 'PRIMA DONNAS' OF MEDICAL PROFESSION — MR. BEVAN
'Making Arrangements for Their Swan-Song'

Mr. Aneurin Bevan, Minister of Health, in the committee stage of the National Health Service Bill in the House of Commons yesterday, described specialists as the 'prima donnas' of the medical profession, and when an Opposition member asked if he suggested that under the new system the medical prima donna would disappear, replied: 'No, we may be making concessions to an intransigent figure, but I am making arrangements for his swan song.'

Mr. F. Messer (Lab.—Tottenham) moved an amendment to delete a sub-section which provides that the Minister may allow any specialist serving on the staff of a hospital which provides hospital and specialist services to make arrangements for the treatment of his private patients.

Mr. Messer said this was a grave departure from the principle held by many Labour members. The Minister would be taking over hospitals which had been used by specialists for the treatment of their own cases, but there was a great danger if specialists who might be servants of the State were entitled to treat their patients privately and were paid by those patients for their services. It would mean better treatment for those who could pay, he said.

He agreed that the Minister would be unable to accept his amendment, but he hoped Mr. Bevan would be able to give them an assurance that as the service developed they could look forward to a really socialised medical service.

Dr. Somerville Hastings (Lab.–Barking) asked why a patient should want to pay unless he expected to get better treatment.

Mrs E.M. Braddock (Lab.–Liverpool) thought that they would lose some of the best specialists unless they had authority to attend their private patients.

Dr. Stephen Taylor (Lab.–Barnet) urged that they should make whole-time practice in the hospitals so attractive that in future every specialist would elect to become a whole-time specialist.

Mr. Bevan, replying, said that this clause had given him more anxious thought than any other part of the bill. 'I would be extremely dismayed,' he said, 'if we created a health system under which the bad principles drove out the good. From the beginning there must be a heavy bias in favour of full-time services. What we are endeavouring to do is to create conditions which will induce specialists to spend all their time at the hospitals – for their own sake, for the sake of the patients, and for the sake of the students.'

Dr. Morgan (Lab.–Rochdale) protested against some of the things that had been said against the doctors whose standard of conduct and ethics is as high as in any other profession, as high as in the trade unions, as high even as amongst M.P.s.

A Member: Beg pardon. (Laughter)

'Therefore so far as I am concerned, I will encourage the specialist to have even his consultations in the hospitals. What would be disastrous would be that by non-acceptance of these principles a racket of nursing homes should grow up. That might happen if this amendment were accepted. Specialists might even "hop away to some other country" and then we should lose their services which were invaluable.'

Mr. Messer agreed to withdraw his amendment and the committee adjourned until to-day.

MR. BEVAN AND SPECIALISTS' FEES IN HOSPITALS
No Exploitation of State Facilities

The Standing Committee on the National Health Service under the chairmanship of Mr. Bowles (Nuneaton) yesterday considered an amendment to omit the power of the Minister to regulate the fees chargeable by specialists to private patients in one of the new State hospitals.

It was moved by Mr. H. Strauss (Con.–Combined Universities) who suggested that this power of limitation was not only bad in itself but was not even good socialism.

. . . Mr. Aneurin Bevan (Minister of Health) said that if he thought the bill as it stood would drive specialists away from the hospitals he would accept the amendment but in fact many of the best hospitals in London already limited the fees chargeable by specialists and the specialists themselves had agreed to this for their own protection.

The amendment was rejected.

PAYING THE DOCTOR
'Competition with Security' – Mr. Bevan

An Opposition amendment to the National Health Service Bill suggesting that doctors in certain scattered areas should be paid an annual salary in addition to capitation fees was defeated by 25 votes to 12 when the standing committee resumed at the House of Commons yesterday and the clause dealing with the arrangements for the general medical services was ordered to stand as part of the bill.

Mr. Bevan (Health Minister) said the argument for a basic salary had been firmly established, but he accepted the proposition that a full-salaried service was not acceptable under existing conditions. He was attempting to introduce into doctors' remuneration two elements. Security for the individual and competition in order to sweeten and refresh the service.

HEALTH SERVICES BILL
Mr. Bevan and the Regional Boards

Mr. Aneurin Bevan, Minister of Health, speaking of the Health Bill to the members of the Royal College of Nursing at the British Medical Association Hall, London, last night, said it would be foolish for a Minister to imagine that he could have universal enthusiasm. 'If you are to make progress you have to tread upon a few corns.'

A statement by Mr. Bevan that some nurses had said they wanted representation upon the regional boards was greeted with loud applause, but the Minister added, 'No one is going to have representation on the regional boards – not even the doctors. These boards are not going to become conferences of different interests.' Nurses, he said, would have their own standing advisory committee.

Voluntary hospital funds would not be taken from the hospitals, he explained: they will be distributed among the regional boards of the hospitals.

NATIONAL HEALTH BILL'S LAST STAGES
An Attentive House

REVIVAL OF OLD CONFLICT ON REMOTE CONTROL

From our Parliamentary Correspondent

Westminster, Monday.

The House of Commons has spent a slogging day on the report stage of the National Health Service Bill. The bill can still compel the attention of a large House – large, that is, for this advanced stage. The attendance at any time this evening would have flattered the second reading of some bills. One could not help contrasting it with the two score members who graced the colonial policy debate a few days ago. A cynic might say that Nigerians have no votes. But that is no explanation of the difference. Not all members can be experts on colonial affairs and the majority of them are willing to leave Nigeria to the experts.

No members can afford to be indifferent about this great measure of health reform, and to do them justice few members have any temptation to be indifferent. Through all the stages of the bill the House – Conservatives as much as Labour – has got down to the job of making it the best possible bill on the lines laid down by the Government. These lines, of course, have not always commanded support of the Tories or even of all Labour members, but there has been precious little that could be described as factious opposition.

We saw again to-day an old conflict revived in all its vigour – the conflict over the diversion of functions from the lesser local authorities. The non-county boroughs, urban councils and rural councils, lose to the county councils the administration of the maternity and child-welfare services and Mr. Lipson, the very Independent member for Cheltenham, moved a new clause that would enable county councils to hand back to these local authorities this responsibility for the maternity and child-welfare services.

LABOUR SUPPORT

Mr. Aneurin Bevan scarcely waited for the arguments to develop. He knew them only too well. He knew also that some Labour members favoured the new clause quite as much as any Tory. The Rev. G. Lang, the Labour member for Stalybridge and Hyde, actually seconded it, and Mr. T.J. Brooks, the Labour member for Rothwell, supported it. Even Mr. Piratin, the Communist, backed it.

The arguments for the new clause were not new, of course. These are that the bill's provision in this respect is all of a piece with the present tendency to whittle away the powers of local authorities and to substitute remote control. In this case the powers are going to the county councils, which (so it is alleged) are often reactionary, and are being taken from county boroughs and urban councils, which are frequently far more efficient and progressive.

Mr. Bevan struck against the new clause with all his force. He delivered himself with great energy and a lot of digging at the impalpable air with his right index finger. The new clause raised a crucial issue. Its incorporation in the bill would wreck it. It would produce a breakdown in the administration. The county boroughs were backward, even though they might have a proud history. Also, they were too poor in the revenue even to discharge their existing functions effectively, much more any new functions.

MR. BEVAN A PROTECTOR

Mr. Bevan repelled with vigour the suggestion that the Government is undermining local government. He presented himself as a protector of the local authorities. Had he not served on every type of local authority? That, as Mr. Bevan urged, was not to say we must not have a reorganisation of local government. That would come, but it would be reorganisation that adapted local government to the demands of the changing circumstances of the times, a process which would vitalise, not devitalise, it.

It was pure Bevan, if one may put it so, and obviously commended itself to many members of the Labour party, though there were some of the Government's supporters who clearly did not find it altogether convincing. Mr. Piratin made the shrewd point that the social legislation the Government is carrying out is bringing about its own reorganisation of local government and that all the Government will have to do later on will be to introduce a bill to legalise an accomplished fact.

Mr. Key, the Under Secretary, advised the Labour critics to have more confidence in the efficiency of the instruments Mr. Bevan had chosen, and with that the division was taken and, of course, the new clause was decisively rejected. It appeared that about a dozen Labour members abstained from voting.

25 July 1946 *p.3*

B.M.A. HOLDS A COUNCIL OF WAR
Plebiscite to be Taken of All Doctors Before 'Fight for Freedom'

The meeting of the British Medical Association acquired a council of war atmosphere when it embarked on a discussion of the National Health Service Bill yesterday.

Delegates spoke of the issue as being one of freedom or death and a battle between good and evil and on two occasions the Chairman of the Council, Dr. H. Guy Dain was spoken of as our general.

. . . it was decided to rally doctors throughout the country aainst the menace of State control by conducting a referendum on whether negotiations on regulations necessitated by the Bill should take place with the Ministry of Health.

25 July 1946 *p.5*

HEALTH BILL

Mr. Churchill made an unexpected move late last night to throw out the National Health Service Bill, which comes up for the third reading tomorrow. With the backing of Mr. Eden, Mr. Henry Willink (former Minister of Health), Mr. James Reid and others, he tabled this rejection motion:

That this House, while welcoming a comprehensive health service, declines to give a third reading to a bill which –
(1) Discourages voluntary efforts and associations.

130

(2) Mutilates the structure of local government.
(3) Dangerously increases Ministerial power and patronage.
(4) Appropriates trust funds and benefactions in contempt of the wishes of donors and subscribers and
(5) Undermines the freedom and independence of the medical profession to the detriment of the nation.

Others who have signed this motion include Sir Henry Morris-Jones (a Liberal National and a doctor), Commander Galbraith, Mr. Linstead, Colonel Stoddart-Scott, and Major Renton.

27 July 1946   *p.5*

MR. BEVAN CROSS WITH TORIES
Health Service Bill

PASSAGE THROUGH COMMONS

From our Parliamentary Correspondent

Westminster, Friday.

The National Health Service Bill got its third reading in the House of Commons today. The measure now goes to the Lords. Today's third reading debate necessarily served up all the old arguments for and against the bill that had been heard in Committee and on the report stage, and the discussion only came to life when Mr. Bevan replied to it.

He was cross with the Conservatives and laid about them with verve. He was annoyed and surprised (and the surprise has not been confined to him) that the Opposition should at this eleventh hour have tabled a root and branch amendment for the rejection of the bill. This amendment amounted to a comprehensive denunciation of most aspects of the measure. It alleged that the bill discouraged voluntary effort and association, mutilated the structure of local government, dangerously increased Ministerial power and patronage, appropriated trust funds and benefactions in contempt of the wishes of donors and subscribers, and undermined the freedom and independence of the medical profession.

Having satisfied his desire for Tory blood, Mr. Bevan had the wisdom in his closing sentences to drop polemics. He conceded that both the Opposition and the Labour members in the Standing Committee had helped to improve the bill though its main structure had not been altered. Better still, he appealed to all concerned to put controversy behind them and to promote that co-operation of medical profession, the people, and the Ministry without which the scheme must fail.

131

His castigation of the Conservatives went far. Once he spoke of the 'foolish and superficial people opposite.' He told them once that a priori prejudices (a neat debating stroke this against Conservatives) had disabled them from understanding the measure. He alleged that the amendment was intended to incite the medical profession and he regretted that some of the leaders of the profession had become identified with this Tory partisanship.

These leaders had become most reactionary politicians, the Minister added. On the whole, however, Mr. Bevan is confident that the medical profession will work the bill with a good heart.

Mr. Willink had reproached Mr. Bevan with having failed to acknowledge all the work his predecessors had put in to prepare the ground for the bill, but Mr. Bevan mordantly retorted to his predecessor in office that even a Conservative House of Commons would have rejected the impracticable measure which Mr. Willink drafted.

8 August 1946   *p.4*

Leader   **PAUSE FOR REFLECTION**

The war cries uttered and applauded at the recent meeting of the British Medical Association are regarded by a correspondent as portents of a breakdown in the health service. But full reports of the B.M.A. proceedings rather suggest that the sabre-rattling was addressed to the Houses of Parliament, where some further concessions may yet be wrung from the Minister, and that, when the Bill becomes law, the medical profession as a whole will not only 'work the scheme whole-heartedly,' as Mr. Bevan anticipates, but may well congratulate itself on having so successfully bluffed its way into a highly privileged position. The issue of continued 'negotiation' with the Minister is shortly to be put to all practitioners in the form of a plebiscite – which the 'British Medical Journal' takes to mean 'a public expression, with or without binding force, of the wishes or opinion of a community.' Its sponsors were agreed that only a negative vote of three to one should be considered binding on the supporters of non-participation. This is very different from the last-ditch spirit of 1912. The difference might have been more apparent if Mr. Bevan had not so long kept the doctors in suspense in the matter of remuneration. His acceptance of the majority recommendations of the Spens Committee will, as the minority report points out, mean a substantial rise, both absolute and relative, in the doctor's financial status. But professional workers in general have fallen far behind the earners of wages and profits in their efforts to catch up with rising costs; they will not begrudge the doctors the privilege of setting a brisker pace.

Leader **THE DOCTOR'S FEE**

'At no time since the inception of National Health Insurance,' says the current 'British Medical Journal,' 'has the capitation fee been regarded by insurance practitioners as adequate payment for the work done and the responsibility involved.' Taking into account this very natural sentiment, the layman may still find it hard to understand why the latest increase of the capitation fee to 12s. 6d. (which is 30 per cent above the pre-war figure) should have provoked a threat of wholesale resignation. The doctors' case is that the Minister of Health had promised to apply the findings of the Spens Committee 'irrespective of the institution of any national health service.' That committee decided that the average doctor's pre-war income was something like 15 per cent too low and that if the whole population were insured the appropriate capitation fee (at 1930 values) would be 15s. 6d. The Minister has offered to negotiate on this basis an agreement covering both remuneration in the new service and the adjustment of current fees, which he regards as inseparable questions. This offer has been declined; hence the provisional award of 12s. 6d., which the doctors consider 'gravely inadequate' and a violation of the Minister's pledge. It is, of course, by no means certain that the 'full application' of the Spens standard would produce a higher figure if the specified increase in the doctor's total income were fairly apportioned as between private and public fees. On the other hand, there is no obvious reason why the Minister should not ask the Spens Committee to interpret a standard in relation to the current capitation fee alone.

'The Doctor's Fee' provoked a great deal of correspondence, of which the following are typical examples.

LETTERS TO THE EDITOR

'THE DOCTOR'S FEE'

To the Editor of the Manchester Guardian

Sir – Your article 'The Doctor's Fee' finds it hard to understand why the latest offer of the Minister, raising the N.H.I. capitation fee to 12s. 6d. a patient a year (which he states is 30 per cent above the pre-war figure), should provoke a threat of wholesale resignation by the doctors. Although few doctors understand the theoretical application of economics, they do understand how the present capitation fee of 10s. 6d. impinges on the present way of living. . . .

. . . The only way I have been enabled to keep solvent, in view of the uneconomic N.H.I. fee, is by charging my private patients too much. The present N.H.I. fee is 14 per cent above the pre-war rate, but my private fees are now 50 per cent above such comparative rate. Translated into cash terms, my private visiting fee is now 7s. 6d. and surgery consultation 5s.: but I compute that the N.H.I. pays me 4s. 2d. a visit and 2s. 10d. a surgery consultation. As I am a rural practitioner I provide drugs for both types of patient, but for my N.H.I. patients I have in addition the work of certification and all the onerous correspondence such a service entails. I have estimated that in order to reduce my private fees to 6s. 6d. and 4s. respectively and at the same time to increase my N.H.I. fees to the same level for the same services a capitation fee of 17s. would be needed.

Such are the practical features of medical practice in a rural area. They probably bear little relation to the deductions of theoretical economics, but they are at least easily understood by the doctors. You may no doubt consider it to be a good thing that the post-war standard of living of the doctors should be on a considerably lower level than the pre-war, but this was not the conclusion of the independent body set up to investigate this matter by the Ministry of Health, the Spens committee. And it is with these cold figures ever in mind that I with many others shall be in the forefront to resign from the N.H.I. service, because I hold the view that good work should be well rewarded, whereas the whole history of the relations between the Ministry and the panel doctors merely proves that the Ministry is actuated by the motto of how much for how little. – Yours, etc.

MANDATARIUS.
September 13.

(Our correspondent misjudges our sympathies. Our leading article suggested that 'the layman' might find the insurance practitioners' attitude hard to understand and tried to summarise their published cases. When the Spens Report appeared we welcomed its proposal to raise the relative financial status of the doctor as the first step in a general improvement of the lagging standards of all professional workers. Most of them will probably read with envy of a spendable income (after taxation) which even without the extra 2s per panel patient offered by the Minister of Health is 8 per cent higher than before the war. – ED, 'Guard.')

THE DOCTOR'S FEE

To the Editor of the Manchester Guardian

Sir – I have seen the various letters complaining that the 12s. 6d. capitation fee is too small and the payment to the doctors out of proportion to the increased cost of living, but I have never yet read any letter which shows the actual work the doctors perform for the fee they already receive. It is a principle of industrial life common to all that payment should have some relation to the work performed.

One would be inclined to sympathise with the medical profession if it could be shown that the numbers of panel patients they were called upon to attend made the task unremunerative. Many doctors in this area have 1,000 or more patients on their panel. It is doubtful if they attend 25 per cent of these in any one year. The present capitation fee for 1,000 patients at 10s. 6d. a head, or £525 per annum, is being paid, for approximately 250 people only, which would appear to be a very fair payment seeing that nothing is provided by the doctor except the prescription.

If a doctor were called upon to examine thoroughly each of his panel patients only once a year, he would have some cause for complaint. One wonders what type of medical attention panel patients would receive if every person on the panel needed medical attention in one twelve months.

The comparative figure of panel patients treated in relation to the numbers on the individual doctor's panel can be quite easily ascertained, and these comparative figures should be published to strengthen the argument put forward for any increase in the capitation fee. The suggested figures would at least enable the ordinary person to view the position in its proper perspective.

I must point out that I am not and never have been an insured person. – Yours, &c.,

F. Mapperley.
Walsall, September 20.

THE DOCTOR'S FEE

To the Editor of the Manchester Guardian

Sir – I am a general practitioner in a Lancashire industrial town. Since 1931 I have kept accurate records of the work I have done.

My list of panel patients numbered 2,509 in 1931, 2,488 in 1939, dropping to 2,244 during the war. The percentage of patients on my list seen in any one year has varied from 56 per cent to 61 per cent (average 58 per cent). Over the fourteen years I have given an average of 4.1 attendances (visits or surgery consultations) for every patient on my list.

Smaller practices will probably show higher attendance ratios because lack of time compels me to do fewer visits than I would like. Also, my crowded surgeries probably keep away patients who would otherwise come to see me more often. A proper, higher capitation fee would enable me to have fewer patients, spend more time on them, and still manage to live reasonably.

At 10s. 6d. a head this allows me 2s. 6½d. for each attendance, which may vary from the mere signing of a 'fit for work' certificate in the surgery to a long night call some miles away, resulting in the loss of two hours' sleep or perhaps ruining an evening's relaxation, which can rarely start before 8 p.m. or, in winter time, 9 p.m.

I must keep two cars because I cannot afford the loss of time if one breaks down. I must have efficient assistance in my house all the twenty-four hours to receive messages. There are light, heat for my surgeries, hot water, rates, &c., and all the essential record-keeping. They make rather a large hole in the 2s. 6½d. gross.

Though private fees are very low in this industrial area, I make considerably more money out of a rather smaller total of private attendances. In other words, the private work has to subsidise the panel income.

In 1944, with a panel list of 2,244 patients, I did 9,243 panel attendances and 9,251 private attendances. After deducting the cost of drugs, &c., used for private patients, my certified expenses were £868. At 10s. 6d. a head, I would receive £1,178 in panel fees. Charging half my expenses for panel work, this leaves me with a net panel income of £744, or 1s 7¼d. per attendance or visit.

In terms of work accomplished, am I overpaid? I do it because I am interested in my work. When the State scheme comes in I shall have no private practice to help me pay my way. It is for the general public to help me to get a fair and proper salary.
–Yours, &c.,

G.P.
September 25.

PANEL DOCTOR'S FEE
Mr. Bevan's New Offer

APPLICATION OF SPENS REPORT

The Minister of Health has informed the Insurance Acts Committee of the B.M.A. that he is willing fully to apply the Spens Report to the current capitation fee, with effect from January 1, 1946, the increase of two shillings recently given being regarded as a payment on account.

Mr. Bevan has invited the Insurance Acts Committee to enter into discussion on the report forthwith, with special reference to the current capitation fee. The British Medical Association stated yesterday that Mr. Bevan has promised that the discussions would be conducted expeditiously.

MR. BEVAN AND B.M.A.

Mr. Bevan, speaking at a dinner of the British Orthopaedic Association in London last night, said it was the task of the public health services to put the best kind of medical apparatus in the hands of the profession, and it was for the profession to use it freely and independently for the benefit of their patients. 'My relations with the British Medical Association,' he added, 'grow more friendly week by week, and before very long I am quite certain we shall reach a cordial understanding and obtain co-operation in carrying out this great work.'

NEGOTIATIONS WITH MR. BEVAN
Doctors' Plebiscite

The British Medical Association has sent a ballot form to every member of the profession in the country seeking an answer 'Yes' or 'No' to the question, 'Do you desire the negotiating committee to either into discussions with the Minister on the regulations authorised by the National Health Service Act?'

The time has now come (it is stated) for a crucial decision by the profession. The Act authorises the Minister now to proceed to make regulations dealing with a wide variety of subjects, including mode and amount of professional remuneration, the terms and conditions of service generally, and the composition of Regional Hospital Boards.

The immediate practical issue which confronts the profession is whether it will or will not enter into discussions with the Minister on the subject-matter of these regulations. This is the issue which the association places before the profession as a whole to determine by plebiscite. To decide this issue is, by implication, to decide others.

13 December 1946

Leader   **DOCTORS DISAGREE**

The British Medical Association has taken a ballot of the whole medical profession on the question 'Do you desire the negotiating committee to enter into discussions with the Minister on the regulations authorised by the National Health Service Act?' About three quarters of the doctors thus interrogated – a remarkably high proportion – have replied and about 56 per cent of the replies are in the negative. What exactly does this mean? What bearing has it on the future of the service which in the Minister's words the people of this country desire and which Parliament has asked him to establish? Before these questions can be answered the circumstances in which the plebiscite was taken must be understood. The passing of the Act determined the general principles on which the national health service should be organised but left most of the questions of immediate concern to doctors as such to be settled by regulations to be framed by the minister in consultation with the profession. For this purpose a 'negotiating committee' had been formed by the B.M.A. and a number of other medical bodies. But the majority view at the last representative meeting of the B.M.A. was that the divergences between the Act and the association's principles were so wide that it would refuse to co-operate in the detailed shaping of the service – provided 'a substantial majority' of the profession at large supported this negative attitude.

. . . The ballot was not secret; indeed it was expressly stated that the B.M.A. would regard a negative vote as an undertaking by the voter not to enter the new service if so advised by the association.

The vote then is primarily a protest against the Government's refusal to take 'doctor's orders' – to swallow a political prescription – in deciding whether or not the people of this country should have the form of health service they want. It means that a small majority of the doctors who voted would sacrifice their opportunity to secure the best interests of themselves and their patients in those matters on which they are professionally qualified to advise rather than acknowledge the right of the people, through

138

their elected representatives, to decide the moral and political issues involved. This does not of course mean that the will of the people is to be frustrated. Dr. Dain, the chairman of the B.M.A. Council, is reported as saying it would be 'quite impossible' to enforce the Act with the co-operation only of those doctors who cast affirmative votes and that there is no way out except through an amending Act – in other words that the Council of the B.M.A. must be allowed to usurp the sovereign power of Parliament. But this is wishful thinking. In the first place the minority of affirmative voters would suffice to get the service started even if they alone were to join it though its development would be seriously hampered. In the second place it is in the highest degree unlikely that the negative voters – apart from those who are already retired or about to retire – will all acquiesce in a boycott of the service when it comes into effect. They have made their protest and many will doubtless be content to let it go at that.

Education

In 1946 the Minister of Education concentrated on speeding up the implementation of the 1944 Education Act through the passage of a second Education Act to give additional powers to local authorities to enlarge the premises of controlled schools in order to take pupils from voluntary schools which were closed down or reorganised. This was an Act which received the support of the Opposition. The main arena for the discussion of education was outside parliament and once again the focus was on the nature and organisation of secondary provision and the shortage of teachers and resources.

28 January 1946   *p.6*

THE NEW SECONDARY SCHOOLS
Not Dumping-Grounds

Miss Ellen Wilkinson, Minister of Education, at the opening of an educational work at Oxford on Saturday, spoke of the Education Act as the blueprint of a wonderful machine which everyone must help to work. There were difficulties arising from the shortage of labour, materials and teachers, but difficulties, after all, were opportunities.

Applications for prefabricated huts providing more than 1,000 additional classrooms and practical rooms had been received from 65 of the 146 local educational authorities, she said. Six training colleges were open, four more would be opened this month, and work was in progress on others.

Appealing to education authorities and teachers to guard against any tendency to regard secondary schools set up under the Act as the dumping-ground for children 'not quite good enough for technical and grammar schools' Miss Wilkinson said: 'To do that will be to leave the modern secondary schools with a feeling of "also-ranishness".'

MISS WILKINSON ON 'WIDER VIEW OF EDUCATION'
Need for Secondary Technical Schools

In a speech to the Lancashire and Cheshire Federation of Head Teachers the Minister is reported as saying that:

. . . For the majority of children secondary education would be provided in the modern school. 'We must make these schools secondary in fact as well as in name,' said Miss Wilkinson.

. . . For children in the modern schools we particularly want to open windows on the world. On leaving school many of them may have to take up jobs which are a bit monotonous. We want them to have interests outside their jobs.'

FREE MILK AND DINNERS
In Grant-Aided Schools

In the House of Commons yesterday, Miss Wilkinson (Minister of Education) announced after question-time that the Government had decided to make school milk free of charge in all grant-aided primary and secondary schools from the date of the introduction of cash family allowances in August next. The whole cost of this benefit will be borne by the Exchequer in accordance with the existing provision for the payment of 100 per cent grant on the school milk service.

'The Government,' she added, 'has also decided to make school dinners free of charge to day pupils at the earliest possible date in all grant-aided primary and secondary schools, but this cannot be until school-canteen facilities are sufficient to meet the expected demand. For the present, therefore, parents' payments will continue. These may not, however, under the regulations, be more than the cost of the food supplied and may be remitted wholly or in part in case of hardship.'

Leader   ## TEACHERS AND SCHOOLS

The various sides of reconstruction war against each other, and more things than houses compete for scarce resources with school buildings and teachers' training colleges. At the conference of the National Union of Teachers yesterday many voiced an anxious suspicion that the Ministry of Education was not fighting for its new Act as vigorously as it ought and that its great reforms might be pushed to one side. Mr. Ralph Morley said there was no shortage of people wishing to become teachers, but room for training sufficient numbers for them had not been found. Was the Ministry, he asked, acting strongly enough in providing temporary accommodation for expanded classes? No one fears that the new leaving age of fifteen will not come into force next April, but without the right number of teachers and school buildings the benefits of the Act will not be gained. Instead we shall have a kind of educational inflation, every child having rather more of something not as good. Behind the schools lie the county colleges, something that we thought we had gained after an earlier war, but lost in a similar post-war scramble. With so much at stake the Ministry of Education should not have to fight its battle alone. It needs the backing of all who desire the Act's promise to become our educational reality.

In May the TUC Congress formulated a demand for the school leaving age to be raised to sixteen years and for a date to be set for its achievement. A 'Guardian' leading article commented:

15 May 1946   *p.4*

Leader   **THE LEAVING AGE**

'Whereas at the present time,' stated six months ago the Ministry of Education in its excellent pamphlet 'The Nation's Schools,' 'there are some half a million pupils in grant-aided "secondary" schools, all the children from the age of eleven plus are now to receive a secondary education, extending later to the age of sixteen.' It is satisfactory that the Ministry should have chosen the first pamphlet to be issued by it as an occasion for reminding local authorities and the public that the raising of the school age to fifteen is merely the initial stage of a single reform which, for practical reasons, must take place by two steps and that the prolongation of the school life of all children to sixteen at the earliest possible date is not a pious aspiration but an essential part both of the nation's educational system and of the Government's policy. All measures of the kind, however, need time to prepare, and there is always a risk that in the period which must elapse before they can become operative the goal may be forgotten in the stress of current business. The deputation from the Trades Union Congress which is to wait on the Minister will render a service to the country in emphasising that danger. Educational like other planning requires as the first condition of its effectiveness a reasonable measure of certainty. It is the barest common sense to insist that, while time must be allowed before a school age of sixteen can become a reality, the task of making the necessary preparations would be greatly facilitated could a date in the future be fixed at once.

The heightened solicitude of the Trades Union Congress for the progress of the most vital of all public services, is a matter for profound satisfaction. . . .

The arguments for raising the age to sixteen are to-day an old story. If all children are to receive an education which is secondary in fact as well as in name they must remain long enough in a secondary school to derive full benefit from it. There is no reason whatever to suppose that if four to five years is the shortest period which will achieve that result in the case of children attending a grammar school, three to four years is sufficient in the case of a modern school. If different types of secondary school, grammar, technical, and modern, are to enjoy equal standing it is necessary that the minimum leaving age should be the same for all. Unless that condition obtains the schools with the lower age will inevitably be regarded as inferior to those with a higher one.

24 May 1946   p.4

Leader   **WAITING TO TEACH**

Kicking one's heels for a year or so is not what the demobilised soldier likes. Unfortunately that is what many who chose teaching for their peace-time work have been doing. It would be unjust to blame the Ministry of Education too much for its failure to have the emergency colleges ready in time, because competition for roofs is fierce. There are, too, difficulties in finding the right staffs, for the well qualified are in great demand from all sides. But the result of these delays is that while only 3,250 students have begun training some 14,750 are waiting to begin, with more being added to the list. Service candidates, who are given priority, may have to wait from eight to twelve months or even more, and civilians must wait longer. There is serious danger that the more lively and impatient will change their minds and enter another kind of work.

'THE NATION'S SCHOOLS' PAMPHLET
Conference Calls for Repudiation

Two resolutions on education were discussed during the afternoon. One called for the repudiation of the pamphlet 'The Nation's Schools,' and the reshaping of educational policy in accordance with socialist principles. The other put forward a 12-point policy to improve educational facilities in view of the 'growing needs for special education among trade unionists, due to the new responsibilities created by the Labour Government's plans for industry.'

Miss Ellen Wilkinson, Minister of Education, said that Labour's guiding aims in education were to see that no boy or girl was debarred by lack of means from taking the course of education for which he or she was qualified, and to remove from education those class distinctions which were the negation of democracy. The latter aim could not be achieved by prohibition, however, and her aim was to make the schools provided by the community so good and so varied that it would just seem absurd not to send the children to them.

THE SCHOOL AGE

Raising the school age in 1947 would mean 350,000 extra places. If every district was to have the type and design of building it desired they lost the advantage of speedy provision of buildings and the economy of mass production. That was why the Government devised its scheme for providing the required building and places.

As to the recruitment of teachers, the N.U.T. had played up extremely well. If some trade unions had had to accept as many dilutees they would have kicked up a fuss. The Government was planning for a net increase of 21,000 teachers in 1948, when the full force of the extra 350,000 children would be felt.

Regarding the provision of milk in schools, Miss Wilkinson said that free milk would be provided at Hoxton and Shoreditch as well as at Eton and Harrow. 'What more social equality could they have than that.'

Mr. W.G. Cove, M.P., said the pamphlet 'The Nation's Schools' was a reactionary document approved during the Coalition, and yet the whole future of education was being based on it. It divided the children into three categories and, to quote only

144

one example, stated that already there were too many places being provided in grammar schools.

Miss M. Herbison, M.P., regretted the continuance of class distinction in education. The best brains, she said, were going to get the academic education, the second best the technical education, and the rest were going to the modern school. An industrial nation could not afford to give only its second-best brains to technical education.

Miss Wilkinson again intervened to make clear her position on the pamphlet 'The Nation's Schools.' She had withdrawn the paragraph on secondary schools, which she did not like, and she undertook to have it rewritten.

The conference did not accept this, however, and carried the resolution. The other resolution was defeated.

The debate was carried into the House of Commons in the Committee of Supply on the Education Estimates.

2 July 1946   *p.6*

MISS WILKINSON'S EDUCATION POLICY
Attack by Labour Member

Mr. Cove (La.–Aberavon), moving an amendment to reduce the Minister's salary by £100, said the Minister had given the impression that she did not understand the drift of the educational policy she was pursuing.

He challenged the Minister to rise and repudiate the policy embodied in the booklet 'The Nation's Schools,' but Miss Wilkinson remained seated. The Minister, said Mr. Cove, now had a Labour majority behind her and had an opportunity of completely repudiating the pamphlet.

When Miss Wilkinson laughed and shook her head, Mr. Cove pointed across the floor of the House and said, 'that is her usual flippancy. That is one of the reasons we keep concerned about her.'

Miss WILKINSON: Tut-tut-tut.

Mr. COVE went on to say, 'The lady is a danger to the whole Labour movement so far as education is concerned. She is not true to the policy we have adumbrated over a period of years.'

VIEWS ON MULTILATERAL SCHOOLS

Dr. Eric James, High Master of the Manchester Grammar School, and Mr. G.C.T. Giles, Headmaster of the Acton Grammar School, and a recent president of the National Union of Teachers, opposed each other on the question, 'Do we need the Common Secondary school?' at a public meeting aranged by the Manchester and Salford District Branch of the English New Education Fellowship, held on Saturday at the Manchester Central Library. Mr. E.G. Simm, headmaster of the Salford Grammar School, presided.

Dr. James, who holds the view that three types of secondary school should be developed, said the replacement of our present secondary system by the common, or multilateral, school would be an educational and a social tragedy. . . .

Mr. Giles contended that unless we raised the whole educational level of this country we should 'go under.' If we deprived children of the chance of learning Greek would it 'terribly matter?' He traced the tradition of a 'liberal education' to Plato, 'about as near a Nazi as was possible in 400 BC.' Our education, particularly that of our grammar schools, dealt far too much with words and books and too little with people and things. One of the weaknesses of the grammar school was its dislike of practical things.

Social Security and Welfare

1946 was the year in which the Social Insurance Act reached the statute book and the system of Family Allowances came into operation. In neither case was there any sustained political debate reported by the 'Guardian', though the issue of the Friendly Societies' place in the administration of social insurance rumbled on for a few months. This was also an important year for the social service functions of local authorities with the publication of the Curtis Report on Children's Services, though legislation was delayed until 1948.

22 January 1946   *p.6*

SIR W. BEVERIDGE
Support for Friendly Societies' Campaign

From our London Staff

Sir William Beveridge is supporting a national campaign which the voluntary friendly societies are starting to protest against the announced decision of the Government not to use the societies in the proposed national insurance scheme. He will preside at a meeting at the Albert Hall on February 11, one of a series that is being held throughout the country. A nationwide petition is also being organised by the National Conference of Friendly Societies.

Speaking in London yesterday, Sir William said that he was giving support to the campaign because the object which the voluntary friendly societies had at heart was an essential part of what he wanted to see done for social security. He wanted security for all as a minimum and encouragement for voluntary action for anyone who wanted to go above it.

Sir William said that the more he looked at some of the administrative reasons which had been given against the use of the friendly societies the worse he thought they were. He believed, he added, that it would be a blot on the social insurance scheme if the societies were not brought in. They seemed to him an invaluable element in the State.

Leader ## SOCIAL SECURITY

Many will share Mr. James Griffith's regret that Sir William Beveridge was not present at the opening yesterday of the second reading debate on the National Insurance Bill. It would have been fitting that the author of the famous report should have participated in the enactment of a measure that so generously crowns his labours and realises his ideals. It would also have been useful if a critic of his authority and grasp of the broad principles could have clarified the major implications of such a complex document. . . .

[Mr. Griffiths] did, it is true, endorse the establishment of a national minimum standard of subsistence as the basic purpose of the Government's scheme but he was not unequivocal about the means whereby it is to be achieved. Clearly he is handicapped by the Government's obstinate determination to go on pretending that a social security system which will ultimately depend on the Exchequer for two-thirds of its funds is still in essence a contributory insurance scheme.

. . . Another serious flaw in the scheme as a whole which gave Mr. Butler an opportunity for damaging criticism is the discrepancy in standard between children's allowances and retirement pensions. The former, as the Rowntree and other investigations have established, are the most important factor in securing freedom from want yet they remain at the niggardly level to which the Coalition reduced Sir William Beveridge's deliberately modest figures. . . .

Some initial economy at the expense of the aged for the benefit of the young would accord better with the realities of our population trend.

INSURANCE BILL
Women Complain of Inequalities

From our London Staff

A number of feminists were called to London this weekend to consider the inequalities of the National Insurance Bill. In the majority view the most serious are the exclusion from direct compulsory insurance of married women and the Minister's undesirable powers (under clause 58) to alter married women's status in insurance by regulation. Said Mrs Abbott of the Open Door Council, 'Ten million married women are not in the body of the bill. You will find them under Miscellaneous Provisions.'

MP'S CASE FOR THE FRIENDLY SOCIETIES
Labour Member and 'Election Pledge'

A strong appeal to the Government to retain the approved and friendly societies in the administration of the national insurance scheme was made when the bill came before the Standing Committee of the House of Commons yesterday. Mr. R.A. Butler (C.-Saffron Walden) intimated that the Opposition was determined to have two separate divisions on the issue. . . .

Mr. Thomas Lewis (Lab.-Southamption), who said he was speaking on behalf of almost all the friendly societies in Great Britain, including the National Conference of Friendly Societies, which represented eight million insured persons and many millions on the voluntary side, asked the Minister to work out a scheme with the friendly societies. Many, he said, had been in existence for a hundred years and they had continued to work National Health Insurance since 1911 in a satisfactory manner.

'OLD SYSTEM WORN OUT'

The societies welcomed the Beveridge Report and the National Insurance Bill. They recognised that the old system was worn out and that the system of differential benefits could not go on indefinitely, and if they thought that their action would jeopardise the carrying out of the National Insurance scheme they would not put their claims forward.

Previous Ministers of Health had expressed their regard for the societies' administration. Why was the Government against their inclusion?

So far the pledge given by the Labour party to the friendly societies had been taken very light-heartedly, especially by the Parliamentary Secretary of the Ministry of National Insurance. Mr. Lindgren, in his week-end speeches, had seemed to have tried to antagonise the friendly societies instead of being conciliatory. He had talked about a slip having been made by Central Office, but he signed the document himself. It was a pledge, and one that should be maintained.

MR. GRIFFITHS AND THE 'FRIENDLIES'
'I would do a lot, but . . . '

Another plea for recognition of approved societies in the National Insurance Bill was made yesterday when the Standing Committee resumed consideration of the clause which makes provision for payment of benefits through the Post Office.

Speaking on a Conservative amendment moved at the last sitting which would allow certain benefits to be paid through friendly societies, Mr. H.V.A. Raikes (Con.–Wavertree) said that if all approved societies were included in the scheme it would not be difficult for the existing machinery to be expanded to enable the societies to make a big contribution to the administration.

Replying, Mr. James Griffiths, Minister of National Insurance, said he could not accept the amendment. 'The issue,' he said, 'is not whether during the past thirty years the approved societies have rendered good service. I say there are many defects in the approved society method of administration. To mention only one, they give the greatest benefit to the people in the best jobs: the people with the least incidence of sickness get the greatest additional cash benefits. I say that is unjust and inequitable and the approved societies have taken no steps to end the situation.

'I would do a lot for the Friendly Societies but there is one thing I would not do – I would not break the unity of this scheme.'

A BATTLE OVER

From Our Parliamentary Correspondent

Westminster, Thursday.

The controversy over the friendly societies and the National Insurance scheme was disposed of in the House of Commons tonight. The Labour amendment that would have permitted the Minister to use the friendly societies in the administration of the scheme was rejected by 279 votes to 184. . . .

Mr. Griffiths rose in a crowded House and he was followed with the closest attention. As a Minister he is popular with all parties and that made his way easier, for he was not long in making it plain that he was not going to give way.

The National Insurance Bill passed its third reading in the House of Commons on 30th May 1946 and received the royal assent on 2nd August 1946.

The following two reports present an interesting contrast, the first looking forward to a 'new Britain', the other concerned with a problem for legislators since the Elizabethan Poor Law.

SOCIAL SECURITY PROGRAMME
Nearly 2,000,000 Applications for Family Allowances Approved

The Minister of National Insurance, Mr. J. Griffiths, was the chief speaker at a meeting at Belle Vue, Manchester, yesterday, at which some five thousand people celebrated the 'famous victory' won by the Labour party a year ago. Mr. Griffiths used it to discuss his own subject, social security; Mr. Michael Foot, M.P., made some strong criticism of the Conservative press; and Mrs. Barbara Castle, M.P., spoke for the most part on food, justifying the Government's policy and warning housewives against insidious anti-Government whisperers in shopping queues.

The biggest crime of the Tories in the twenty years between the wars, said Mr. Griffiths, was that they very nearly made the British people a people without hope. From now on, however, the burden of the poor would be borne by the nation until the day came when they had built a new Britain in which there would be no poverty.

Mr. Griffiths dealt briefly with various aspects of the Government's social security proposals. He announced that of the two million applications for family allowances received so far (another half-million is expected) 98 per cent have been approved. Illustrating how the allowances would relieve many households from grinding poverty, he referred to a mother of 18 children, 11 of whom are under 14. This women will receive £2.10s. a week from August 6. 'We are spending £16,000,000 on this scheme,' he went on. 'It is not really being spent; it is an investment by the nation in the greatest asset of all – the boys and girls who will be the citizens of to-morrow.'

WORKMEN'S COMPENSATION

The proposals in connection with workmen's compensation would do more to sweeten relations between labour and management than anything else in our lifetime,' while the National Insurance Bill would, for the first time, bring within its scope as contributors virtually the whole of the population. It introduced into insurance a new class – the self-employed man, who was sometimes called the 'little man.' Lord Beaverbrook talked about the 'little man'; the Labour party helped him.

MR. BEVAN'S ADVICE ON TRAMPS
'Firmness with Work-Shy'

A system of rehabilitation for tramps, of whom, in April, there were 807, is advocated by Mr. Aneurin Bevan, Minister of Health, in advice he has issued to Public Assistance Authorities on problems of vagrancy, pending new legislation designed to abolish the existing Poor Law.

The logical development of war-time policy seems to be the establishment by local authorities of a system of reception centres to provide food and shelter for a short period while consideration is given to the best means of dealing with each individual – whether anything can be done for him by way of, for example, employment, training, rehabilitation, or, if he be aged or sick, long-term institutional care. The casual would be encouraged to stay in the centre until this question is determined. The hard core of habitual vagrants, including men who are work-shy, anti-social, or recalcitrant, should also be given suitable treatment. For the limited number of men in this group firmness must, when necessary, be applied if reasonable discipline is to be maintained and a spread of idle vagabondage discouraged.

In the new legislation it is contemplated that general responsibility for dealing with vagrancy will be transferred to the Assistance Board, though it is proposed that the Board should discharge part of this responsibility through local authorities – and possibly other bodies – acting as their agents.

The Family Allowances Act came into operation on 6 August 1946, and the 'Guardian' maintained its earlier stance on the level of benefit.

30 November 1946 p.6

Leader **FAMILY ALLOWANCES**

Increases in the allowances for dependent children paid to people who qualify for unemployment assistance or supplementary pensions are shortly to be submitted to Parliament. The debate will reveal how remote even now is the ideal of an integrated system of social security based on consistent and accepted principles. Much indignation has been expressed because the recipients of these increased payments, whose total income is assessed on a bare subsistence standard, do not benefit from the Family Allowances Act. The complaint is misdirected, for the measure merely extended to the rest of the community in a restricted form a benefit that was already enjoyed in full by the groups in question, whose standard of living it had raised above that of some employed workers with many children to support. To draw attention to the anomalous working of the Act is not to justify the payment of children's allowances twice over in some cases, what it does justify is a demand that all children's allowances should be fully adequate to maintain a child at a decent subsistence standard. The Government prefers the cheaper course of raising the public assistance scale to the required extent and leaving the general family allowance at a level too low to bridge the gap between a low wage and the minimum needs of a large family. The same difficulty will arise on a much larger scale when the forthcoming Public Assistance Bill is introduced. Either the principle of a national minimum standard of living must be applied uniformly throughout the social security system or we must resign ourselves to another series of patchwork adjustments and persistent anomalies.

25 March 1946   *p.4*

Leader   **TRAINING IN CHILD CARE**

The Curtis Committee of Inquiry into the care of children deprived of normal home life, which was set up last year, has found certain aspects of the problem so urgent that it has published an interim report, 'Training in Child Care.' The group of workers for whose training the report makes specific proposals is the residential staff of the 'house mother' (or 'father') type, in charge of groups of children in small cottages or 'scattered' homes, or as part of large establishments. Training for this particular work is not comprehensively covered, except by certain voluntary bodies for their own staffs. To put it on a professional basis a Central Council for Training in Child Care is recommended, which will draw up a curriculum, arrange for teaching centres and tutors, and award certificates. The house mother or assistant matron should not be less than eighteen or more than thirty-five years and should have 'sufficient education to profit by the course.' A three years' course is suggested, but this might be less if the student were already partly trained. Such a system would not only provide better candidates but would be a safeguard against the introduction of unsuitable people. That the committee urges that 'a beginning should be made without delay' is a measure of the importance of this matter. It is to be hoped that all three departments concerned, the Home Office and the Ministries of Health and Education, will take prompt action.

The full report of the Committee was published on 15 October 1946 as a White Paper (Cmd. 6922) and on 16 October the following leading article appeared:

16 October 1946   *p.4*

Leader   **THE CURTIS REPORT**

The Curtis Committee on the care of children deprived of a normal home life describes the by now familiar confusion and overlapping of functions of Government departments and local authorities. About that it suggests certain radical alterations. But what stands out most vividly from this detailed and patient report is the description of some of the places where children whose birthright is a normal, happy life are leading lives of great misery. . . .

The worst conditions have been found in some public assistance institutions and nurseries and in particular in workhouses where for lack of separate accommodation healthy children are kept in confinement amongst idiot children and sick adults without occupation or opportunities for play.

. . . The number of children at present being cared for in one way or another is 124,000. The administrative reforms suggested in the report would actually increase this number by bringing under the scope of public care certain categories of other children including those in voluntary homes now unregistered.

. . . While it is said that the ultimate responsibility should be with one central department which should have a children's branch making a special study of child welfare it is emphasised that the local authorities should continue to be responsible for their own children. They must not be regarded as entries in a card index. There should therefore be a special committee to deal with all questions of child care and the responsibility should be definitely laid on a children's officer. In the revised organisation which is recommended the Children's Officer would be 'the pivot.'

20 November 1946   *p.6*

CARE OF CHILDREN REPORT
Government Taking All Possible Administrative Action
— Mr. Greenwood

In the House of Commons yesterday

Mr. WILSON HARRIS (Ind.–Cambridge University) moved an amendment to the Address regretting that no mention was made in the King's Speech of any intention to give effect to the recommendations in the recent report of the Care of Children Committee (the Curtis Report). He said that action must be taken to put an end to conditions which ought never to continue for a single day longer. Parliament was responsible for the care of these children. They could not talk one day about the supremacy of Parliament and the next day repudiate the responsibility which flowed from that supremacy.

The committee had been set up because of the suspicions aroused about the condition of children under public care by the case of Denis O'Neill, who when boarded out in Shropshire underwent such treatment that he died and his foster-father was now undergoing six years' imprisonment.

These children were described as 'deprived children' and he found a great deal of poignancy in that description. They were deprived of all those things which a happy home provided to make a child's character. The report both allayed public anxiety and accentuated it. He paid tribute to staffs of institutions who came under a shadow after the O'Neill case and to the many devoted men and women who were doing their utmost to supply to these children what ought to be supplied in their own homes.

He said there was a large number under the Home Office who must not all be regarded as delinquents. He asked what Government department should be made ultimately responsible for them. The Curtis Report itself was unanimous that there should not be any more divided responsibility between three or four different departments, and that one department alone should be responsible. The children had no means of making their voices heard and it was essential that there should be action, and action now.

Mr. G. NICHOLSON (C.-Farnham), seconding, said he could scarcely believe that the Government was unaware of the deep sense of disquiet felt by every section of the population as a result of the Curtis Report. There should be legislation this session and the maximum amount of action. A melancholy and ugly picture had been presented and the whole volume was a sorry condemnation of the inspection system and of the Ministry of Health which had received the inspectors' reports and had done nothing about them.

The first thing to aim at was to see that each individual child had someone to look to. Each 'deprived' child should have a 'god-parent' who would visit it and help it. We should get away from institutional treatment and favour a system of boarding-out. He spent the week-end reading the report and on Sunday night went to see his youngest daugher, aged four months. 'The contrast between her and the wretched children I had been reading about was almost more than I could bear. Imagine by some malicious turn of fortune's wheel any of our children being put into this position. I say may God protect us from it and lead us to do our duty to the helpless.'

155

Leader   **THE CARE OF CHILDREN**

Tuesday's debate in the House on the problems of the care
of homeless children reviewed in the Curtis Report brought out
again the main distressing facts and emphasised yet again the
deplorable administrative confusion behind them. That so many
opinions were heard about which of the three departments
concerned would best be made solely responsible is proof in itself
of the complexity of the question. Mr. Greenwood in his reply
reasonably pointed out that when the report was presented less
than a month before the King's Speech legislation could hardly be
prepared immediately. Obviously legislation, when it comes,
should be carefully prepared, but there are immediate
administrative improvements that can be made without much loss
of time. A circular going out within the next few days from the three
main departments concerned will urge action upon all local
authorities. The important thing now is that the Government should
still regard the problem as immediate and urgent and should not
be allowed to forget it. A letter in our columns yesterday from the
Doncaster and District Council of Social Service drew attention to
the plight of children whose parents are sent to prison for neglect
and urged that special centres should be set up for them and that
the parents while serving their sentence should receive some
training in the care of children. This is only one instance of the many
reforms to which the Government should attend without delay.

CARE OF CHILDREN
Improvements Need Not Wait for Legislation

From our Labour Correspondent

London, Sunday.

The Home Office, the Ministry of Health, and the Ministry of
Education sent out a joint circular yesterday to all authorities
concerned with the care of children, instructing them to review their
existing arrangements in the light of criticism made in the Curtis
Report and to consider at once what improvements can be made.

The purpose of the joint circular is to try to get something done
without waiting for legislation, and it is pointed out that such defects
as lack of co-operation between departments and lack of care in trying to meet a child's needs as an individual 'need not await legislation or major schemes of reorganisation.' But legislation is also

promised, although we are not told anything more specific than that the Home Secretary, the Minister of Health, and the Minister of Education have the Curtis Report 'under active consideration' and that 'there will be no avoidable delay in making a statement on those recommendations which involve action by the Government.'

The joint circular from the three Ministries should do good by calling attention to the urgency of making brighter the pitifully drab lives of many children who are committed to public care. It does well to emphasise that the meeting of a child's physical needs is by no means all that matters and that 'an atmosphere of security, personal interest, and affection' is equally important. But the main obstacles to bringing about major improvements in the care of children are lack of buildings and of suitably trained men and women. There is a sad lack of foster parents who are willing to give children homes. These are problems which cannot be solved overnight.

13 December 1946   *p.5*

NEW RULES FOR CARE OF CHILDREN
Bringing the Two Responsible Departments Into Step

From our Political Correspondent

Westminster, Thursday.

Mr. Attlee told the House of Commons to-day that the Government had not yet decided which department should in future hold general responsibility for the welfare of children deprived of a normal home life. He added that he did not know whether administrative reforms were being carried out before a decision was made on the general issue.

It seems that Mr. Attlee had not been fully informed, for to-day the Home Office and the Ministry of Health are posting to local authorities a joint memorandum on the boarding out of children and young persons, a joint circular and separate rules and orders.

Although the Home Office, acting under the Children and Young Persons Act, 1933, and the Ministry of Health, acting under the Poor Law Act, 1930, still must observe their own departmental procedures, the joint circular suggests that wherever possible 'all boarding out work for which the local authority is responsible in any area might be undertaken by, or under the same officer, or that in any case there should be closer association of the officers responsible for boarding out . . . this work would also require co-ordination with that of the health or

157

other visitors who supervise foster-children under child life protection requirements. It may also be possible by co-operation and agreement to secure that voluntary organisations make use of foster homes approved by local authorities in boarding out children in their care.'

(1947)

Housing

1947 was a year in which the housing programme faced severe difficulties. One of the harshest winters in the twentieth century curtailed the building of houses in the first three months of the year and the economic crisis of the summer forced the Government to cut back on investment in housing. To these circumstances may be added the continuing shortage of raw materials, particularly timber, and the black market 'leakage' of labour and materials. The Government was able to make a significant contribution to future housing policy by the passage of the Town and Country Planning Act.

8 January 1947   p.5

LAND DEVELOPMENT VALUES FOR THE STATE
Proposals Under New Planning Bill

COMPENSATION FUND OF £300,000,000 TO PREVENT HARDSHIP

From our Political Correspondent

London, Tuesday.

The Town and Country Planning Bill, which has now been published, makes four major changes in the law.

1. It transfers from private property owners to the State the 'development value' of land. All development by private owners will involve the payment to a new Central Land Board of a 'development charge.'

2. Property owners who lose development value as a result of the bill, are denied compensation as a right, but a fund of £300,000,000 is to be set up from which payments will be made to landowners in England, Scotland and Wales, who would otherwise suffer hardship.

3. Local authorities below the status of county or county borough councils are to lose their planning powers, though the larger bodies may delegate to them powers for the execution of

161

plans. The councils of counties and county boroughs may combine to form a joint planning board.

4. The principle of the Town and Country Planning Act, 1944, which provided grants to local authorities towards expenditure on the acquisition and clearing of land for the re-development of areas of extensive war damage, is extended to cover areas of 'bad layout or obsolete development that require to be developed as a whole, and areas of derelict land acquired for the purpose of being brought back into use.'

LAND TENURE

The bill is not so radical as one had been led to expect. It nationalises nothing except the speculative development value and it provides £300,000,000 as compensation for 'hardship.' It interferes little with the existing use of land, and it is estimated that 85 per cent of land units in this country will be wholly unaffected by the bill, since they have no development value.

The bill introduces a new element in land tenure: it virtually abolishes freehold in the sense that the property owner will no longer have an automatic right to do what he likes with it, beyond its existing use. The Coalition Government's White Paper on 'The Control of Land Use' went so far as to propose restrictions on development, with compensation, and a development charge of 80 per cent of the improved value of the land when consent to develop had been given. 'The Control of Land Use' was never discussed in the House of Commons.

9 January 1947   *p.6*

REACTION TO PLANNING BILL
Liberal Support: Tories Think Compensation Scheme Too Vague

From our Political Correspondent

London, Wednesday.

The general political reaction to the Town and Country Planning Bill, published this morning, is one of caution. Both the Conservatives and the Liberals are committed to some extent to parts of the bill, and it may indeed be that the sharpest comment on the measure will come from the extremists of the Labour party on the ground that it is not radical enough.

Mr. Clement Davies, the Leader of the Parliamentary Liberal party, made the following comment to-night:–

'Taxation of land values due to public improvements is in accordance with Liberal policy for the last fifty years, and the country might like to be reminded that the Liberals introduced it in 1909. It is true that this taxation was abolished by the Coalition Government in 1918, but, except for the Prime Minister, Lloyd George, all the important officers in that Government were Tories, with Austen Chamberlain as Chancellor of the Exchequer.

'Liberals welcome, of course, the greater power for local authorities to acquire land for public services, whether to be utilised by private individuals or by public authorities. One question that is worrying me is that so much is left to be done by Orders in Council to be drawn up at some future dates.

'Liberals also approve town and country planning being on a much wider basis than it has been so far. It is right that the planning authority should be the county council.'

The Conservatives have referred the bill to the Town and Country Planning Committee of their Parliamentary party, of which Mr. W.S. Morrison, a former Minister of Town and Country Planning, and Mr. Henry Strauss, formerly Parliamentary Secretary to the Ministry, are members. The Conservatives will examine the bill carefully before committing themselves to official criticism since the bill is largely based on the reports produced for Mr. Churchill's Coalition Government.

There will be a strenuous attempt to prevent Mr. Herbert Morrison from putting the bill into the agenda of the House of Commons in the second week after reassembly, as he has threatened to do, perhaps playfully. The Opposition hopes for longer than that to consider the bill and 'to consult the constituencies' which in this case means, in a major degree, the local authorities. When the Police Act was before Parliament in the first session the larger local authorities applied pressure on the Government effectively, and Conservative members were among those who fought for the interests of the smaller authorities who lost their police powers.

At first glance, Conservative opinion has fixed on three subjects in the bill which seem objectionable:

1. The compensation proposals, which lack definition and which are bound up with the sum of £300,000,000 arrived at by unspecified means;
2. The proposal to acquire development value for the State for all time, with no indication as to the basis on which it will be assessed;
3. The widening of the purposes for which land can be acquired compulsorily on 1938 values.

NEW SYSTEM OF LICENSING

From our London Staff

To tighten up still further the black market in building, the Ministry of Health has decided to empower local authorities in England and Wales to take proceedings against offenders in their areas. Such prosecutions will not be limited to classes of work for which the authority is empowered to issue a licence, but will cover all infringements of the regulations, including any breaches of licences issued by the Ministry of Works. The Minister of Works will himself continue to take proceedings against 'black market' offenders in any cases which he thinks fit.

Another alteration in regulations which will make evasion of the existing orders more difficult is the cancellation of a clause which excludes from licensing work carried out on private dwellings by unpaid labour. The abuse of this privilege has led to a grave dissipation of materials needed for more vital purposes, and so the clause is to be withdrawn though licensing officers are being instructed to 'give sympathetic consideration to applications made by persons who genuinely intend to carry out building work by unpaid labour.

Leader ## BLACK MARKET BUILDING

The measures by which the Minister of Works hopes to nip in the bud the black market in building that has for months past been absorbing more materials than the housing drive would have been welcome indeed a year ago. Their announcement at this stage is a frightening confession of futility — or worse. It has always been obvious that the Ministry of Works had not and could never have the means to police effectively the privately controlled distribution of building materials; that the division of responsibility for the licensing of housing work between local authorities and the Ministry of Works was an open invitation to the law breaker; and that until they had full knowledge of the amount of non-housing work licensed by the Ministry of Works the local authorities could not possibly tell how much private housing and house repair work they could license without directing materials and labour from their own house-building contracts. It had been taken for granted that there must be technical difficulties, unfamiliar to the layman, which made the equally obvious remedies impracticable. If that is the case their adoption now is so much eyewash. If not, what conceivable excuse can there have been for not adopting them a year ago?

PLANNING BILL
Mr. Churchill Tables Rejection Motion

Mr. Churchill, with the support of other Opposition front benchers, last night tabled an amendment asking the Commons to reject the Government's Town and Country Planning Bill, which comes up to-morrow and Thursday. The reasons for opposing the bill are set out in the amendment, which reads:

That this House, while desiring a further measure of town and country planning, declines to give a second reading to a long and complex bill making great changes in the powers of local authorities before time has been given to those authorities and other interests vitally affected to study its provisions; which fixes for compensation an arbitrary sum not purporting to be just and not determined by independent inquiry, and lays down no principles for its allocation to individuals; which gives no sufficient indication of the principles to be followed in levying development charges; which continues to provide for the compulsory acquisition of land by reference to a basis of money values which changed conditions have rendered invalid; which makes possible discrimination against proper development by private persons; and which, by leaving for decision by subsequent orders matters requiring definition in the bill, will create uncertainty and so will hamper and delay sound development.

Leader **THE PLANNING BILL**

As a means of making possible the use of our land in the public interest Mr. Silkin's Bill is widely welcomed. From this point of view it takes us an immense step forward leaving far behind the frustrations that made pre-war planning little more than the passive registration of unplanned trends and carrying us almost to the point where the general good may determine the design and layout of our towns and countryside. Almost, but not quite. Comment on this aspect of the Bill, therefore, must be concentrated on shortcomings which, though relatively small, are in themselves important and regrettable. It is evident, however, that criticism in the Commons will be concentrated not on improving the Bill as an instrument of good planning but on contesting the justice of its financial provisions. . . .

29 January 1947   *p.4*

Leader

HOUSING PROGRAMME

Mr. Bevan's 'Housing Programme for 1947' might more
accurately have been called a housing labour and materials
programme. It shows (on favourable assumptions about softwood
imports and coal output) how many new houses he hopes to enable
the building industry to erect, and therefore considers it reasonable
to expect it to erect, not how many he proposes to see that it does
erect. Is this good enough? His reluctance to go even so far a year
ago was understandable. Until the local authorities were ready to
employ building labour it was right to issue licences freely for its
employment elsewhere and meanwhile to encourage the local
authorities to develop all the sites they could. It was also inevitable
that some time should elapse before the 'concentrated' building
materials industries got into their stride and the peace-time balance
of the labour force was restored. Because local authorities
responded so well, the meagre supplies of materials and labour
became too thinly spread over too many contracts, the completion
rate slowed down, and costs went up – how far the White Paper
does not disclose. That, however, was better than running the risk
of the housing programme failing to keep pace with the expanding
supply of labour and materials. But this excusable maladjustment
was inexcusably aggravated by the continuing 'leakage' of labour
and materials. By August Mr. Bevan was apparently confident that
the priority system and the zonal conferences instituted by the
Ministry of Works had got this black market under control, for he
then expected to finish by Christmas the 25,000 municipal houses
already at eaves level. In fact only 13,800 were finished. He now
says that means of strengthening the Government's control over
scarce materials and components are being sought. If the search
is not soon rewarded his 1947 programme has no better prospect
of achievement than his autumn roofing drive.

30 January 1947   *p.4*

Leader

MR. SILKIN'S DAY

In his efforts to make the national planning of land use in
the public interest a reality Mr. Silkin has had a long hard and not
always successful struggle. He has had to meet his party's apathy
and the obstruction of departments as well as private interests and
he has been handicapped always by the weakness of a Ministry
that was set up as a sop to importunate critics of the Coalition
Government's inability to make up its mind. Yesterday, however,

166

he came into his own. The two-hour speech in which he moved the second reading of the Town and Country Planning Bill was an excellent piece of lucid exposition. . . . he has gone on to improve out of all recognition the machinery and technique of local and national planning – short of establishing a unified control over the use of land by Government departments and statutory undertakings.

11 March 1947   p.4

Leader   **HOUSING IN 1947**

The great frost of the last six weeks brought building almost to a standstill. Its onset is reflected in the housing returns for January, which show a general decline in the monthly rate of completion. Throughout February, aggravated by intermittent blizzards, it made the digging of foundations and service channels in the rock-hard ground impossible and arrested all operations that depend on water remaining in liquid form. But the temporary setback for which the frost has been directly responsible is of small account when compared with the continuing frustration that must result from the fuel crisis, and from the redeployment of our national resources which it has enforced upon us. There is no escape from the necessity to seek our economic salvation in measures that must play havoc with the housing programme. This transformation of the outlook is not immediately apparent from the Government's 'Economic Survey,' for the building targets it lays down are the same as in Mr. Bevan's White Paper of the previous month. But the emphasis is radically different. Hitherto our main problem has been to increase the labour and materials available for house-building so as to give effect to the popular desire that a decent dwelling for every family should be the first improvement in our national standard of living. We are now bluntly reminded that we could, at a pinch, live without new houses altogether, but not without imported food or electric power – and that the pinch if not upon us, is just around the corner. The question is no longer whether we can manage to reach Mr. Bevan's housing targets (which is more than doubtful) but whether we can afford to try.

The possible output of new houses this year is limited by the possible output of coal. Because we cannot offer the timber-exporting countries the coal they want in exchange, our supplies of softwoods this year will be 'only some 75 per cent of requirements'. . . . Moreover, the shortage 'will last for some years.' Structural steel and clay products are also scarce and will become scarcer if their producers cannot get all the fuel and power they can use. . . .

If the housing programme is kept bigger than the supply of materials warrants in order to keep a large labour force employed, progress will be interrupted, more time will be spent on each house, costs will rise and the desired increase in output per man-year will be discouraged. All this will postpone the day when we can afford to build as many houses as we want even further than would a reduction in the building labour force. If, on the other hand, the surplus labour is released for building work other than house-building it will inevitably compete with housing for scarce materials and add greatly to the difficulties of controlling the black market.

1 April 1947   *p.4*

Leader   **HOUSING STANDARDS**

When enough new houses have been built to ensure that every family may have a separate dwelling to itself we can make a start on the much larger task of rebuilding or reconditioning those houses which are no longer fit to live in. In anticipation of that time the Ministry of Health has circulated to local authorities a report which recommends that the standard of fitness for habitation issued for their general guidance in 1919 should become the statutory minimum and should be replaced as a target by a list of sixteen requirements 'essential to comfortable domestic life.' This advice reflects the change in the popular estimation of housing values. Its acceptance by the Ministry as a basis for future legislation reflects a still more significant change from the official attitude in the last post-war 'economy crisis.' Indeed, the most satisfactory feature of an otherwise gloomy housing situation is Mr. Bevan's refusal to be stampeded into lowering quality for the sake of larger numbers. His only serious lapse in this respect has been his undue emphasis on the standard three-bedroom house at the expense of special forms of accommodation for single persons and elderly couples. This, however, is soon to be corrected by new legislation and a revised manual sanctioning a range of plans which will more closely correspond with human needs. At the same time 'housing medals' are to be awarded annually to the local authority and architect responsible for the best-designed scheme.

23 April 1947   *p.8*

GOVERNMENT'S CASE FOR CUTTING HOUSING PROGRAMME
Local Authorities' Fuel Disappointment

Mr. John Edwards, Parliamentary Secretary to the Ministry of Health, yesterday addressed a conference of Lancashire and Cheshire local authorities, in Manchester, and explained why the

Government had to impose restrictions upon local housing programmes. The conference was organised by the National Housing and Town Planning Council.

Mr. Edwards said that by the end of 1946 it had become apparent that the number of houses for which contracts had been let was in excess of the building capacity. Therefore the Government worked out the new programme for 1947. The allocations to local authorities had now been made, and it was hoped to publish them in the next monthly housing return. He was afraid that the final figures would come as a disappointment to local authorities, but the restrictions were not on the amount of accommodation to be provided but only on the amount to be put on paper.

'The housing need cannot be met by half-finished houses, and this is all we shall get if we go on letting contracts which it is beyond the existing resources to fulfil in a reasonable time.'

9 May 1947   *p.5*

CHECK TO THE HOUSING PROGRAMME
Bad Weather: Shortage of Materials

AUTHORITIES TO CONCENTRATE ON EXISTING CONTRACTS

From our Political Correspondent

Westminster, Thursday.

The Government has abandoned the hope, which it held in January, that 240,000 permanent houses would be completed by the end of this year. At the end of March, 218,783 houses were being built, and the Government's new plan is to complete this year as many of them as possible. No estimate of the number likely to be completed before the end of the year can now be made.

This check to the housing programme is described in a preface to the March housing return, published as a White Paper today, and was mentioned by Mr. Aneurin Bevan in answer to a question in the House of Commons this afternoon. The preface explains that the total effect on the housing programme of the continuing shortages in material, of the fuel crisis and the bad weather 'is undoubtedly very serious indeed.'

The White Paper also makes clear that the country's economic dislocation has upset the ratio between houses completed and houses under construction, and states that 'the rate at which new tenders can be approved during the rest of the year must be reduced . . . to maintain a balanced building programme.' The Ministry of Health is anxious to avoid a recurrence of conditions in which so much of the labour and materials available are spread over work in progress that few houses get finished.

Leader **OUTLOOK FOR HOUSING**

There was little sign in yesterday's Commons debate on housing that the speakers were conscious of an impending crisis. The debate took place on the morrow of our failure to get timber from Russia – timber is the scarcest of housing materials – and in the shadow of an almost inevitable choice between building as many houses as we can next year and eating as much as we need to keep going, Mr. Bevan was presented by the Opposition with his favourite Aunt Sally, the demand for free private building. The real complaint against this policy hitherto has been that he allowed the housing programme to get out of balance by driving with too loose a rein. This he admits but claims to have been unavoidable: he is now seeking to correct it by rationing tenders and keeping the number of houses started down to the number which the industry's resources might enable it to complete without needless delay. As yet, however, tenders approved and houses put in hand still outrun the monthly figures for houses finished and the probability is that we shall soon be unable to afford the labour and imported materials which have made even that modest rate of completion possible. The first need for the future is to cut down the cost in resources and time of each house that is built. The welcome adoption of payment by results on local authority contracts will go a long way to achieve this, but only if both the housing programme and the labour force engaged on it are restricted to such proportions as will correspond with the rates at which the scarcest materials can on a realistic appraisal be expected to flow to the sites after the 'twelfth hour' has struck. Mr. Bevan's peroration did not suggest a willingness to accept that limitation.

Leader **CRISIS FOR HOUSING**

It was unfortunate that the general debate on housing in the Commons should have come just before, instead of after, the Government statements on the national economy. For the main issue now in the housing field is not whether we are building as many houses as we could but whether we can afford to go on trying to build as many as we are doing. On this issue the Government has yet to make clear its decision – if indeed a decision has been reached. We know that some preference in housing is to be given to the mining and agricultural areas to which it is urgently necessary to attract recruits, but that announcement may refer only to the scheme (excellent as far as it goes) for allotting to such areas an extra 15,000 aluminium houses. We know, too, that timber imports are to be cut and that softwoods constitute the great bulk of the timber we pay for in dollars, but we cannot judge the effect of this cut on housing until we also know whether the competing claims on softwoods for railway wagons, farm equipment and factory and ship building will be given the priority which the trading situation would seem to demand. Hitherto it has been the Government's policy to expand the building labour force, though latterly at a diminished rate. But is not building one of the industries from which man-power must now be induced to flow into the import-saving and exporting trades? And can the constructional needs for those trades be met if 60 per cent of the building labour force remains engaged in housing?

Granted that some curtailment of the housing programme is inevitable and that there is at least a case for carrying it farther, in the circumstances of the moment, than the shortage of imported materials will make necessary, the next main problem is to make the cut in such a way as will involve the least delay in completing those houses now under construction and the least impairment of the industry's capacity to get back into its stride when the crisis has passed.

19 August 1947   *p.4*

Leader   **BUILDING LABOUR**

By restricting the issue of licences for private house-building and pressing for a speedier acceptance of contracts to erect Airey rural houses, Mr. Bevan has begun the selective pruning of his building programme. That process must soon be applied also to municipal housing in the non-priority areas if it is to bear fruit in the form of a good crop of finished houses this year and an adequate contribution thereafter to the nation's economic recovery. The effects desired are first a higher output of houseroom per man in the mining and farming areas, where extra accommodation can best help to restore our trade balance; secondly a transfer of labour from builders in search of new contracts to those who lack the men to finish quickly the work they have in hand; and finally to throw some building workers in non-priority areas out of employment in order that the labour exchanges may divert them to jobs which more immediately serve the country's over-riding needs. But this last effect will by no means automatically follow. So long as every bricklayer is free to set up as a master builder many of those who become unemployed will prefer the black market to the Labour exchange. Everything therefore depends on the success of the new system of controlling scarce materials to be introduced next month.

On 23 October Sir Stafford Cripps announced in detail the measures to be taken in order to alleviate the economic crisis and the dollar deficit. One of these measures was a slowing down in the housing programme. A 'Guardian' leader commented on the plans:

25 October 1947   *p.4*

Leader   **THE HOUSING CUT**

How much, and how soon, is housing to contribute to the pool of labour needed for diversion to more urgent tasks? We need one more figure than Sir Stafford Cripps gave in his otherwise lucid statement before we can answer these questions. There are now 260,000 houses under construction and 90,000 more under contract. About 20,000 of these are likely to be finished in the next two months, bringing this year's total to perhaps 110,000. Next year, said Sir Stafford, we can expect to finish more. But how many more – 20,000, say, or 120,000? The latter figure would give a total which falls short of that which, in Mr. Bevan's view, could have been attained this year if there had been enough timber and plenty of fuel for the industries producing other materials. Next year, we are told, the supply of these other materials will be 'matched up' to the available timber, and there is timber already in hand for 'many' of the 330,000 houses that will then remain to be completed. If 'many' means two-thirds, and if the Government's decision to complete all these houses 'in the shortest possible time' means what it says, it should not be difficult to get 230,000 finished next year. Of the remaining 100,000, according to Sir Stafford's figures, 70,000 will be completed by mid-1949, leaving 30,000 still under construction. To reach the planned level of 140,000 under construction at that stage, therefore, it would be necessary to start work on 110,000 houses not yet under contract. With the 90,000 now under contract but not yet begun, this means that for the next twenty months we should go on starting new houses at the same average rate (10,000 a month) as in the first eight months of this year. On that basis, it is clear, no labour at all would be released from house-building or from the production of materials for housing. If, however, the real intention is to hold down the rate of completion next year to something between that realised this year and that planned for 1949, then the projected number of houses under construction by mid-1949 can be reached by starting new houses at an average rate of only 5,000 a month, and a substantial labour force would be released next year from house-building as well as from the materials industries.

2 December 1947   *p.4*

Leader   **HOW MANY HOUSES?**

The White Paper makes clear the extent to which expenditure on buildings is to be reduced during 1948. It also indicates how many houses are expected to be finished during 1949. What it still leaves indefinite is the number to be completed during 1948 and hence the rate at which new houses must be started in order to fulfil the promise of 140,000 under construction by mid-1949. Since timber imports are to be cut the amount available for new houses in 1948 will presumably be greater than that which we are told will suffice to finish 140,000 during 1949. It should therefore be possible to complete that number next year in addition to the hundred thousand or so which are already roofed and require no more timber. If that is the intention – as the reiterated undertaking to finish all the houses now in hand 'as quickly as possible' suggests – the average rate at which new houses are begun during the next year and a half cannot be much lower than it has been in the recent past. In that event the cut in housing labour and expenditure will fall largely on work other than the construction of new permanent houses which in fact will be curtailed only to the extent that would in any case have been necessary in order to balance the programme. From the standpoint of social needs that would certainly represent the best distribution of the necessary saving in resources, but whether workers freed from repairs and conversions will become 'available' while master-builders' licences can be had for the asking is another question.

Health

In the area of health 1947 began with an examination of the consequences of the BMA's plebiscite decision not to enter into negotiations with the Minister. During the rest of the year the two parties gradually came together, though the profession's fears were never far below the surface.

10 January 1947   *p.8*

'THE LANCET' ON B.M.A.'S 'UNHAPPY DECISION'
An Appeal to Reverse It

A call to the B.M.A. to reverse its provisional 'unhappy decision' not to discuss the National Health Service with Mr. Bevan is contained in the current issue of 'The Lancet.'

Negotiation to secure the best possible arrangements for both patients and doctor was surely the only course 'for reasonable people,' the paper says. Current discussion on the National Health Service Act suggested that there was a danger of thinking too much about the doctor and too little about the patient.

The essential fact to be kept in mind is that everyone who has studied medical practice in this country agrees that the patient is not getting anything like the full benefit obtainable from modern medicine. In many modern hospitals he has to be content with care which by modern standards is second rate, or worse, and general practice, for all its excellencies, too often resembles the small business which sells the customer what it has in stock rather than what he needs.

The National Health Service scheme was the outcome of discussion and planning over many years and embodied many features of schemes it superseded. Although administrative decisions would be taken by laymen, lay boards had a way of paying attention to the doctor, who at every level was enabled and encouraged to express his views, and if necessary his grievances. There would be medical members and committees at hospitals and the various bodies envisaged by the Act.

'If with all this the voice of medicine cannot make itself heard or is suppressed by the Minister it can be switched over to loud-speakers provided by the British Medical Association and other medical organisations, can be translated into print by the medical press, or can be raised in Parliament.

'Returning to the spirit of the Medical Planning Commission in which it played an impressive part, the British Medical Association should reverse last month's unhappy decision – based as it was on incomplete figures. Nothing short of a new lead from the council or its more cautious members will induce the representative body on January 28 to retrieve an impossible situation.'

On 2 January the Presidents of the Royal Colleges, Lord Moran (Royal College of Physicians), Sir Alfred Webb-Johnson (Royal College of Surgeons) and Mr. William Gilliat (Royal College of Obstetricians and Gynaecologists) wrote to Aneurin Bevan requesting clarification of certain points and assurances about many of the fears which the medical profession had, particularly with regard to the general practitioner service. The main points of this letter were published in the 'Guardian', along with the Minister's reply. Their letter, dated January 2, said:

MR. BEVAN'S REASSURANCES TO DOCTORS
'Free Discussion Without Prejudice'

ANXIOUS FOR THEIR HELP IN SHAPING NEW HEALTH SERVICE

We believe that behind the opposition of members of the profession is the fear that to enter into discussions would compromise their position by implying their approval and acceptance of the main provisions of the Act.

The Presidents raised three points on the general practitioner part of the service –

The first is the method of remuneration. There is general agreement that there are circumstances in which a basic salary or a guaranteed minimum may be necessary, but this is not regarded as justifying a universal basic salary. Cannot the circumstances in which a basic salary is appropriate be left open for discussions?

Secondly, a large element in the opposition is the fact that if the tribunal recommend the expulsion of a practitioner from the service his appeal is to be judged by the Minister, who has appointed two of the three members of the tribunal.

In the third place, there is a widespread and not unfounded fear that there will be serious interference with the liberty of movement of general practitioners. The whole profession regard it as essential that independent practice should continue and that independent practitioners should have the necessary facilities for the treatment of their patients.

The Presidents emphasise their anxiety to induce specialists to do virtually all their work inside hospitals, feeling that 'the importance of the cause justifies this step.'

10 January 1947   *p.5*

MR. BEVAN'S REPLY

Mr. Bevan replied on January 6:

Every doctor will have to decide for himself when the proper time comes whether or not he should take part in the new service, and the profession as a whole will be free to determine their views on the service when they know what it is to be. The resumption of discussions now would not prejudice these eventual decisions.

The issue for the medical profession today is not whether they will join a service, the final shape of which cannot yet be known, but whether they will accept or forgo the opportunity to influence its shaping.

I want to have their help and advice in this task, and I can certainly assure that, if discussions take place, I shall endeavour to meet any views of the profession which do not conflict with the principles of the Act.

'It has been said that I have not consulted the profession and that I have been unwilling to negotiate with them. That is not so. I and my officers had full discussions with the Negotiating Committee and were throughout in close touch with the representatives of the profession. Thus the Government were at all stages fully informed of the views of the profession and the original proposals were modified in many important respects to meet those views.'

Mr. Bevan gives these answers to the questions about general practitioner work–

Remuneration – The Government have accepted the view of the profession that remuneration should be based substantially on capitation fees and have thus rejected the conception of a full-salaried service. I have had it in mind that the remuneration of all general practitioners should include an element of salary but that the element should be small. As you yourselves recognise there are circumstances in which a guaranteed minimum is necessary, and my own view has been that administratively the most convenient method of achieving this object is to make the basic element universal. But this is essentially a matter which I should like to discuss with the profession.

The Tribunal – The question to be decided by the tribunal is whether the retention of a doctor in the medical list would be prejudicial to the efficiency of the service, and I regard the setting up of an independent tribunal as an addition to the safeguards which have prevailed under the National Health Insurance for the last 35 years.

The function of the General Medical Council is to determine whether a doctor has been guilty of unprofessional conduct and that remains unaffected. I will gladly discuss with representatives of the profession the procedure to be followed before deciding an appeal to me from a decision of the tribunal to remove a practitioner's name from the list, with a view to providing any additional protection possible within the framework of the Act.

Liberty of Movement – There is no power to direct a doctor to go anywhere or do anything. There is a provision in the Act the sole object of which is to avoid an undue concentration of doctors in any one area.

What I have in mind as the everyday procedure is that in the case of a partnership or group of doctors the partners or members of the group will have the initiative in selecting a doctor to fill an approved vacancy and normally their selection will be confirmed as a matter of course. Similarly, in the case of a single-handed practice the initiative in selecting the incomer will lie with the local medical committee.

Of specialists and independent practice, Mr. Bevan says it is a basic principle of the new service that 'there should be no interference with the clinical freedom of any doctor – specialist or general practitioner.'

'I am confident,' he adds, 'that round a table we shall be able to make satisfactory arrangements which will encourage specialists to work within the precincts of hospitals – a point to which, like you, I attach the utmost importance.'

DOCTORS TRY AGAIN
A Second Vote?

RECOMMENDATION TO NEGOTIATE

The Council of the British Medical Association yesterday agreed to enter into discussions with the Minister of Health about the National Health Service Act provided that certain conditions are fulfilled and subject to the consent of the association as a whole.

On January 6 the Minister addressed a letter to the presidents of the three Royal Colleges in which he gave certain explanations and reassurances to the medical profession about its position under the present Act. This letter followed on the results of the BMA plebiscite (which showed that 64 per cent of general practitioners in Great Britain had voted against participating in the new service) and on the B.M.A. Council's resolution on December 11 recommending that there should be no negotiations with the Minister on the regulations to be made under the Act. The Council of the B.M.A. yesterday carefully examined the situation created by Mr. Bevan's letter, as regards both its tone and its substance. The council finally passed the following resolution –

That the British Medical Association, having considered the final results of the plebiscite, and the Minister's letter of January 6, and desiring to secure for the people the best possible health service, is willing that discussions be entered into with the Minister to that end, provided that such discussions are comprehensive in their scope and that the possibility that they may lead to further legislation is not excluded and that after the conclusion of these discussions a second plebiscite of the profession be taken on the issue of entering the service.

This resolution, which was passed without opposition, will go forward to the special representative meeting of the Association to be held in London on January 28. It will be for this meeting to decide whether to confirm or reject the council's recommendation.

PROMISE OF NEW PLEBISCITE

By 252 votes to 17 doctors from all parts of the British Isles at a special meeting called by the British Medical Association in London yesterday decided to discuss the national health scheme with Mr. Bevan, 'provided that the possibility of fresh legislation is not excluded.' About 300 representatives were present. . . .

Dr. Guy Dain, the chairman of the council, said two things had happened since it was decided to have no negotiations with the Minister. The presidents of the royal colleges had written a joint letter to the Minister asking a number of questions, and the Minister had replied. It was obvious that the letters, the plebiscite, and the council's strong resolution refusing negotiations had produced in the Minister a more conciliatory attitude than he had hitherto shown. and his letter did contain for the first time an offer to talk to them.

Following the exchange of letters, to refuse any negotiations would put them in the wrong with the press and the public and it was up to them to see that any negotiations were on their terms. They were anxious to provide the best possible health service, and they did not want any spanners in the works to prevent that. This alteration in the position, he insisted, did not mean any weakening of the council's policy to the Act. It was in no sense a climb-down. They must leave no doubt that the discussions would be fruitless unless the Minister was prepared at the end to make such alterations as would meet the principles to which they were firmly attached.

31 January 1947   *p.6*

THE DOCTORS' CASE
Appeal to Mr. Bevan

The current issue of the 'British Medical Journal,' discussing the special representative meeting of the British Medical Association in London on Tuesday, says: 'The Minister of Health and the public generally do not seem to us yet fully to have understood the reasons why so many thoughtful members of the profession criticise the present Act and are apprehensive because of its implications.' The article continues:

It is clear that the representatives, coming from all parts of the country to give voice to the views of the doctors in their divisions and branches, were fully seized of the gravity of the present position, fully determined not to yield on principle, and quite clear about what is meant by the endorsement of the Council's recommendation to enter into discussions with the Minister.

If Mr. Bevan rejects the association's offer, then a complete deadlock will be reached. . . . If we are to be just we must, as a profession, recognise the fact that Mr. Bevan has already made compromises which are not wholly acceptable to his own party. We must recognise, too, that if the Minister agrees to include clauses of the Act in the scope of further discussions he will probably have to face opposition from his own side of the House of Commons. Nevertheless, this is what the profession is asking him to do and asking the public, through Parliament, to do. . . .

We therefore appeal to the Minister of Health to show high political courage by accepting with all its implications, the invitation now extended to him by the representative body as the mouthpiece of more than three-quarters of the doctors of this country.

Thus the BMA and the Ministers finally commenced negotiations and the issues involved, for the time being, disappeared from public view with only the slightest hint at the progress of the discussions.

23 July 1947   *p.3*

B.M.A. DISCUSSIONS ON HEALTH ACT
'No Points Conceded'

No points have been conceded in recent discussions from the position the British Medical Association has taken up on the National Health Service Act. This was disclosed by Dr. H. Guy Dain, chairman of the council, at the annual meeting of the B.M.A., which opened in London yesterday.

Reporting on discussions which B.M.A. committees have had with the Government, he said: 'There has been no attempt on the part of the Minister's officers to tie us down in discussion. Reports we have had were very free, and we have spoken to our principle and have put forward our arguments as vigorously as we know how.'

A written statement of the B.M.A. arguments was being prepared for submission to the Minister as they felt his own officers' reports might put them 'in a milder form.' The final stage was likely to be reached in the autumn, and until then he asked members to leave matters in the hands of the negotiating committee.

A demand to know what has been going on 'behind the closed doors' was made by Dr. H.H. Goodman, of Newcastle. Moving a resolution asking for an early report on the discussions, he declared that there was a very strong body of opinion in the Labour party opposed to the length the Minister had gone in appeasing the medical profession.

During the six months' lull the public had been led to believe that the medical profession was in full agreement with the Government, and had written off the profession as a fighting force. Doctors had been played into the hands of the Minister, and would ultimately be jockeyed into a position from which there was no turning back.

The motion was lost by a large majority.

MR. BEVAN MEETS THE DOCTORS AGAIN
Profession's Dilemma on Health Act

From our London Staff

Fleet Street, Tuesday.

The Minister of Health, Mr. Aneurin Bevan, and Mr. Arthur Woodburn, Secretary of State for Scotland, met the negotiating committee of the medical profession to-day to discuss points relating to the National Health Service Act. The meeting was to have been held last month, but the statement which had been prepared by the doctors was so long and detailed that the Minister asked for more time in which to study it.

A further meeting will be held to-morrow, after which both the statement and the Minister's replies will be made available to the members of the medical profession. A plebiscite will then probably be held among the doctors to decide whether or not they will cooperate in that part of the scheme which applies to general practice.

EARLIER DISCUSSIONS

A Medical Correspondent writes:
The negotiating committee consists of representatives of the B.M.A., the English Royal Colleges, the Scottish Corporations, the Society of Medical Officers of Health, the Medical Women's Federation, the Association of Non-teaching Voluntary Hospitals, and the Society of Apothecaries. A plebiscite of the whole profession was held at the end of 1946 to decide whether the negotiating committee should discuss with the Ministry of Health the regulations and orders to be made under the Act, which received the royal assent on November 6, 1946.

The result of the plebiscite was fairly even, with a slight majority for those voting for no further negotiations (37 per cent votes yes, 44 per cent no). There followed a brief period of stalemate. Then a fresh approach was made possible after correspondence between the three presidents of the Royal Colleges and the Minister of Health. Discussions with the Minister were resumed in February on the clear undertaking that 'such discussions are comprehensive in their scope and that the possibility that they may lead to further legislation is not excluded.' Then Mr. Bevan became conciliatory and the profession, led by the B.M.A. less intransigent.

The negotiations over the past ten months have been conducted without publicity and in a fairly cordial atmosphere by sub-committees of the negotiating committees concerned respectively with general practice, hospital and specialist services, public health, mental health, ophthalmic services, and superannuation. Discussions were with officers of the Ministry and in varying degree each sub-committee achieved a measure of agreement on many topics and a failure to agree on a few points.

DIFFICULT QUESTIONS

All these last few difficult questions on which agreement has not been reached are now being put to the Minister himself in a two-day discussion. It is understood that the profession is particularly concerned about section 35 of the Act, relating to partnership agreements, which it regards as unworkable and requiring considerable amendment. The method of remuneration of doctors under the Act is still unknown. The doctors would like a capitation fee only.

The Minister will probably insist on a capitation fee plus an element of basic salary. Any basic salary is objected to by the profession as a first step towards a full-time State-salaried service. The profession is still worried, too, about what is called 'negative direction,' the right given by the Act to the Medical Practices Committee to exclude a doctor from practising in a fully doctored area.

Once the two-day meeting is over a summary of the representations of the negotiating committee will be published, with the Minister's considered reply. There will follow central and local discussions and a final plebiscite of the whole profession to determine whether it will or will not take service under the Act.

Under the Act as it stands the Minister, or any future Minister, could convert the profession to the wholetime fully salaried service which many doctors fear. This would transform the whole character of medical practice as a free profession and might profoundly alter the relations between doctor and patient. The right to own and therefore to sell a practice, payment by capitation rather than by salary, and freedom to practise anywhere are all essential parts of the present structure.

On the other hand, for a fully co-ordinated and comprehensive service some central direction and control is necessary. The medical profession, in fact, is facing the dilemma familiar to other professions and trades – no planning with all its gaps and inequalities, or planning with certain inevitable restrictions on the individual.

The results of the negotiations were finally published on 18 December in the form of two documents – the Negotiating Committee's statement to the Minister and the Minister's reply.

Leader **TIME FOR DECISION**

All the doctors in the country are about to receive two documents representing from both sides the final outcome of the protracted discussions between the Minister of Health and the profession's negotiating committee. At the end of next month they will be invited to say whether they collectively wish the British Medical Association to advise them individually not to enter the new health service and in a pugnacious statement last night the council of the BMA left no room for doubts that it hopes they will. After reading both documents those doctors who do not share the council's expressed distrust of the Minister's good faith – a compliment he refrains from returning – may well wonder what the fuss is all about. . . .

. . . In many instances definite assurances are given that should be regarded as satisfactory in view of the limits imposed on the field of legislative action by constitutional procedure and practical experience. Among the main outstanding issues are whether the Act invalidates existing partnership agreements and, if not, how compensation for loss of goodwill can be apportioned between partners. On the first Mr. Bevan promises amendment if his legal advisers are found by the experts to be mistaken and on the second he proposes to remove uncertainties by regulation.

. . . Surely this is a flimsy foundation on which to base a demand for the retention of the traffic in practices. . . .

. . . It is not on such grounds that the average doctor will be induced to forgo a great opportunity to devote himself in well-paid security to the real purpose of his profession.

31 December 1947 p.4

THE HEALTH ACT

To the Editor of the Manchester Guardian

Sir,–In your issue of December 19 you state that, after reading the two documents on the discussions just concluded between the Minister of Health and the Medical Negotiating Committee, 'the doctors may well wonder what the fuss is all about.'

The National Health Service Act entails a fundamental revolution in medical tradition and practice, and the doctors have wisely not been content, as you seem to have been content, to read only these two documents, but have studied the terms of the Act itself, and two salient provisions leap to the eye, which, combined, give the present Minister of Health and his successors a more absolute control of the liberties, personal and professional, of individual doctors than obtains anywhere outside the regimes recognised as totalitarian.

(1) Section 86 reserves to the holder of the office of Minister of Health (and I have myself seen that office held by five different persons in the last seven years) the power of determining, by regulations which have the force of law, and offer no possibility of successful challenge, 'the qualifications, remuneration, and conditions of service of any officer employed under the Act'. It will thus be entirely possible for this Minister, or his successors, so to change the 'remuneration and conditions of services' as to transform the present system of partial basic State remuneration into a full-time salaried State service, and it was made abundantly clear during the debates on the N.H.S. Bill that this is the ultimate and unalterable aim of the Socialist party, to be implemented when as Mr. Bevan said, 'the time is ripe' to achieve it. It is the equally unalterable resolve of the medical profession, recorded in repeated resolutions with majorities approaching unanimity, by its accredited representatives, during the past four years, to resist this ultimate aim.

(2) Section 42 provides that when a member of one of six named classes of employees, including doctors, dentists, and pharmacists, is dismissed from the service (and his livelihood thereby endangered) his prescriptive right of appeal to the Law Courts is refused, the Minister alone being constituted the final judge. The history of this section is significant. A motion to allow appeal to the Law Courts was carried in the committee stage of the bill, but this decision was subsequently reversed on report stage, the Minister protesting that he could not tolerate possible reversal of his decisions by any outside body, and his protest was of course endorsed by the subservient Socialist majority in the Chamber.

I submit, sir, that these considerations warrant 'some fuss being made' by those concerned to defend their essential liberties as citizens of a free country.— Yours &c.

E. GRAHAM-LITTLE
House of Commons
December 27.

Education

Education remained curiously dormant again in 1947, the year in which the school leaving age of fifteen years came into effect. What debate there was tended once more to be extra-parliamentary and confined to the educationalists and the parents of children about to embark upon, or already in, secondary education. The issues of primary education, the curriculum and the control and administration of education simply did not arise. The year did, however, bring the debate about multi-lateral schools to the fore, as local authorities began to unveil their plans for future development, and on a sadder note also brought the death of Ellen Wilkinson, Minister of Education.

1 January 1947   *p.8*

SECONDARY SCHOOL CLASSIFICATIONS
Assistant Masters' Views

From our Special Correspondent

Blackpool, Tuesday.

A resolution by the London branch expressing alarm at the tendency shown in recent Ministry of Education circulars to divide children into types, was rejected by the council of the Incorporated Association of Assistant Masters in Secondary Schools to-day, after Mr. A.W.S. Hutchings, the secretary, had described it as 'most dangerous' in its implication.

Mr.E.J. Wynburne, the proposer, called for a rigid examination by competent educational bodies, on which the association was represented, of the validity of the underlying assumption in the circular. 'Are the children of eleven who come to us of three fundamental, differing types,' he asked, 'or is there a hangover from the past to train children to be members of particular classes of society with particular economic functions? To what extent is this vile vocationalism perpetuated in current circulars in order to aid administrative convenience?'

Mr. Hutchings said that if the resolution were passed it would be interpreted as support for politcal attack upon the Ministry's views. 'It is probably the most dangerous one we have to consider.'

Discussion then turned upon multi-lateral schools as opposed to secondary grammar, modern, and technical schools, and whether children's minds did conveniently fit into one of the three classifications. Mr. R.E.R. Evans said that local education authorities were dividing children into three types without allowance for variation. 'The three types is sheer nonsense,' he said,' and it is ruining the whole future of secondary education.'

17 January 1947   *p.6*

OLDHAM'S £2,000,000 SCHEME FOR EDUCATION
Multilateral Secondary Schools

The multilateral secondary school has been accepted as the basis of the development plan which Oldham Education Committee has submitted to the Minister of Education. Its proposals, embodied in a £2,000,000 scheme, provide for six county multilateral secondary schools – each with accommodation for approximately 1,000 pupils – and for a similar Church of England school, approval for which has been given by the Church authorities. There will also be two new Roman Catholic secondary schools in Oldham and a third in Middleton will take some Oldham children.

The Oldham authority has rejected the Govenment suggestion – reinforced in pamphlet and in circular letter – that in large urban areas secondary education should be given in three distinct types of school – grammar, technical, and 'modern.' Under the borough plan there is to be no separation. Except for two bilateral – modern – technical – Roman Catholic schools, all the secondary schools will be multilateral, receiving children without any examination or test directly from the primary schools and offering each type of education.

Between them, the schools will be able to offer every sort of alternative course at Higher School Certificate standard, and, at the same time, each school will be big enough to offer special treatment to backward children in classes limited to single age ranges. . . .

In an interview with a 'Manchester Guardian' representative yesterday, Mr. Maurice Harrison, Director of Education in Oldham, replied to certain points raised by Dr. Eric James, High Master of the Manchester Grammar School, in a recent speech. He 'entirely disagreed' with Dr. James that certain subjects which were just practical in the grammar school – Greek, advanced mathematics, and science, for example – would drop out of the curriculum of the community school.

'Dr. James,' he said, 'is able to offer any course in Higher School Certificate because he has 1,450 boys. But in the average grammar school you are asked what you would like to do and then the headmaster tells you what you have got to do. We will have Higher School Certificate work in every one of our schools although not every type of work, but we will have every type in the seven schools together, and we will use them as a group, basing our Higher Certificate work on the sixth forms in the schools as a whole.'

Mr. Harrison also referred to the criticism that there would be an insufficient number of boys of the 'grammar school type.' That might be, but 'we will have a large number of boys who, under the present system, never see the inside of a grammar school but who are well able to do grammar school work in one or two subjects. Only a multilateral school can give them that opportunity. We will have much bigger numbers working in our higher forms than Dr. James realises.'

LETTERS TO THE EDITOR

27 January 1947   *p.4*

SECONDARY SCHOOLS

To the Editor of the Manchester Guardian

Sir,–The Oldham Education Committee's development plan, described in your issue of January 17, stands out as being one of those which, in practice, is most likely to meet all the requirements of the Education Act concerning secondary education. The proposal appears to be to build six multilateral schools of approximately 1,000 children each, an arrangement which should solve some of the most pressing social and educatinal problems of the school system to-day. First, the 11 plus examination, with all its attendant evils, will be finally abolished as unnecessary. Second, every child will be guaranteed an equal opportunity of obtaining the best educational facilities provided. Third, all children from a given area, with their differing aptitudes and interests, will attend the same school, a factor which is bound to lead to a richer school life and a closer contact between the school and the community than could otherwise be obtained.

In his interview with your correspondent the Director of Education for Oldham crossed swords with Dr. James on the important question as to whether a multilateral system could provide specialist education of a standard equivalent to that now reached in the sixth forms of the grammar schools. He points out that, using the multilateral schools as a group, it will be possible to offer an even wider range of specialist work than is often possible in the average grammar school. Since the argument that the multilateral school is bound to lower standards and to lead to a more limited choice is one of the main planks of the grammar school protagonists, it would be interesting to see their objections to the Oldham scheme on this point.

It is encouraging to find a Lancashire town, leading educational progress. Development plans have still to be issued in the case of 14 more local authorities in Lancashire, and perhaps some of them will follow Oldham's example.– Yours &c.

Brian Simon,
16, Moorfield Road, Manchester 20, January 19

30 January 1947   *p.4*

SECONDARY EDUCATION

To the Editor of the Manchester Guardian

Sir,–Although letters are not, perhaps, the most satisfactory way of carrying on education controversy, since Mr. Brian Simon in his comments on the Oldham plan has specifically referred to my views on the question of multilateralism, I fee that some rejoinder is called for. It would, of course take too long even to summarise all the arguments against the multilateral school which includes in a common school at the secondary level children of all intelligences.

The particular point which Mr. Simon raises concerns academic standards and the range of specialist work. Briefly, the position is this. In multilateral school of 1,000 pupils perhaps 200 will be of grammar-school type – that is, of verbal or academic ability capable of learning a foreign language fairly easily. This will mean that of these children one age-group will be put together in one or at most two classes, instead of being distributed according to their abilities and intersts into four or even more classes, as in most grammar schools. Such a concentration violates the principle of fitting the education to the child, and must sacrifice both the most and least able members of the group. . . .

It should, however, be remembered by the layman that there is almost complete unanimity among those who have had first-hand experience of the grammar schools (and not all who write about them have had such experience) that neither on grounds of social justice nor national expediency can the multilateral experiment be justified. We are in danger both of removing the chance which the grammar schools give to children of every class to enjoy the academic opportunities of the wealthy and of destroying the vital contribution these schools have made to our national life.-Yours, &c.,

ERIC JAMES,

The Manchester Grammar School, January 27.

3 February 1947   *p.4*

Leader   **NEW SCHOOLS**

April 1, 1947, when the school-leaving age goes up to 15, will be a milestone in the history of English education. The metaphor is hackneyed but apt in this instance. For a few steps carry one past a milestone and the character of the road does not change abruptly with the mark; yet something measurable has been reached and passed. Anyone who expects obvious symptoms of a revolutionary change on April 2 will be disappointed. But a new revolutionary principle will have come into education – the attempt to provide secondary education of three distinct types embodied in the grammar school, the junior technical school and the modern school respectively. Hitherto the school system has hardly gone beyond trying to find large pegs for large holes: the cleverer children were given the chance to stay at school longer. The new scheme tries to provide round holes for round pegs. Human beings have ability not only in differing degrees but of different kinds. . . .

The commonest though not the only special lines can be labelled 'verbal' and 'mechanical.' The Ministry of Education's scheme assumes that what is known to be true of adults is also true of children, that special aptitudes are, before the age of fifteen, already well enough differentiated to be worth special training.

The article goes on to consider the variety of schemes which local education authorities had proposed in order to accommodate the pegs in the appropriate holes:

Some (for instance, Dorset and East Suffolk) conform to the official intention and submit schemes based mainly on 'unilateral' schools, specialising in one type only of curriculum. At the other extreme, Middlesex has announced its intention to set up 'common schools' to which all children in an area will go and will take roughly the same course. Birmingham plans unilateral schools for most of the city, but multilateral in one district. Bristol and Rotherham seem to distinguish grammar from modern schools, but to lump technical in with modern. Others rely on 'multilateral' schools, in which the three types of education will be kept distinct, but given side by side under the same roof and the same head master. Surrey, the West Riding of Yorkshire, Coventry and Oldham are following this principle: Bradford Education Committee has just gone over to it, after starting on the ulilateral path. This solution gets over the superficial social difficulty; if every boy wears the same cap, no matter what he learns, differences in schooling will not be translated into social distinctions. That may satisfy some political critics. But it does not go far to meet the technical problem. It will still be necessary to determine when a child enters the school at 'eleven plus' which 'side' he is to go on; and in practice it is not found very much easier to switch a boy from one side to another than from one school to another. If the problem is really there the multilateral school conceals rather than solves it. And then, as Dr. James, the High Master of the Manchester Grammar School, has pointed out, the multilateral school has another defect. Unless it is on an enormous scale there may not be on any 'side' enough pupils of both the age and the ability to make up a class for the more specialised studies appropriate to the older children. With such a variety of options before it the Ministry will be wise not to insist on strict uniformity in all areas. The next five yeas are bound to be in some measure experimental, and we may learn more from the experiment if there is variety in the data. This is no field for fixed ideas. Neighbouring authorities must not be too proud to learn from each other.

LETTERS TO THE EDITOR

3 February 1947   *p.4*

SECONDARY EDUCATION

To the Editor of the Manchester Guardian

Sir, – Whatever may be the merits of the multilateral school, Mr. Brian Simon, in your issue of January 27, is surely going too far when he claims as one of them that 'all children from a given area, with their different aptitudes and interests, will attend the same school.'

So long as we have in this country independent schools (including the public schools, which are mainly boarding) and direct-grant schools (which are mainly day schools) most parents who can afford the fees will use every effort to place their sons in them. By the much higher standard of ability and attainment which these schools, especially those of the direct-grant type, can now through the increased demand require for admission, and by the scholarships which they offer for boys needing financial help, they take off the cream of the intellect in the county or in the area which they serve. I do not wish to see their privileged position weakened.

190

Mr. Simon seems to think that the multilateral school will achieve that 'parity of esteem' which is to-day one of the main problems of education. It may succeed in doing so among the different types of State-maintained schools, but it will be at the cost of creating a new class cleavage, based on education, which will be wider than any existing before the Education Act of 1944.

The Act, of course, illustrates the British genius for compromise, but until its leading advocates in politics and in educational administration send their own children to the State schools one cannot feel completely convinced of their sincerity in some of the claims which they make for it or regard the Act as truly democratic.—Yours, &c.,

Headmaster,
January 28.

Ellen Wilkinson died on 6 February 1947.

7 February 1947   *p.4*

Leader   **ELLEN WILKINSON**

The death of Ellen Wilkinson will be felt nowhere more than in Manchester. Here she was born and bred and though the city has seen little of her in these later years she carried a tang of Manchester with her wherever she went. She brought to public affairs an acute mind, an ebullient spirit, and – the dominant thing in her – a passion for social justice, an intuitive and devoted partisanship for the poor and the weak which found a fertile field in the dismal years of deflation and unemployment between the wars. It was by a finely dramatic stroke of history that she became at last the member for Jarrow, most tragical and hopelessly smitten of all the victims of the great slump. She had a vein of intransigence, she could be an uncomfortable colleague as well as a ruthless opponent. She could write with force, wit and pith. Letters or journalism lost a craftswomen to politics. But it is hard to think of her making her career in anything but the Labour movement. . . .

Her last years have been given to the drive to train teachers and build classrooms enough to make possible the raising of the school-leaving age without postponement; though she will not see it she lived long enough to ensure that it should be so and to know that it would be so. Meredith bade us 'plod on, and keep the passion fresh.' Plodding was not much in Ellen Wilkinson's line, but all politics are something of a plod, and few politicians have ever kept the passion fresher.

DEATH OF MISS WILKINSON
Government's Loss

HER WORK FOR EDUCATION

From our Political Correspondent

Westminster, Thursday.

The much regretted death of Miss Ellen Wilkinson, the Minister of Education, is not only a personal loss to the Government – both Mr. Attlee and Mr. Churchill spoke of her energy and conscientiousness to-day – but imposes on Mr. Attlee the task of making changes in his Ministry at a moment when he is hard pressed with major problems.

No announcement of Ministerial changes is to be expected for some days, but the appointment of a successor cannot long be delayed, since the Ministry is immediately concerned with the raising of the school-leaving age on April 1.

It is difficult to judge of Miss Wilkinson's work as Minister of Education, since she was handicapped in two respects. Her health has not been good while she has held this office, and probably a less dogged person would not have attempted to perform such arduous duties as long as Miss Wilkinson did.

In the second place, she succeeded to the Ministry at a time when it was just beginning to apply the Education Act of 1944 – a major measure which had been piloted through Parliament by Mr. R.A. Butler, a Coalition Minister. Miss Wilkinson therefore had the heavy but unrewarding task of devoting herself to somebody else's legislation. She did introduce an amending bill, but it raised no great points of principle.

It should, however, be recalled that Miss Wilkinson's last important public act was to end the widespread rumours that the Government might defer the raising of the school-leaving age by stating bluntly that it would be raised on April 1.

Miss Wilkinson's death causes a by-election at Jarrow, which she held against a Liberal National at the general election by 22,656 votes to 11,649.

MISS WILKINSON'S SUCCESSOR

The appointment of Mr. George Tomlinson as Minister of Education is excellent. He has vigour and judgment, he knows the administrative machinery of education well, and has served as president of the Association of Education Committees. He is just the man to make the new Education Act work. Mr. Attlee has paid Lancashire a compliment in choosing one Lancashire-born M.P. to follow another at the Ministry of Education. But in one respect Mr. Tomlinson's path to the office has been even more remarkable than Miss Wilkinson's. She worked her way from a primary school to the university. He never went to a secondary school at all; at the age of twelve he went into the weaving shed as a half-timer. He will appreciate, even more vividly than she could, the meaning of secondary schooling for all.

LONDON SCHOOL PLAN WILL INVOLVE EXPENDITURE OF £187,000,000
Clean Break with Ministry Recommendation

The 'comprehensive high school' providing a 'many-sided education in an atmosphere of social unity,' is the main instrument chosen for the London School Plan to carry out the programme of development called for by the Education Act of 1944. The plan was published yesterday and will be considered by the LCC shortly.

The plan will involve a capital expenditure of £187,000,000 and an addition to the rates of about 4s. in the pound. It will provide for about 190,000 children in secondary schools (when 16 becomes the leaving age), for 216,000 children in primary schools, and for 54,000 children in nursery schools.

ORIGINAL FEATURES

The most original feature of the plan is the method proposed for getting round the problem of the existing 'voluntary' secondary schools – formerly known as 'aided' and now as 'assisted' schools. Many of these are too small, or too restricted in scope, to form self-contained units in the County Plan. On the other hand, the LCC has no power under the Act to enlarge or make building grants to voluntary schools.

It is therefore proposed 'in order to realise the comprehensive school as nearly as possible, to provide as near as may be to each of them a county school which will provide the accommodation necessary to complete the unit.' . . .

EQUAL OPPORTUNITY

The development plan should aim,' the plan says, 'at providing all pupils with equal opportunity for physical, intellectual, social, and spiritual development. . . . The education proposed can best be described as a liberal education. Each course will consist of two parts:

(a) A core common to all, which will include religious education, physical education, English, social studies, general science, mathematics, languages, music, art and craft.
(b) More specialised work and study, related to groups of professional, industrial, or commercial occupations, and chosen according to the age, aptitude, and ability of a group of pupils.'

Besides coming out strongly against the tripartite division of secondary education the London Plan also avoided the term 'multilateral' in favour of 'comprehensive.'

RAISING THE SCHOOL AGE
Shortage of Books and Furniture the Main Difficulty

From our London Staff

Fleet Street, Monday.

Apart from a broadcast by Mr. George Tomlinson, the Minister of Education, to-night, nothing will be done officially to mark the fact that to-morrow the school-leaving age goes up to 15 without exemptions.

An official of the Ministry said to-day that the forecasts of difficulty in putting into effect the new Education Act would prove, on the whole, unnecessarily gloomy. Not only would there be enough teachers by 1948 (when the full effect of the Act will be felt) to deal with the raising of the school-leaving age, but there would be others available for the almost equally important reform of reducing the size of classes.

In all, 130,000 children who would normally have left school at the end of next term will have another year's education and will go back to school in September. By September, 1948, there will be another 260,000 extra children in the classrooms but they will not impose any strain on the staffing resources.

TRAVELLING TEACHERS

The provision of places for these extra children is not so easy. One third of them can be accommodated in existing schools but the others will have to be taught temporarily in prefabricated huts or by such improvisations as travelling teachers and mobile units containing cinema and radio apparatus. By September this year it is anticipated that about 90 per cent of the temporary schools needed will have been provided though it is not possible to be quite as confident on this point as it is about the numbers of teachers available.

The travelling teachers and mobile units will be needed not so much to make up for absence of classrooms as to help small schools to fit small numbers of extra pupils of the 14–15 age group into the curriculum. By far the most serious obstacles to completing the programme will be equipment and books. Although the amount of extra furniture needed could be made in four-and-a-half weeks under normal conditions, its manufacture will have to be spread over eighteen months and will be subject to delays caused by the fuel cuts as well as by the shortages of timber and steel.

The cuts have also had a most serious effect on the printing of additional books. By arrangement with the Board of Trade and the Ministry of Supply, paper has been made available to educational publishers at rates between 37½ per cent and 80 per cent of the amount used in 1939. Recent stoppages in the paper mills have reduced this amount and delays in printing are serious. Even this difficulty, however, is not as bad as it might have been. It will be September before additional books are needed in really large quantities and by that time the effect of summer production (at a time of reduced demand) will have been felt. . . .

'The raising of the school age makes possible the development of a system under which every child will have an equal chance to become the best sort of man or woman that each has it in him or her to become,' said Mr.George Tomlinson, Minister of Education, in a broadcast last night.

Until buildings and teachers were available to meet all requirements less than the best would have to be put up with, but the additional year was going to be worth while. By the end of August, when the first real need for additional accommodation would be felt, they were hoping to have the 'hut' programme very largely complete. The 13,000 teachers whom it was estimated would be needed for the raising of the school-leaving age were guaranteed by the emergency training scheme alone. 'We expect to have a substantial margin for reducing the size of the classes by September, 1948,' Mr. Tomlinson added. 'The success of this scheme for the training of teachers to meet the emergency has been phenomenal.'

SCHOOL-LEAVING AGE
An Investment for the Future

Mr. George Tomlinson, Minister of Education, speaking at the conference of the National Union of Teachers at Scarborough yesterday, defended the raising of the school-leaving age. He looked upon the extra year as an investment which would pay dividends for the whole of the rest of the child's life.

The purpose of education was the greatest cause in the world and was the making of men and women of the future who would build a new world to heal the sickness of the old, the Minister said. 'We all know that now as never before, if the future generation do not make a better job of it than we have done, there will be no future at all for their successors or for civilisation as we have known it,' he added.

Too often in the past education has been the first and easiest victim of false economy. They were not going to let it happen again and had proclaimed their faith in education by raising the school-leaving age at a time of great difficulty. In that process the teacher was the vital link.

'At a pinch you might be able to do without Parliament. You could do without the Minister, you could certainly do without civil servants and almost as certainly without local education authorities. Without any or all of them the world might not seem very much the worse. But if there were no teachers the world would be back in barbarism within two generations. That simple fact is the measure of the responsibility and privilege which every good teacher should carry with a sense of pride.'

MEANING OF EQUALITY

'We all want equality of opportunity and we mean to see that it becomes a reality. But more than anything else that means that the child who is born in a tiny remote village must be taught with the same skill and devotion as his brother who grows up in one of the great cities.'

GRAMMAR SCHOOLS' FUTURE
No Autocratic Control

A circular on multilateral and other kinds of secondary schools is being issued by the Minister of Education on June 17, and on June 10 a pamphlet will be published on 'What we mean by secondary education.'

Mr. George Tomlinson, the Minister, addressing the Association of Education Committees at Brighton yesterday, said that these were very important documents and he thought they would dispose of accusations that the Ministry wanted to discourage experiments and that it was trying to put the grammar schools in a strait jacket of autocratic control.

'The grammar school has occupied a unique place in the British education system,' he added, 'but we want to make equality of opportunity a reality and give an equal chance to those children who don't go to the grammar school.'

The last thing he wanted to do was to lower the standards of the grammar schools or subject them to bureaucratic control; his aim was to weaken nothing and strengthen everything. Nor did he want to discourage experiment in multilateral and other similar kinds of schools. Every type of secondary school had its own distinctive contribution to make.

Leader ## THE GRAMMAR SCHOOLS

The grammar schools will be grateful to Mr. George Tomlinson, the Minister of Education, for his assurance given yesterday to the Association of Education Committees that 'the last thing he wishes to do is to lower the standards of the grammar schools' or to 'put them in a strait-jacket of automatic control.' They will look forward to seeing this doctrine expounded in a fuller and more concrete form in the promised circulars on secondary education which his Ministry is to issue this month. The grammar school is threatened by two foes. One is the ambitious director of education, eager to extend his field of control as widely as he can, often with colourable [sic] grounds of administrative efficiency. The other is the zealous equalitarian, not uncommon on education committees where the Labour party holds a majority, who in his zeal for equality of opportunity is willing to risk sacrificing the quality of the best schooling given or even to justify lowering it for the sake of a higher over-all average. (It is not suggested that all directors or all Socialists take these views, but where they do they are a formidable combination.) The Labour party's policy, quite rightly, is one of equal opportunity. But this is a target to be aimed at and gradually attained as the new schools, which are to be called into being in the next five years or so, can be equipped with adequate buildings, strong staffs, and a corporate spirit of their own. It is a matter of decades before the tree now planted comes fully to fruit. In the meantime there may be in some places a certain lingering jealousy of the direct-grant schools and a readiness to detract from their position and to take away from them some of the privileges to which they owe part of their peculiar virtues. This, Mr. Tomlinson rejects as 'plain madness.' But it may follow inevitably from measures which in themselves appear perfectly sane.

The circulars referred to, 'The Organisation of Secondary Education' and 'The New Secondary Education,' were commented on by a leading article the following month.

14 July 1947   *p.4*

Leader   **A NEW SERVICE**

. . . The lead which these documents offer comes at the right moment. It was evident from the start that the universal secondary education which was the core of the Act would amount to the creation for the majority of a completely new educational service. The full magnitude, however, of the changes involved and the numerous alternative possibilities between which, in order to give effect to them, a choice must be made could not at once be grasped. The first necessity, therefore, was to translate the idealism of Mr. Butler's White Paper into the pedestrian realities of administrative arrangements. That stage, though not completed, is well advanced. The need for schools of different types has been estimated, difficulties measured, objectives stated, qualified and re-defined and – though there are still some laggards – the development plans of most authorities submitted to the Ministry. . . .

The pillars of the New Order are, in short, to be two. The first is equality of conditions in respect of staffing, buildings, equipment, libraries, playing-fields, and all other essentials. The second is a wide variety of provisions 'designed', in the words of the late Minister, 'to suit different children not different income groups.'

Given these guiding conceptions, both till yesterday not only defied in practice but challenged in principle, and both – though obviously time will be needed to make them a reality – today generally accepted, their possible applications are of great diversity. The threefold classification of which most is commonly heard was never intended to imply, as the recent circular points out, that only three types of secondary education are practicable or desirable. Not only separate grammar, modern and technical schools but multi-lateral and bilateral schools, 'comprehensive' schools and 'school-bases' all have claims to consideration. The essential need at the moment is for experiment. . . .

1 August 1947 *p.5*

£213,000,000 TO BE SPENT ON EDUCATION
Minister Advised to 'Grip Essentials'

By our Parliamentary Correspondent

Westminster, Thursday.

For the first time since he became Minister of Education, Mr. George Tomlinson today introduced the Estimates of his department – £213,000,000 – in the House of Commons. Between thirty and forty Labour members heard him. A party that is supposed to be passionate about education might have done better than that. The Opposition supplied about the same number of auditors.

Education can always be counted on to fill any part of the House except the Chamber. Mr. Tomlinson was worth a better audience for his own sake. He is humorous, humane and rich in commonsense. He was not content to talk only about the work of his department. He talked about life in general and life in a Lancashire weaving shed in particular.

He had things to say about 'tackling' and tacklers and about neglecting tackling in order to read 'Hamlet.' He made this personal confession to illustrate the superiority of a liberal to a technical education. There was also a word about 'the little town of Accrington,' the ajective clearly being a term of affection and not intended in the least to subtract from the vast importance of Accrington. No Lancashire man would dream of doing that. . . .

On the subject of grammar schools he warmly repudiated suggestions made by some critics that the Government is seeking to reduce their standard. He counselled the friends of the grammar school 'not to cry stinking fish lest it should begin to stink.' He argued that the value of a school is not to be seen in its relation to other schools and that the status of the grammar school could not be endangered by bringing the secondary schools up to the standard of the grammar schools, which was the simple aim of the Government.

It was when referring to 'further education' that Mr. Tomlinson dared to insist on the higher values of a liberal as opposed to technical education though he did it without in the least depreciating technical education for its own specific ends.

Mr. R.A. Butler, the author of the 1944 Act, who followed Mr. Tomlinson, did not think the Minister had sufficiently allowed for the possible effect of the economic crisis on education, but he advised him to grip essentials and insist on a certain order of priorities being met, though that might necessitate warning the country that some educational reforms could not be carried out as quickly as could have been liked.

Social Security and Welfare

In the area of social security and welfare services 1947 was a relatively quiet year. Preparatory work was undertaken in the provision of services for children deprived of a normal home background and the commitment to legislation, in this area and in national assistance, contained in the King's speech finally sounded the death-knell for the Poor Law. The major legislation for income maintenance had been passed, though it was not yet fully operational, and neither the proposed Children Bill nor the National Assistance Bill stimulated any sustained political debate at a time when the Government's handling of the economic crisis provided the real focus for the Opposition's attack.

25 March 1947   *p.5*

GOVERNMENT ACCEPTS CURTIS REPORT
New Branch of the Home Office for Child Welfare

From our Political Correspondent

Westminster, Monday.

Mr. Attlee told the House of Commons to-day that the Government had accepted the recommendations of the Curtis Committee (for England and Wales) and the Clyde Committee (for Scotland) that the welfare of children deprived of a normal home should be supervised by a single separate department.

The Home Office, with a new children's branch, will be responsible in England and Wales, and the Home Department in Scotland. A standing advisory committee, representative of the Ministries of Health, Education and Labour, and other interests, will assist the Home Office. The special duties now held by the Admiralty, the War Office, and the Ministry of Pensions for orphans are not affected by the new arrangements.

County councils and country boroughs are to be the local authorities responsible for the welfare of all deprived children and will have to prepare schemes for the approval of the Home Secretary and the Scottish Secretary. 'It is proposed,' said Mr. Attlee, 'that unless there are exceptional reasons to the contrary the local authority should, at least for a period of three years, exercise their responsibility through a children's committee on the lines suggested in the Curtis and Clyde reports. It is also intended that the schemes should make provision for the appointment by each local authority of a children's officer who would be in general charge of the work of providing a home background for homeless children.'

Legislation will be needed to wind up the Poor Law (under which some homeless children are provided for) and to require local authorities to submit schemes. No clear statement has been made by the Government about how soon legislation may be introduced, but it must be enacted before the new national health arrangements come into full operation in April, 1948.

25 March 1947   *p.4*

Leader   **THE CARE OF CHILDREN**

The Government's decision to bring the task of caring for children deprived of a normal home life under one central department should do away with much of the inefficiency caused by the shared responsibility of three Ministries. The responsibility will now belong to the Home Office, which will have a new and enlarged children's department and a much larger staff of inspectors. These changes would not, however, in themselves ensure that any one homeless child was properly cared for. The test of the matter is in the local administration. The Curtis Report spoke strongly on this, and the Government also accepts its recommendations that the county councils and county borough councils should be the responsible local authorities and that they should work for three years at least, through an ad hoc children's committee. Here there is likely to be some criticism. The Association of Education Committees has urged that the special children's committee 'would perpetuate the worst features of the existing system' and would cause these children to be still classed apart. It would prefer to see the Education Committee taking over the care of all children over two. It might be well if this question were considered further before legislation is presented. It is essential that the local arrangements, upon which all depends, should be satisfactory, now that the Government has at last taken the first step towards a real reform.

CHILD WELFARE
Miss Myra Curtis on Home Influences

From our London Staff

Fleet Street, Tuesday.

Miss Myra Curtis, principal of Newnham College, Cambridge, addressing the annual meeting of the N.S.P.C.C., presided over by Princess Elizabeth in London yesterday, said that the work of the Curtis Committee should make an important difference to the welfare and happiness of our children.

She thought the essential features of home life were affection, security, confidence in the future, and a sense of being backed in one's adventures in life. Miss Curtis emphasised the importance of the co-operation of local authorities. She urged every area to appoint a 'children's officer' and make provision for the first reception of children who were removed from their homes and she hoped that by this means the Poor Law stigma would finally disappear. 'The worst things the members of the committee saw in their travels were in the workhouses,' she said. 'We do not want children to be in workhouses at all except in the direst emergency.'

Miss Curtis was not in favour of the care of homeless children coming wholly under public control. She thought that voluntary societies and public authorities should continue to work side by side.

NEEDS OF 'NOBODY'S CHILDREN'
A Liberal View of the Curtis Report

From our London Staff

Fleet Street, Thursday.

A committee appointed in September by the Liberal party executive to consider the findings of the Curtis Committee issued its own report, 'Nobody's Children,' to-day. The committee was under the chairmanship of Mr. Russell Vick, K.C., and included among its members Lady Violet Bonham Carter and Lady Rhys Williams.

Mr. Fothergill, chairman of the party executive, expressed dismay at a press conference this afternoon that the Labour Government had been so slow in taking action to carry out the Curtis

Report. The Labour party had given the impression before it came into power that it had shared the humanitarian outlook of the Liberals. The Government's record of the last two years had exploded that idea. The social conscience of the country was now aroused and again the Liberal party had come along with a statement of what ought to be done.

The Government's decision to place on the Home Office the ultimate responsibility for the care of homeless children is warmly welcomed, as also is the decision to retain the day-to-day provision of care in the hands of the local authorities. The report emphasises that the Home Office should have the power to bring a defaulting authority into court.

October brought what Sir Stafford Cripps called a 'Battle for Democracy' when announcing stricter food rationing, cuts in capital expenditure and production of luxury goods for export only in a bid to reduce the dollar deficit to £250,000,000 a year by the end of 1948. A 'Guardian' leader commented:

24 October 1947   *p.4*

Leader   **BITTER TRUTHS**

Slowly and painfully the Government has been brought to admit the truth that social progress must be halted and our standard of living reduced. This is what the Government refused to face all through the summer. It has now to admit it bleakly, and Sir Stafford Cripps yesterday gave no crumb of comfort that there is any other way out.

. . . The programme Sir Stafford Cripps sketched is finely balanced. If anything it is too optimistic and assumes that our production and our exports will rapidly mount, in spite of the dislocation that the change-over must cause. In any case it is only an interim programme. We can make few long-term readaptations for another twelve or eighteen months in such things as food and mechanical equipment. All the struggles that are before us are 'to buy time.' A dollar crisis will remain with us and the cuts in our standard of living will, in large measure, be permanent. It is doubtful whether the political implications of this have been worked out. Certainly they have not been worked out by some members of the Government and of the Opposition.

Only by careful study of Sir Stafford's speech will ordinary men and women take in the bitter truths. If they do not economise on coal and tobacco there will soon be less of either. Our food rations are to be cut. The housing programme is to slow down. Factory building will drop away to nothing. Only by increases of output unlikely to be achieved quickly will home supplies of consumer goods be kept up and some classes of goods must in any case become very scarce. Everywhere we see a tightening of the restrictions on imports and a forced draught to export. The consequences will be felt in every home and factory. It remains now to get these truths home to the people on whom it falls to work and to suffer. That will be done best in a clear political atmosphere when first things are put first and goodwill is mobilised, unspoiled by rancour and sourness. But the Government will have to make its contribution too.

In spite of this the 'Guardian' found some cause for optimism in the National Assistance Bill.

1 November 1947   *p.4*

Leader   **RELIEF AND WELFARE**

'The final break-up of the Poor Law' is described as a fundamental object of the National Assistance Bill. This in itself would be no great achievement for the scope of that heavy statute has been whittled down to insignificant proportions. Every insurable cause of poverty is covered by national insurance and separate provision has been made for every substantial class of persons whose misfortunes cannot be brought within an insurance scheme. The local authority's duty as legatee of the Elizabethan parish to relieve the destitute has been retained only as a catch-all for cases that defy both actuarial treatment and statutory classification. It is not the mere transference of these vestigial obligations to the state that makes this Bill important nor is it the symbolic value of the concluding step in a protracted social revolution. The point is that henceforth a single national agency operating a uniform code will accept on the nation's behalf the responsibility for preventing any citizen from falling involuntarily below a minimum subsistence standard of living. The duty remaining to the local authority will be the very different one of providing positive welfare services for people in need of help for reasons other than financial; those who are destitute as well as handicapped will be enabled by the National Assistance Board to take advantage of such provisions on the same footing as those with private means. In this way local welfare services will be cleansed of the 'Poor Law taint.' It only remains to ensure that the spirit and standard of these services will prevent them from acquiring a taint of their own that would defeat their purpose.

THE LAST OF THE POOR LAW

Westminster, Monday.

Two notes were struck in the second reading debate on the National Assistance Bill in the Commons to-day. On the one hand, there was a jolly valedictory to the last remnants of the Poor Law now extinguished by the bill, on the other, the bill was hailed as putting 'the copingstone' (thus Mr. Aneurin Bevan in one of his more prosaic moments) on the nation's social services.

Mr. Bevan introduced his bill with remarkable sobriety. He has never so risen above party. Indeed, he was obviously prepared to make a love feast of it if the Opposition was willing. A Minister has not often introduced such a bill and claimed so little credit for it on behalf of his Government, which is all the more remarkable remembering Gravesend. He spoke in praise of Beatrice and Sidney Webb's work, but added that there were others who had helped in the abolition of the Poor Law and that they belonged to all parties. That was generous enough.

Colonel Walter Elliott 'welcomed the bill' on behalf of the Opposition, but it was a grudging welcome. It was hardly in the spirit of welcome that he plunged into an attempt, which would not have been worth while had it been successful, which it was not, to show that in 1940 the Labour party was fighting to keep out-relief in the hands of the local authorities and out of the hands of the Assistance Board, whereas now Mr. Aneurin Bevan is using the Assistance Board for all he is worth. Then, while justly claiming a share in building up the social services for Lloyd George, Asquith and Neville Chamberlain, he seemed more concerned to diminish the Government's credit for the present measure than to obtain recognition for the three dead statesmen. Surely Colonel Elliott, if he wished to welcome the bill, might have done it more generously than this.

TWO WAYS OF ASSISTANCE

Mr. Bevan explained how the bill seeks to deal on two lines with the 'residual categories' left outside the National Insurance and the National Health services – 400,000 on outdoor relief, 100,000 in institutions, and 30,000 'deprived' children. First, the National Assistance Board, as it is now to be called, is to provide monetary help for those who remain ineligible for insurance benefit or unemployment benefit or need financial help in other ways, while the local authorities are to be made responsible for welfare services. The latter services will apply to the blind, the deaf, the tuberculous, and old persons.

Mr. Bevan, who never lacks imagination, spoke of the problem of the old as the peculiar problem of our time, appealing in support of his dictum to the 'staggering estimate' that by 1970 people of seventy years of age would be one in five of the population. . . .

(1948)

1948 was the year in which what has subsequently become known as the Welfare State came into being, in the sense of actually beginning to provide services to the population. For the most part it was a painless birth, though the Health Service continued to be the source of considerable pre-natal agony. Indeed it was the Health Service which was overwhelmingly the dominant issue and this section will concentrate on the disagreements between the Minister and the medical profession which threatened the viability of the new service up to the eve of its promised starting date. It will therefore be necessary to give somewhat more cursory treatment to the other areas of social policy. This is not meant in any way to deny the importance of other policy developments; rather it is to reflect the relative coverage of these topics which the 'Guardi ' provided for its readers during 1948.

Housing

In 1948 the Government's performance on housing continued to be affected by the economic crisis, and shortage of raw materials. But there was no major change in policy and the debate continued to centre on whether or not the Government was set to achieve the targets set by the Coalition. The following extracts give some of the flavour of the debate.

17 May 1948   p.5

MR. BEVAN ATTACKS THE PRESS
'Pumping Deadly Poison Into the Public Mind'

Master builders were among Government opponents who made a minor demonstration outside a cinema in which Mr. Aneurin Bevan, Minister of Health, addressed a public meeting in Scarborough yesterday, on the eve of the Labour party conference. They paraded with a cart on which was a placard bearing the message, 'Do you want a house? Now is the chance to say so.'

Mr. Bevan was interrupted several times and there was some booing mixed with applause. He told the booers, 'Be careful, boys. This is our meeting, you know.' Referring to the placard he said: 'They are demonstrating and demanding that the housing policy be changed. If I had allowed them to have their way they would have been bankrupt long ago. The fact is that I am the patron saint of the speculative builder. By next October we shall reach the target of 750,000 houses in Great Britain. That was the target laid down by the Coalition Government, but these are houses and that was wind.

'In the last three years we have not turned our back on any of our promises. We shall carry them all out, one after the other. One of the greatest difficulties now is the shortage of steel. It is held up because, between the wars, the steel owners made money by not producing steel. We have nothing at all to apologise for. On the contrary, we have a record to be proud of.'

After mentioning the Government's Health Scheme, Mr. Bevan said: 'Why should we, who are clearing up the muddle, allow ourselves to be scared by headlines in the capitalist press? It is the most prostituted press in the world, most of it owned by a gang of millionaires. These newspapers and employers and owners are engaged in diverting the social will. That is their job. The national and provincial newspapers are pumping a deadly poison into the public mind, week by week. If you listen too carefully to it and allow it to weaken your will the consequences will be disastrous.'

An interruptor: For you, yes.

'For me?' retorted Mr. Bevan. 'Don't be such a damned fool. I know there are some people in this nation who are worse off, but we have always intended that they should be worse off. You cannot have social justice and everybody be as well off as before.'

'We have nothing but confidence in the result of the 1950 general election. We have saved Britain from irretrievable disaster.'

22 May 1948   *p.5*

ANXIETY OVER HOUSING
Mr. Bevan's Claims

MAJOR ISSUE AT NEXT ELECTION

From our Political Correspondent

Scarborough, Friday.

The Minister of Health was unable to send delegates away from the Labour Party Conference to-day with the kind of news about housing which many of them would have found most helpful in their constituencies. The best he could do was to promise that the building industry would be brought 'up to date' when the results of inquiries made or being made into the industry by the Ministries of Works and Health had been studied. Mr. Bevan suggested that the Monopoly Bill might also be used for this purpose.

He reasserted the familiar claims for the administrative success of the housing programme, but though a detailed motion which declared that the 'housing drive is still not being prosecuted with the efficiency the situation calls for' was defeated on a show of hands there is evidently great discomfort among constituency workers caused by pressure from the homeless in their own areas. The waiting list in Bucklow was reported to be increasing faster than the completion of houses. It looks as though housing is expected to be the chief issue at the next general election.

212

The special problem of tied cottages in rural areas illustrated uneasiness in extreme form. This year, as last, the conference refused to support Mr. Bevan's plea to allow the Government to judge the best time for legislation in this subject. The Minister of Health was nettled by the hostile vote. He argued that the whole Labour movement accepts in principle the need to abolish tied cottages, but no legislation will be introduced apart from general legislation on rent restrictions and he was unwilling to handle rent restriction generally until more houses have been built – he wanted 250,000 to 500,000 more. He argued that until there is a larger pool of houses, changes in the Rent Restriction Acts might have a bad effect on rents.

24 June 1948   *p.3*

LARGE AS WELL AS SMALL HOUSES
Mr. Bevan's Promise

Mr. Aneurin Bevan, Minister of Health, told the Urban District Council's Conference at Eastbourne yesterday that the housing programme was not running down as had been suggested. It was smoothly and harmoniously turning out large numbers of houses, and the whole programme was in balance.

'Last year I had to tell local authorities not to start too many houses. Local authorities insisted that I was stopping them building. What we were doing was adjusting our building plans to our building abilities. The result is that we are now completing 20,000 permanent houses a month. A large programme is under way and I am now approving more houses again.'

'Before very long we shall be putting up some large houses and some smaller ones,' he added. He visualised bigger houses for the family man and smaller ones for bachelors and old people.

26 June 1948   *p.4*

Leader   **THE NEXT HOUSING BILL**

The Ministry of Health is now working on details of a bill to be introduced in the next full session of Parliament – not during the freak session for the Parliament Bill – which will permit the reconditioning of rural houses and the conversion of city terraces into smaller but self-contained dwelling-places. Mr. Aneurin Bevan promised last July to bring in legislation, which so far as it affects rural housing will be based on the findings of the Hobhouse Committee. It looks as though Mr. Bevan has decided to reverse the earlier policy of the Government towards the renovation of cottages, but presumably he will attach conditions to the grant of funds which will enable him to justify the change to his supporters.

Conversion of city terraces will be based on the report of the committttee set up by the Coalition Government at the beginning of 1945, of which Mr. Lewis Silkin, now Minister of Town and Country Planning, and Mr. Charles Key, now Minister of Works, were members. Conversion cannot be attempted unless planning authorities have power to vary restrictive covenants and local authorities have power to acquire outstanding leases.

26 June 1948   *p.4*

Leader   **HOUSES AND EXPORTS**

For a time at least we are to go on building as many houses as we are doing now. Mr. Bevan has gained enough of his own way to make a sorry mess of the Government's plans for economic recovery. Next month workers were supposed to begin to leave the building trade as the number of new houses was cut to 140,000 a year, by December 164,000 men were to have been freed for more important jobs. Instead work will continue on 200,000 houses and the labour force still remains almost as large as it was at the beginning of the year. This can only mean that the export industries will not get the extra workers they need. That the new houses are to be more varied with a fifth of them again built for private owners is welcome but it is no compensation for slackening our efforts to curb the imports we need far more.

26 July 1948   *p.2*

HEALTH MINISTER'S HOUSING FIGURES

Mr. Ernest Marples, Conservative MP for Wallasey, speaking in his constituency on Saturday, accused Mr. Aneurin Bevan of 'uttering a false statement' about housing figures, and threw out a challenge to the Health Minister.

'Our Parliamentary system is in danger from outside by pressure from totalitarian Russia and from inside by Ministers who are incompetent or untruthful,' said Mr. Marples. 'The untruthful Minister is the more dangerous. Here is an example of a lie which should be nailed. Mr. Aneurin Bevan, when winding up a debate, said: 'We have built in the first two and a half years at the end of this war more houses than were built in ten years at the end of the 1914–18 war.'

214

'This,' said Mr. Marples, 'is a lie. We actually built not "more houses" but 821,951 less. In the two and a half years after the end of this war we had built 372,769 homes, including temporary prefabs. In the ten years after the end of the 1914–18 war 1,194,720 houses were built.

'In the House of Commons I accused him of "one of the greatest falsehoods," and official documents supporting my figures were handed to his Parliamentary Private Secretary. Mr. Bevan had neither the courage to answer nor the decency to withdraw. I publicly accuse this Cabinet Minister of uttering a false statement at the Dispatch Box. Let an independent arbitrator be appointed and his decision be accepted as final. If Mr. Bevan's statement is proved a true one, I will agree to donate £500 to a charity providing he will give £500 if his statement is proved false.'

The rising costs of housing led at least one local authority to seek economies.

22 October 1948   p.8

HOUSES WITHOUT 'GADGETS'
Council's Economy Cut

In spite of strong protests Paddington Borough Council decided last night to 'cut all gadgets' from their Fulham Place housing scheme, six blocks of flats. Some are to be reduced one storey in height.

To reduce costs, brown asphalt is to be used for flooring in place of the jointless floors, serving hatches between kitchen and dining-room, and the tradesmen delivery hatches are to go; there will be no picture rails, heated towel rails in bathrooms and laundries, and storage accommodation will be omitted. Cycle and store sheds and some perambulator sheds will be left out, and lifts which were to have carried eight persons will be reduced in size to carry a smaller number.

Councillor Mrs V. Lane (Conservative) said: 'All the cheese-paring of this council seems to be done at the expense of women. The council should look at homes from a woman's point of view.'

Councillor A. Barrett (Conservative) said: 'Mr. Bevan calls service hatches old-fashioned, snobbish inventions, but perhaps he has never helped his own 'trouble and strife' to get the dinner. The women of this country have been kicked around quite enough. (Cheers from the gallery). Give them the labour-saving hatch, and if it is going to cost too much, at least leave them a hole which they can drape with curtains. How much would a hole cost? Any man worth his wife's love would soon get a bit of wood and saw and fix up a door for it.'

215

HOUSING PROGRESS
September Total Second Highest of Year

From our Political Correspondent

Westminster, Tuesday.

The number of new permanent houses finished in Great Britain during September was 20,402 – the second highest monthly total for the year. Excluding requisitioned houses, 768,292 'units of accommodation' have been provided since the war. This is the basis of Mr. Aneurin Bevan's claim that he has passed the first target of 750,000 homes fixed by the Coalition Government in its post-war housing plans.

The rate of house-building in 1949 can still not be settled because of uncertainties about the timber supply, but local authorities have been told to work on the assumption that the number of houses under construction on May 31 last, about 180,000 can be maintained.

The special treatment of miners and farm workers in need of houses has produced this result – from April 1, 1947, the miners have had 18,831 new houses (permanent and temporary), and since April 1, 1945, the farm workers have had 10,833. Fifteen thousand aluminium bungalows are being produced this year, and most of them will go to miners. At the end of September 7,540 had been finished and 4,897 were being built. Farm workers are to get a two-storey house built of concrete blocks and posts. Twenty thousand have been allocated to rural authorities, and about 18,600 were in contract at the end of September.

Health

The BMA's plebiscite requesting opinions on the terms offered by the Minister and a decision on whether or not to enter the Health Service provided the central issues in this area.
   The BMA's attitude was quite clear.

9 January 1948   *p.5*

B.M.A.'S ADVICE ON HEALTH SCHEME
Rejection Urged

A special representative meeting of the British Medical Association after a full day's discussion last night passed a resolution unanimously declaring that 'in their considered opinion the National Health Service Act in its present form is so grossly at variance with the essential principles of the profession that it should be rejected absolutely by all practitioners.' The declaration is to be issued to the whole of the medical profession. . . .

The council of the B.M.A. last month indicated two main grounds of criticism of the Minister of Health. These were:

(a) His decision to pay a basic salary of £300 to all general practitioners entering the scheme, as well as capitation fees for each patient on their lists. The Council feared that this basic salary could be raised without legislation so as to convert the service into a full-time salaried State service.

(b) His refusal to introduce amendments to clarify the part of the National Health Service Act affecting partnership in practices unless it is decided by the courts that the Act will not bear the interpretation which he puts upon it. The B.M.A. Council regarded this point as 'the crucial test of the genuineness of the Minister's declared intention, if convinced by argument, to amend the Act' and commented 'He has declined to amend. Did he ever intend to amend?'

    THE DOCTORS' VOTE

. . . the result of the plebiscite will undoubtedly bear on the successful launching of the service. It may not give a very reliable measure of how many doctors now practising will join but it will do a great deal to determine the policy of the B.M.A. If it is evident from the plebiscite that enough practitioners will join to give the service a good start the B.M.A. may be expected to accept the position with good grace, continuing indeed at all times to press for adjustments in the interests of its members (as it is entirely right for it to do) but not setting itself against the service in principle or discouraging its members from joining it. If, on the other hand, a large majority disapprove of the terms the B.M.A. will be encouraged to unrelenting hostility which will handicap the service at every turn. 'Whether the service is good or bad,' as the 'Lancet' points out, 'depends chiefly on what we (the doctors) choose to make it. 'Whatever its faults the new scheme clearly has within it, as Mr. Bevan has claimed, the seeds of 'the greatest health service this or any other country has known.' If it is frustrated or mutilated by the unwillingness of doctors to collaborate it will be poor consolation for them to say afterwards 'It was all the Minister's fault' – even if it were true.

The main issues outstanding are the basic salary, the legal position of partnership agreements and the right to appeal to the law courts. The problem of the basic salary goes deepest. The sum proposed, £300 a year, is not a big share of a practitioner's prospective earnings but many doctors fear it is a first step towards a full-time salaried service (which Mr. Bevan would certainly have preferred). They fear that a doctor with a paymaster might be unable to give his patients the undivided consideration they get from him now. It has not been easy for the ordinary man, accustomed as most of us are to work for wages, fully to share this horror at the prospect of salaried employment or rather at the distant shadow of it. No doubt there is something of a 'mystique' about this which the layman cannot appreciate and it would be impertinent of him to tell the doctors what they should think about their own status. But there is another side of the question on which he can reasonably speak. It is the cardinal point of the B.M.A.'s attitude that payment by salary is against the patients' interests. On this should not the patients' opinions count?

. . . They know that the stiffest obstacle to good doctoring is often the inability of patients to pay for it and they see that this service removes that obstacle from the doctor's path. Doctors are fully entitled to dispute whether the terms offered are unfair to them. But if they claim to base their decision on whether the scheme is fair to their patients they should remember that, by and large, the patients have everything to gain from the success of the new service.

HELP FOR DOCTORS WHO VOTE 'NO'
'Substantial Funds'

A warning that the Minister of Health, Mr. Bevan will not be able to operate the National Health Service Act if sufficient doctors vote against its adoption is given in the 'British Medical Journal.' Urging doctors to vote on the merits of the case, it says that what medical men most fear is the 'loss of freedom.' By standing firm, it is claimed, they can retain it.

The paper contends that Mr. Bevan thinks he has a trump card in denying compensation to those general practitioners who do not enter the service on July 5, and says: 'The association will advise general practitioners not to enter the service only if the number who say 'No' is sufficient to defeat Mr. Bevan. The strength of the profession will lie in the size of the majority against the Act.

'The doctor who votes "No" may temporarily suffer because a doctor in the next street votes "Yes." The B.M.A. has substantial funds at its disposal to tide him over this difficulty. In any case the "Yes" man is unlikely to be a superman nor even, may it be said, a better doctor.'

B.M.A. ANSWERS MR. BEVAN
'A False Charge'

Dr. H. Guy Dain, chairman of the British Medical Association Council, yesterday issued a statement replying to Mr. Aneurin Bevan, Minister of Health, who said at Pontypridd on Saturday that the Health Act, which comes into force on July 5, could be launched smoothly in the interests of the people, or stormily, 'surrounded by prejudice, poisoned by misrepresentations, and fragmented by partisan passions.' Dr. Dain's statement said:

The charge that the medical profession is defying Parliament is false. Parliament has imposed on the Minister of Health the obligation to bring in a comprehensive health service. In so doing Parliament must have expected the Minister to conduct himself in such a manner that he secured the co-operation and goodwill of those concerned, who believe in a comprehensive health service as much as he does. Has Mr. Bevan in this vital matter met Parliament's wishes? The public can judge, but there is no doubt what the average doctor's answer would be.

Parliament has imposed no obligation whatever on doctors to join the service. On the contrary, Parliament has expressly given the profession the right to enter or to stay out as it chooses. Mr. Bevan himself has explicitly admitted that this is so. He has also admitted that doctors, like other workers, have the right to make up their minds collectively, as well as individually. Why does he now pretend that we are defying Parliament? Why do his supporters in the press continually raise these untrue and malicious charges of 'sabotage'; Reasoned criticism – however violent – of B.M.A. policy is one thing, but damaging and malicious imputations of this kind are another matter and we are watching the situation closely.

As for 'partisanship' – if it is partisanship for the medical profession to stand for the freedom which is the public's as well as their own, then we are guilty of partisanship. If it is 'prejudice' to stand for a principle – the integrity of medicine – then we are guilty of that too.

'PARLIAMENT HAS SPOKEN'

Mr. Bevan, speaking at the opening of the East Glamorgan County Hospital at Pontypridd on Saturday, said:

This ceremony is taking place at a time when controversy is raging in the medical world concerning the merits of the new Health Act. The atmosphere is charged with partisan feeling. A little later on I shall certainly find it necessary to make a statement in the hope of creating a better sense of proportion in the minds of those who will be responsible for making the Act a success. In the meantime I would say this to the doctors:

Do not allow yourselves to be too much influenced by the statements made by a few persons who claim to be speaking for the whole profession. Read with care, and as dispassionately as possible, the statement that I have circulated to the profession and which each doctor has already received. Keep in mind that the emotions of the moment will pass but that the obligations to provide an efficient health service for the British people will be permanent.

The new Health Act will start on July 5. That is the will of Parliament, and Parliament, after all, is still the supreme authority in Britain. The new health service can be launched smoothly in the interests of the people or it can be launched stormily surrounded by prejudice, poisoned by misrepresentations and fragmented by partisan passions. The responsibility for deciding between these two rests largely with the profession. Parliament has spoken; the country now awaits, and expects the co-operation of the medical world.'

NOT A FULL-TIME SALARIED SERVICE

From our London Staff

Fleet Street, Thursday.

It is not the Government's intention to convert the national health scheme into a full-time salaried service so far as doctors are concerned declared Mr. Aneurin Bevan, the Minister of Health, to-day.

His statement was made in response to questions submitted by the 'Lancet,' and is published in to-day's issue. Speaking of the £300 basic salary proposed for doctors under the scheme, he says:

> Some doctors have expressed the fear that this is merely the beginning of a full-time salaried service. I cannot read into the mind of any future Minister, or prophesy what may be done by future Governments, but that is not our intention. Our intention is that the main source of a doctor's remuneration shall be by capitation.

MEDICAL PARTNERSHIPS

Mr. Bevan points out that the £300 basic salary does not affect the prospects of a fully salaried system, which could be brought about 'with or without this £300 element, which makes no difference.' A full-time, salaried service has been possible under existing legislation for some 36 years.

To clear up doubts on the legal position of medical partnerships under the Act, the Minister proposes to obtain 'a collective legal opinion of high standing,' by appointing at once a committee of legal experts to say whether or not a partner in an existing partnership is fully protected. The Minister states that he would like the profession's co-operation in the selection of this committee. He will consider its report, and if there is evidence that existing partnerships are unfairly prejudiced by the Act he will proceed at once to seek an amendment of it.

TRIBUNAL'S POWERS

Commenting on the claim that a doctor should be able to appeal to the law courts against dismissal, Mr. Bevan says that a doctor will have exactly the same rights as any other citizen to go to the courts on the question whether or not he has been lawfully 'dismissed the service.' He points out that the Minister has no power himself at any stage to remove a doctor from the list. The most he can do is to uphold his removal by an independent tribunal.

30 January 1948   p.5

THE DOCTORS' PLEBISCITE
'No Intimidation'

BMA ANSWER TO MR. BEVAN

The British Medical Association last night denied that there would be any intimidation of doctors in connection with the postal vote which the association is taking on the National Health Service scheme. This statement was made in reply to Mr. Aneurin Bevan, Minister of Health, who said in the House of Commons yesterday that the B.M.A. was engaged in a campaign to induce doctors to vote one way.

The B.M.A. plebiscite forms on the national health service were ready for dispatch last night to nearly 56,000 doctors in England, Wales and Scotland, and every practitioner should receive his copy by Saturday morning. The result of the plebiscite wil be announced to a special meeting of the council of the association called for February 18, and will be published towards the end of February.

When Mr. Bevan was asked in the Commons yesterday about the nature of the plebiscite, he stated: 'I understand that each doctor has to sign his name on the voting paper with his address and professional particulars and that the association conducting the ballot is itself engaged in a campaign to induce the doctor to vote one way. This House may well feel this procedure is a long way removed from the secret ballot and the workings of democracy as we know it in this country.' (Loud Labour cheers and Opposition counter-cheers.) He added, amid Opposition cries of 'Oh!': 'And it is bound to cast doubt on the validity of the result.'

Asked by Mr. J. Baird (Lab., Wolverhampton E.) if the House would have an opportunity of expressing its views 'on this attempted blackmail,' Mr. Bevan said that was a question which should properly be addressed to the Prime Minister or the Leader of the House.

When the Minister said later, 'As I understand it open votes of this description always give rise to the possibility of intimidation,' Mr. Churchill asked, 'Intimidation by whom?'

Mr. Bevan replied: 'It was because open votes of this sort were removed from our constitutional practice that the secret ballot had been established. Fear of intimidation is the reason for the secret ballot.' . . .

Commenting on the plebiscite the 'Lancet' says:

Without graver cause than its present pessimistic fears the profession would be wrong to engage in a major political struggle. It is a plain if deplorable fact that a proportion of the profession are now objecting to the service chiefly because they object to Mr. Bevan. We may be sure that the Government would not readily surrender in any way to what they would regard as a deliberate attempt for partly political reasons to thwart the will of Parliament. Their probable reaction would be to assert that organised medicine was once more standing in the way of a useful public service.

A statement issued by the Liberal Party Committee yesterday says:

It is of vital importance to the people that the National Health Service should begin to operate in July in the most favourable circumstances possible. The Liberal party therefore deplores the fact that there should have arisen a dispute between the Minister and the B.M.A., which is likely, if unresolved, to prejudice the service and the public interest, and calls upon both the Minister and the medical profession to reopen negotiations in a public-spirited attempt to settle their outstanding differences.

31 January 1948   *p.4*

Leader   **THE PLEBISCITE**

Every doctor in Britain is today to be invited to vote in the plebiscite on the National Health Service organised by the British Medical Association. Many of them would prefer a modified form of service, but do not intend to carry their protest to the length of withdrawing from public practice. These will welcome yesterday's assurances from the B.M.A. that 'there will be no intimidation' and that (as the plebiscite form itself indicates) 'how individuals vote will not be divulged.' This removes any doubts inspired by the reply of the chairman of the B.M.A. Council when reminded that a large proportion of the doctors who pledged themselves against the National Health Insurance Act later accepted service under it. 'We have better organisation now,' he said, 'and we will jolly well see it does not happen this time.' There is, however, still considerable uneasiness among the refugee doctors, who were referred to at the recent B.M.A. meeting as 'potential blacklegs,' and who are being sent forms of a different colour – presumably to simplify the task of classifying answers. Most of these doctors have only recently secured admission to the permanent register. Others await the opportunity to apply. Some have painful recollections of plebiscites in their native lands. All are conscious that there is no appeal to the courts from the decision of the General Medical Council. Their anxieties are, of course, groundless, but it would not be surprising if those who are least accustomed to British ways should be persuaded by this unfortunate distinction in colour not to vote if they cannot accept the B.M.A.'s advice.

LETTERS TO THE EDITOR

31 January 1948   p.4

THE HEALTH SERVICE

To the Editor of the Manchester Guardian

Sir,–We the undersigned medical members of Parliament are deeply concerned at the situation which has developed between the B.M.A. and the Government. There is general agreement that a comprehensive National Health Service should be established as an integral part of a complete scheme of social security for the whole nation.

The present National Health Service Act has been endorsed by the House of Commons and the House of Lords without substantial amendments, and there is no evidence of any feeling against it among the general public. Yet the leaders of the British Medical Association entrusted with negotiations on behalf of the entire medical profession have attempted to organise and exploit an outburst of mass hysteria among doctors in order to set up a privileged class exempt from the will of Parliament and dictating the terms on which it will serve the community.

This is a recrudescence of syndicalism in its most crude form, and one has only to consider what would happen to the railways or the mines if those engaged in these vital industries were to make similar attempts to hold the nation to ransom. The series of meetings at present being held by doctors is characterised in almost every case by the intolerant shouting down, sometimes organised, of any doctor who attempts to put a point of view in favour of the scheme, and by the definite though somewhat incoherent emergence of a Tory party standpoint in the more acceptable speeches.

We seem to have passed the stage when the prime consideration is the welfare of the patient, and the deepest

224

emotions become evident when there is a rallying to the defence of the sacred right to buy (and sell) practices and to practise at will in over-doctored areas.

We find it difficult to believe that all the humanitarian idealism of the doctor can be canalised into this kind of self-centred thought at a time when the community, particularly the poorer section, is short of doctors, when the doctor is to be well compensated for the loss of the right to sell his present practice, when he is given a very large share (a much larger share than has ever been given to any vocational group) in the management of the service, and when the amount of his remuneration is not even in the forefront of the dispute.

Nor can we believe that the mass of the people can be persuaded to emulate those slaves who, in the American Civil War, fought on the side of the South in order to preserve the right of their masters to own, to buy and to sell.

Can it be that the B.M.A. leaders are committing themselves and the profession they lead to be used as the spearhead of an anti-Labour campaign?

Lastly, we do not regard the plebiscite now being held as a democratic one. The condition that each voting paper must be signed lays the whole thing open to the kind of intimidation, persecution, and victimisation now associated only with totalitarian countries where such supervision of voting has been the general rule.–Yours &c.,

S.W. JEGER,
SOMERVILLE HASTINGS,
L. COMYNE,
M.B. MORGAN,
House of Commons, January 30.

4 February 1948   *p.4*

To the Editor of the Manchester Guardian

Sir,–The letter from four of the medical members of the Government on January 31 would seem to have no better object that that of discrediting the medical profession in general and the B.M.A. in particular. While in the case of many who are ill-informed on the facts of the present lamentable disagreement it might well achieve its object, so far as the most discriminating are concerned it is rendered impotent by its own extravagance. The groundless accusations of 'mass hysteria,' 'organised shouting down of opponents,' 'Tory party standpoint' &c, and the calculated imputation of base motives are the hall-mark not of balanced reasoning but of the less savoury type of political propaganda.

225

Out of the welter of unsupported insinuation and calculated innuendo there emerges one direct accusation which demands rebuttal. The writers categorically state that the B.M.A. has attempted to organise doctors in order to 'set up a privileged class exempt from the will of Parliament and dictating the terms on which it will serve the community.' Mr. Bevan himself has answered that by admitting that the doctors have the right to make their choice not only individually but also collectively.

As regards the plebiscite, the general public can rest assured that the doctors recording their votes this week are doing so entirely uninfluenced by intimidation or mass hysteria and without the slighest fear of persecution or victimisation. The prime consideration which is guiding them in their choice is whether the Act in its present form does or does not imperil their scientific and clinical freedom.–Yours &c.,

G. RUTHVEN MITCHELL, Chairman, Blackpool and
Fylde Division British Medical Association,
Drumreaske, Wood Street, St. Annes-on-Sea, February 1.

4 February 1948   *p.4*

To the Editor of the Manchester Guardian

Sir,–The statement in your leading article of January 31 that 'most' of the 'refugee doctors,' to whom plebiscite forms of a distinctive colour are being sent 'have only recently secured admission to the permanent register' is untrue. Under the Medical Practitioners and Pharmacists Act, 1947, temporarily registered Practitioners and alien practitioners who have served in his Majesty's forces have become eligible to make application to the General Medical Council for permanent registration, but up to the present time no permanent registration has been completed.

As was stated in my press release sent to you and other newspapers on January 29.

The form is being sent to 1,200 alien doctors not yet on the British permanent register in order that they may express their opinion. The returns in respect of this group of practitioners, however, will not be included in the main figure.

Doctors, British or alien, who are on the permanent British register receive the ordinary plebiscite forms.

Since your allegation of 'uneasiness' and 'anxieties' among these doctors rests on the foundation of an incorrect statement by you, I am astonished that you should have seen fit to give currency to these reports without verification of the facts. It has been repeatedly stated – in the 'British Medical Journal,' on the plebiscite form itself, and in the B.M.A. answer to Mr. Bevan's statement in the House of Commons – that 'how individuals vote

226

will not be divulged.' This is so whatever kind of practitioner is voting, British or alien, on the permanent register or on the temporary register.—Yours &c.,

JOHN PRINGLE, British Medical Association,
Tavistock Square, London WC1.

6 February 1948   *p.5*

UNUSUAL MOTION FOR HEALTH SERVICE DEBATE
Support for Recent Legislation

GOVERNMENT UPSET BY THE B.M.A.'S CAMPAIGN

From our Political Correspondent

Westminster, Thursday.

The Government and the Labour party are more upset by the attitude of the British Medical Association to the National Health Service Act than by any campaign conducted by any other organisation against provisions of Labour legislation introduced during this Parliament.

This is the only explanation of the unusual course taken by the Government in providing Government time on Monday for a debate on a motion asking the House to approve once more the purposes of an Act so recently passed. The debate is obviously timed to take place before the B.M.A. plebiscite closes. One cannot recall any precedent for such a motion in support of recent legislation.

The motion, which stands in the names of the Minister of Health and the Secretary of State for Scotland, reads thus:

That this House takes note that the appointed day for the National Health Service has been fixed for July 5, welcomes the coming into force on that date of this measure which offers to all sections of the community comprehensive medical care and treatment and lays for the first time a sound foundation for the health of the people, and is satisfied that the conditions under which all the professions concerned are invited to participate are generous and fully in accord with their traditional freedom and dignity.

It appeared from questions that were asked in the House this afternoon that something may be said during the debate of the now famous meetings between Mr. Bevan and the Negotiating Committee of the B.M.A. An account of the impression left on some of the negotiators has already been published, but Mr. Herbert

227

Morrison did not respond to a question about the publication of a transcript of the meetings. He did not know if it existed, and even if it did he was sure there would not be time to publish it before the debate.

TORY AMENDMENT

Mr. R.A. Butler, for the Opposition, will propose that the government motion be amended by leaving out the reference to the conditions in which the professions will work under the National Health scheme and by substituting the following words: 'But declines to prejudice in any way the right of individuals in any of the professions concerned to express their opinions freely, according to their traditions, and in the interests of their patients, upon the terms and conditions of service of the proposed National Health scheme.'

The Opposition does not dissent from the Government's welcome of the establishment of a National Health Service.

'TRUE FACTS' FOR DOCTORS

Wing Commander N.J. Hulbert (C.-Stockport) asked the Minister of Health in the House of Commons yesterday if his attention had been drawn to the fact that medical consultants and specialists at a meeting at the headquarters of the B.M.A. on January 28 rejected his proposals for a National Health Service by 766 votes to 11 and what action he proposed to take to make the scheme acceptable to the medical profession.

Mr. A. Bevan, in a written reply, said: 'Yes sir, I think that if professional men and women were allowed at organised meetings of this kind a little enlightenment as to the true facts of the new scheme they would certainly find it acceptable to them.'

10 February 1948   *p.4*

Leader   **THE HEALTH SERVICE**

. . . The B.M.A. speaks as if it was an immense concession for the doctors to consider coming into the scheme at all and that nothing further was called for on their side. This is quite wrong. There is an overwhelming case for the introduction of the service, the dispute is a dispute on terms and on terms the Minister (though he may, as Mr. Butler said, lack the 'bedside manner') has gone much farther to meet the doctors than they have yet gone to meet him. If the leaders of the B.M.A. are so hopelessly committed against anything like the present terms of service that they cannot make a move one must hope

228

for the intervention of some fresh party of a high enough moral standing to put the problems still at issue in their proper perspective. It will be a reflection on the Government no less than on the B.M.A. if the mess continues. If a Minister is personally difficult and has allowed a hostile atmosphere to grow the Cabinet must step in to save a scheme that is a bigger thing than any one Minister's prestige. The one thing which must not happen is to risk letting things come to a deadlock which might imperil the success of the service.

16 February 1948   *p.4*

THE HEALTH SERVICE

To the Editor of the Manchester Guardian

Sir,—Your leading article on the Health Service of February 10 maintains to the full the high reputation of your paper for impartial statement and balanced judgement. There is, however, one point which calls for clarification. In supporting the view that the B.M.A. should make the first move towards conciliation, you repeat the claim put forward by Mr. Bevan that he has already made large concessions. That assertion, though true in substance, needs amplifying if misconception is to be avoided.

It is necessary in the first place to understand that, in framing the Act, and negotiating upon it, the Minister has had by the nature of things to deal separately with two distinct groups of doctors – on the one hand, the consultants and specialists; on the other, the general practitioners. The present dispute is concerned wholly and solely with the latter group. Since negotiations began Mr. Bevan has conceded some points raised by the consultants and specialists; to the general practitioners, he has made not a single concession, but has remained immovable on the assumption that the doctors have no right to negotiate on matters of principle or conscience, nor indeed on any matter which is not directly related to the monetary aspect.

The marked contrast between the sweetly reasonable reception which met the specialists and consultants, and the arrogant inflexibility accorded the general practitioners has given rise to a suspicion that the Minister has been trying to exploit the necessary division of doctors in order to weaken opposition by creating disunity in the profession. The realisation that, in spite of the preferential treatment meted out to them, the consultants and specialists intend to remain loyal to their colleagues may possibly account for Mr. Bevan engineering a debate which, though impotent to help the situation in any way, may well have seemed worth while, if only to bolster up his own morale.—Yours, &c.,

G. RUTHVEN MITCHELL, Chairman, Blackpool and
Fylde Division, British Medical Association,
Dumreaske, Wood Street, St Anne's-on-Sea, February 11.

19 February 1948   *p.5*

DOCTORS' OVERWHELMING VOTE AGAINST HEALTH ACT
Only 4,084 Ready to Serve Under It

B.M.A.'S NEXT MOVE TO BE DECIDED IN MARCH

The British Medical Association's plebiscite on the National
Health Service Act has resulted in an overwhelming vote against
it and against accepting service under it.

Of general practitioners alone 17,037 voted against accepting
the scheme as it stands and only 2,300 were in favour. Of
practitioners, consultants and specialists in Great Britain 25,340
voted against and 4,004 for accepting service under the Act.

The preamble to the ballot paper stated that if the majority
against accepting service included approximately 13,000 general
practitioners out of a present total strength of 20,500 the association
would advise the profession not to enter into any contract under
the Act in its present form but continue their services to patients
or other professional work.

The next step will be decided at a meeting of the B.M.A.
representative body to be held on March 17.

'AVALANCHE'

Out of 55,342 forms issued covering all branches of the
profession 40,814 doctors disapproved of the Act and only 4,735
approved. To the question whether consultants and practitioners
would abide by the decision of the majority and undertake not to
enter the service if the answers disclosed a majority against 24,066
agreed and 4,494 disagreed.

The result of the plebiscite is not so much a 'landslide' as
an 'avalanche,' states the B.M.A. In no single category of all the
14 groups was there a majority in favour. The nearest to acceptance
among civilian doctors was 'whole-time research workers,' where
the majority against fell to two to one. Even doctors who have
chosen for themselves the career of a permanent commission in
the forces disapproved of the Act by more than 16 to one. Six out
of every seven doctors in full-time Government employment were
opposed to the Act.

'Repeatedly the charge has been made that it is mainly the
older doctors who are against the present health service,' states

the B.M.A. 'For lack of time and because of the complex work involved in an analysis of the three-part voting no breakdown into age-groups has been attempted. But a fairly accurate estimate of how the younger practitioners feel about the Act can be obtained from the voting among general practitioners' assistants, who recorded 2,323 votes against and only 306 in favour. The general practitioner's assistant is generally not over forty and normally is much younger.'

The number of ballot papers returned was 45,549, 82 per cent of those issued.

19 February 1948   *p.5*

RESULT A SHOCK FOR GOVERNMENT

From our Political Correspondent

Westminster, Wednesday.

The result of the plebiscite has been a shock to the Government and has caused dismay among many members of the House, which as a whole approves the establishment of the national health service. There is, however, no sign yet that the Government will change its course, and it could scarcely move yet from the position it adopted in the emergency debate on the plebiscite held only a week last Monday.

The only official, or rather semi-official, comment on the plebiscite came from a Ministry of Health spokesman to-night. It was this:

The House of Commons has recently reviewed the new health scheme. By a large majority it has reaffirmed that it welcomes the beginning on July 5 next of this new scheme as one which lays for the first time a sound foundation for the health of the people. Parliament also declared itself satisfied that the conditions on which professional people are invited to participate are generous and fully in accord with their traditional freedom and dignity. The Act will come into operation on July 5 in accordance with Parliament's decisions. Before July it will therefore rest with the individual doctor, as with everyone else, to decide for himself what part he cares to play in the new arrangements.

As soon as the full effects of the plebiscite become evident – the B.M.A. has a representative meeting next month – and as the appointed day for the operation of the national health scheme draws near, there will be increasing anxiety and increasing pressure on the Government to end a state which may by then appear to have reached deadlock.

There is not at the moment any ground for supposing that the government will make any more concessions to the doctors, though some Opposition members take the view that much good might follow from an amendment of the Act to the effect that the basic salary would not be changed by regulation but only by a new Act of Parliament. This, it is argued, might relieve the doctors of their greatest dread – the use of the basic salary as the first stage in creating a salaried service. The result of the plebiscite may encourage the doctors to be still less accommodating, but Parliament intends that a national health service shall be set up.

DOCTORS 'STAMPEDED'

'The Socialist Medical Association does not believe that the B.M.A. plebiscite figures will make any difference to the start of the National Health Service,' says a statement issued by the association. It continues:

Doctors have been stampeded into a vote on an emotional and political basis which does not indicate at all accurately whether they will actually follow the B.M.A. lead to stay out of the service or not. Most general practitioners will discover between now and July 5 that they can best serve the sick by joining the service on the generous terms they have been offered. The public will, in any case, be paying for the service and they will expect their doctors to join it. The present 'no' vote is no higher than in 1911, but most doctors joined the panel system, and they will do so again.

Clearly the Minister of Health cannot be expected to alter an Act of Parliament under pressure from a small section of health workers for the B.M.A. vote represents only about 8 per cent of the total people employed in the health service. There is ample scope for experiments and modifications within the Act, ample opportunity for future action to improve it and the public must back the Government to get this magnificent scheme started.

13 March 1948   *p.6*

MR. BEVAN EXPECTS AN OUTCRY
As Health Service Begins

Mr. Aneurin Bevan, Minister of Health, at the annual meeting of the Institute of Almoners in London last night, painted a word-picture of the operation of the new Health Service after July 5, 'Every time a maid kicks over a bucket of slops in a ward the echoes will reverberate right through Whitehall,' he said. The Minister elaborated the picture:

For a little while there will be a perfect outcry, a cacophony of complaint. Newspapers will be full and I am sure that some doctors will make irate speeches. The order paper of the House of Commons will be filled with questions and for a while it may appear that everything is going wrong, but as a matter of fact everything will be going right because people will be able to complain. They complain now but nobody hears about it much. What the Health Act will do after July 5 is to put a public megaphone in the mouth of every complainant.

'When things have settled down,' said Mr. Bevan, 'we shall find this period of interrogation – this public examination – will have been an essential pre-requisite for the proper integration of the Health Service. I hope that the acerbities that surround certain polemics will soon disappear and that we will all of us be able to work for the sick and needy and helpless.'

17 March 1948   *p.4*

Leader   **AFTER THE PLEBISCITE**

Since the British Medical Association's poll of the doctors in February there has been no move by either side towards the settlement of the dispute over the terms of the national health service. That was to be expected; the B.M.A.'s Representative Body is to meet to-day to consider its next step and the Minister of Health has naturally waited to see what the next step would be. The main resolution which the Council of the B.M.A. has put before the meeting might be described as firm but mild. It expresses the hope that 'the Government will make it possible for the profession to co-operate by making such changes in recent legislation as will maintain the integrity of medicine and prevent doctors being turned into state servants.' It does not specify the changes which would satisfy this definition (though it is well enough known what the B.M.A. would like them to be) and so leaves more room for give and take. The Minister himself has declared that he has no intention of turning the doctors into state servants and it should not pass the wit of man to find some way of putting this intention into statutory form. But there is not much time to spare. The terms of service offered to the general practitioners over which most of the controversy has arisen are not the only questions to be settled before the new service can come into operation in July. The Spens Committee has not yet announced its recommendations on the payment of consultants and specialists on which agreement, though probable, is not to be taken for granted; nor on the payment of dentists who have also to play an important part in the scheme and who present some problems peculiar to themselves. There is certainly no time for the Minister and the B.M.A. to dig themselves in for a war of attrition if the service is to get a fair chance in July.

PHYSICIANS' HINT TO MR. BEVAN
A Safeguarding Act?

The Royal College of Physicians has passed a resolution which may help to end the deadlock between Mr. Aneurin Bevan, Minister of Health, and the medical profession about the proposed National Health Service.

A principal cause of professional discontent with the service is the power possessed by the Minister to change its character by regulations. The resolution of the Royal College of Physicians of which Lord Moran is President, states:

> The College affirms its desire for unity and recognises that the comprehensive health service cannot be successful without the willing co-operation of all branches of the profession. The College believes that this can be furthered if the Minister of Health makes clear in an amending Act that a whole-time service shall not be brought in by regulation so that if any future Government desires to introduce such a service a fresh Act of Parliament would be required.
>
> The College reaffirms its opposition to a whole-time medical service.

NEW HEALTH SERVICE
B.M.A. Welcomes Physicians' Resolution

The Royal College of Physicians' resolution that the Minister of Health should make it clear in an amending Act that a whole-time service should not be brought in by regulation, so that if a future Government desired to introduce such a service a fresh Act of Parliament would be required, was welcomed by the British Medical Association yesterday as a step forward without going the whole way to meet doctors' objections to the new Health Service.

A spokesman of the association said it had always been willing to meet the Minister to find a way out and ensure the success of the health scheme so long as doctors' interests were safeguarded. What the profession is afraid of is not only the threat of a full-time salaried service in the future but provisions in the present Act which will prevent it from doing its job effectively.

MINISTERS AND DOCTORS

Our London Correspondent

The Government is pleased with the intervention of the Royal
College of Physicians in the controversy about the National Health
Service. The college has an influential voice in the affairs of doctors,
and has cleared away a good many hazards by dwelling on one
major issue – whether doctors in the Health Service are to
become whole-time salaried officials or not. It has, moreover,
chosen an issue on which Mr. Bevan could satisfy the profession
without budging an inch from his position. He has been as specific
as a Minister could be, short of putting a clause in a bill, in asserting
that neither he nor the Government intends the basic salary to be
the thin end of the wedge.

It remains true that many doctors are suspicious and if the
amending bill for which the college asks would secure the working
of the Health Service it does not seem much to pay. There is no
news today of Mr. Bevan's next move but it is most likely that he
will say something in the House before taking any action outside.

NO FULL-TIME STATE MEDICAL SERVICE
WITHOUT LEGISLATION

The recent proposal of the Royal College of Physicians that
it should be made statutorily clear that a whole-time salaried State
medical service would not be brought in by regulation but would
require further legislation to make it possible was accepted on
behalf of the Government by Mr. Aneurin Bevan, Minister of Health,
in the House of Commons yesterday.

He told the House that he had studied the resolutions sent
to him by the Royal College of Physicians and the British Medical
Association, which have been published. 'I have been trying to
determine for myself what it is that is really and sincerely worrying
the doctors. It seems to me that the key to the doctors' unease and
restlessness is some instinctive fear, shared by many most well-
meaning men and women, that although the Act does not propose
it, and although the Government have themselves denied it, the
real objective is a full-time salaried State medical service. It is this
fundamental point which I want now to tackle once and for all.'

It seemed clear that something more than his spoken
assurance was needed. He was certainly quite willing to do

anything to banish this apprehension for good. 'The Royal College of Physicians has made the useful suggestion, with which the other royal colleges associate themselves, that I should now make it statutorily clear that a whole-time service will not be brought in by regulation, but would require further legislation to make it possible. My colleagues and I accept that most cordially. In short, we propose that it should be clearly impossible to institute a full-time salaried service by regulation alone. It would then need express legislation if it were ever proposed.'

16 April 1948   *p.4*

Leader   **SECOND OPINION**

The British Medical Association has been prompt to respond to Mr. Bevan's change of attitude on the Health Service scheme, and the doctors who rejected the terms of service with such emphasis, only two months ago, will be asked to vote again within a fortnight. They will have before them the Minister's answer to fourteen questions posed by the B.M.A. council, and its comments on them. The questions and answers are now published. The council has not yet made known what advice it will give. But one may fairly suppose that, if it was as wholly dissatisfied with Mr. Bevan's answers now as it was with his previous answers in December, it would not be calling on the doctors to vote again. And if it is not going to advise them to vote against the terms this time, its soundest line tactically is to advise acceptance. The B.M.A. has to consider its position not only in the current negotiations but as the continuing spokesman of a large part of the profession. It has built up today (with some unintended help from Mr. Bevan) a remarkably solid following which will stand it in good stead in any further questions which may arise in the operation of the scheme. The doctors can now enter the service confident that the association is strong enough to protect their interests in its working and interpretation as effectively as it has conducted their case at the outset. But this remains true only so long as the association retains their support. If a good number of doctors are brought by Mr. Bevan's belated concessions to change their minds and enter the service in any case (as seems probable) while the B.M.A. and the rest stay outside, its present strength would dwindle; if it leads its following solidly into the scheme it keeps its strength and its negotiating power.

DOCTORS NOT SATISFIED
B.M.A. Council View

NEW ASSURANCES INADEQUATE

From our Correspondent

Shrewsbury, Sunday.

Dr. Guy Dain, Chairman of the B.M.A., addressing the Shropshire Montgomeryshire and Radnorshire Medical Independence Committee and representatives from the western counties of England at Shrewsbury to-night, said that Mr. Bevan's modifications of his plan for the National Health Service had created a new situation, but the B.M.A. council had decided that they were not enough.

Doctors would receive on Monday or Tuesday a full statement from the council on the new situation, and would see that in the council's opinion the proposals of the Minister 'do not sufficiently safeguard the freedom of the profession.' When doctors voted in the plebiscite they would realise that those who had studied the matter most did not consider that doctors would be properly safeguarded by the proposals the Minister had made.

'We are ready to see this campaign through,' he said. 'We have all the material ready. We have the organisation going. You have the opportunity of standing fast in the position you took up at the last plebiscite.' . . .

'If you deal with this plebiscite as you did with the last, we can obtain everything we think necessary for the freedom of the patient and ourselves, before we go into the service,' he said. No further negotiations with the Minister would be entertained, either with or without a meeting of the representative body, if doctors gave the council the necessary majority there will be no need to call a representative meeting, because the deal is off.'

'IF 13,000 VOTE AGAINST'

After the meeting your correspondent asked Dr. Dain this question. 'If the majority of the general practitioners vote "No," is it certain that the B.M.A. will resist the new service?'

Dr. W.A. Callaghan, speaking on behalf of Dr. Dain, said, 'If 13,000 or more general practitioners vote against it, the fight goes on.'

SOCIALIST DOCTORS AND B.M.A.
Advice to Mr. Bevan

Members of the Socialist Medical Association, at their annual meeting in London yesterday, voted unanimously in favour of a resolution which urged the Minister of Health not to make any compromise with the British Medical Association which would 'imperil the principles of the National Health Service Act.'

Moving the resolution, Dr. Stark Murray, vice-president, said that the B.M.A. had tried to 'manoeuvre the doctors into a position against the Government. They have not the faintest idea of what the term "democracy" stands for.' He did not think that the concessions already made by the Minister had imperilled the principles of the Act. They were just an attempt 'to convince the stiff-necked group of men and women at B.M.A. House that the Act is not going to do the things they consider it is going to do.'

Dr. H.B. Morgan, M.P. for Rochdale, Dr. S.A. Winstanley, a member of the Manchester branch of the British Medical Association, and Dr. S. Freeman, of the Socialist Medical Association, were the chief speakers at a Manchester meeting yesterday when the new National Health Service was discussed. Dr. Morgan thought it would be a pity to wreck the whole scheme for the sake of the small part to which the B.M.A. objected. Dr. Winstanley said he opposed the scheme largely because he believed in the system of the family doctor and the relationship which it encouraged beween doctor and patient. He admitted that the National Health Insurance Act had been a benefit to the public and to the profession. Dr. Freeman said that Dr. Winstanley should remember that almost the same arguments were used against that Act as were being used now.

VOTE SHOWS LESS OPPOSITION TO SCHEME

The Council of the British Medical Association has decided to accept the invitation of the Minister of Health to enter immediately into discussions on the amending bill and other matters arising out of the National Health Service Act and is to recommend that the profession should join the Service.

This decision was reached after considering the results which were announced last night of the latest plebiscite of the medical profession. On each of the three questions on which a separate vote was taken there was a majority unfavourable to joining the service, but the opposition was smaller in each case than in the February plebiscite and more doctors abstained from voting.

In accepting the Minister's invitation to enter into discussions, the B.M.A. Council has drawn its attention to 'the large section of the profession which is still opposed to service and whose goodwill is essential if the service is to succeed.'

6 May 1948   *p.4*

Leader   **JULY 5**

The National Health Service is saved. That is the upshot of the doctors' second plebiscite which the Council of the British Medical Association made public last night. The Service still has many obstacles before it; it will be years before it becomes all that it is planned to be. But at least it should start promptly on July 5. It should not be held up at the outset by lack of general practitioners to work it. In fact a majority of the profession are still against the terms of service. But the adverse majority has diminished so markedly since the February vote that the B.M.A. Council has decided to advise the doctors to co-operate.

. . . It is important first, that people should not expect a magical transformation on July 5 and, secondly, that they should not blame the doctors if at first things fall short of expectations.

. . . One must be grateful especially to those who within and without the ranks of the B.M.A. have striven through what seemed at times almost hopeless estrangements to keep alive the spirit of compromise and co-operation. Blessed are the peacemakers.

15 May 1948   *p.4*

Leader   **DENTISTS' PAY**

The Spens Committee's Report on the payment of dentists under the National Health Scheme, long awaited and made public yesterday, leaves unanswered the main question which most dentists have been asking themselves. It meets the question 'How much?' but it does not meet the question 'How?' It puts forward no scale of fees for dental operations: it is content to indicate the total amount which these operations should bring in to a capable and experienced man, working as hard as man should be expected to work at this very arduous and responsible labour. One must presume that the scale of fees is to be embodied in regulations to be made by the Ministry of Health, and it is a fair complaint that, if the service is to start on July 5 or anything like it, the dentists will have very little time to consider and discuss the terms offered. The Spens Report makes the important point that payments for particular operations should be so balanced that, over a period, a man's pay would not be affected by the amount of time he spent on different types of work: the scale should not be so calculated that, for instance, a man would earn more by drawing teeth wholesale than he would if he spent more time on more conservative slow and skilled operations. Many dentists have feared that when the scale of fees was published it would be found to put a premium on the more rapid and less painstaking forms of treatment. They will be glad to note what the committee has said in this respect: but their doubts cannot be satisfied until they have seen the actual scale of fees proposed. In general terms the Spens Committee's recommendations should be found generous enough to draw in the additional dentists whom the country needs if teeth are to be properly cared for under the new scheme. But the quality of dentistry counts as well as the quantity and that depends on the details as well as on the general outlines of the new arrangements.

5 June 1948 *p.5*

The Spens Committee's report on the remuneration of consultants and specialists in the National Health Service was published to-day (Cmd. 7420, price 6d.). Mr. Aneurin Bevan announced yesterday that the Government had accepted the committee's recommendations in principle and that he himself would start talks quickly to discover the best means of applying the principles, and particularly in the case of pay for teaching duties. However long these talks lasted, the final scheme would be deemed to operate from July 5.

Proposed scales of pay are based on evidence of incomes earned in 1938–39. The Spens Committee has not attempted to convert 1939 values into present values, but points out that when this calculation is made allowance should be made not only for the change in the value of money but for the increases which have taken place in incomes both in the medical and in other professions. It is recommended, too, that all specialists engaged either whole-time or part-time in the Health Service should receive, in addition to their pay, 'expenses necessarily and reasonably incurred in the course of their work.'

10,400 DOCTORS JOIN
Dentists to Seek Assurances

The Minister of Health announced last night that 10,450 general practitioners in England and Wales had joined the medical lists of executive councils under the Health Service Act. This was the total up to Saturday. A week earlier the figure was 6,209.

Representatives of the Dental Consultative Committee are due to discuss with the Minister of Health the possibility of including in the amending bill provisions to allay opposition to the dental scheme as it stands. The committee will ask for assurances concerning increased clinical freedom and the establishment, if possible, of a system of 'grant in aid' whereby some reward would be made for enterprise and skill.

SPECIALISTS UNDER HEALTH ACT
Spens Report Approved

From our London Staff

Fleet Street, Tuesday.

Two resolutions were passed by a meeting of consultants and specialists held yesterday at the Royal College of Physicians, the effect of which is that the royal colleges, the Scottish medical corporations, and other bodies represented at the meeting have decided to maintain their own machinery, independent of the B.M.A., to watch the setting up of the new consultant service under the National Health Act.

The first resolution approved the Spens Report in principle, recommended its adoption, and expressed the hope that the government would implement it. The second was to the effect that the joint committee of consultants and specialists should continue in existence in order to consider matters of special concern to members of the profession represented on it.

OPTICIANS ADVISED TO ACCEPT
Health Service Terms

Opticians are advised to enter the National Health Service scheme. It was announced last night that the Joint Emergency Committee, the negotiating committee representing the optical profession, after its long negotiations with the Ministry of Health, is advising members that the terms, while not entirely adequate, form a basis on which the profession can enter the supplementary ophthalmic scheme of the health service on July 5. Negotiations are still proceeding on the permanent scheme which is planned to replace the supplementary one.

Branch associations of opticians will now discuss the final results of the negotiations, but the individual optician will make his own decision whether to enter the supplementary scheme.

PROMISE TO DENTISTS

Additional details of the Minister of Health's assurance that there is no intention of introducing a salaried service for dentists working in private surgeries are disclosed in a letter issued to the press last night.

The letter, sent on Wednesday to the British Dental Association, the Incorporated Dental Society, and the Public Dental Service Association states that the Minister will review the question of clinical freedom in consultation with the profession but not before the Act becomes operative on July 5. He will sympathetically consider the suggestion that dentists should be free to proceed with treatment except that involving the provision of dentures before obtaining the approval of the Dental Estimates Board to the estimate of costs. While it is intended to review the scale of fees within a year, the review woud be primarily directed to the times normally taken for the various operations.

The Merseyside and North Wales branch of the British Dental Association, representing about 400 dentists in the North-west, decided last night to stay out of the Health Service scheme.

B.M.A. FIGHT 'OVER'

Dr. Guy Dain, Chairman of the British Medical Asociation Council, speaking at Exeter last night said, 'The fight is over. The public after July 5 will get the very best service that doctors can give. We shall make the public medical service of this country the finest that is humanly possible.'

Leader **DOCTORS' LISTS**

It is a pity that the coming into force of the National Health Service scheme should have had for a curtain-raiser the tiresome little squabble which developed in the House of Commons yesterday. Some doctors have left until very late their adherence to the scheme. The local executive councils in some districts have therefore not been able to post lists of doctors in post offices and other public places as early as they had hoped to do. (Manchester's should be available today.) In consequence, some people in these places have not been able to register yet, because they could not get hold of a list of doctors in the scheme. This is a nuisance, but it will soon right itself: for patients can join at any time – it is only doctors who must be in by July 5. In a few weeks it will have been generally forgotten. But a foolish attempt to make political capital out of it, on both sides, brought out an ugly flash of tempers in the Commons. Mr. Bevan, disclaiming responsibility for the delay, thought fit to have a stab at the British Medical Association for advising doctors (quite a long time ago now) not to rush too hastily into the scheme: a Conservative M.P. retorted no more temperately that the whole cause of the delay was 'the Minister's intense obstinacy in conducting negotiations.' These exchanges are futile and tactless. The Minister and the B.M.A. were both obstinate, and both have a share in the blame for any delay there has been. But allotting the blame does not matter. The spirit in which the scheme is carried out is what matters. The Minister and his critics should remember that the scheme needs everyone's goodwill to make it go. Fault-finding, even if justified, is at this point a hindrance to the good work.

Leader **JULY 5**

Today the National Health Service comes into force and the passing of the milestone will be hailed with a chorus of praise, some of it perhaps complacent. We are in process of making a great move forward. But only the first step, the legislative part of the move, is now completed. The larger part of the task is to come. It is a moment of opportunity not of achievement. The health service which comes into being today is only the ground floor of the building. The rest will come but it still wants building, not by M.P.s or civil servants in Whitehall but by doctors and nurses and opticians and many more, by members of the regional hospital boards and the local hospital committees. There is now something solid to build on. The Act puts the hospital services as never before on a sound rational base, the regional boards will be able to make the best use of what hospitals there are. But they know better than anyone that new and better planned hospitals (and many more nurses in them) will be needed before we can call the hospital services wholly satisfactory. The whole population becomes, for the first time, entitled to the medical services hitherto available only to insured workers, the scandal of 'under-doctored' areas will slowly disappear. But the full fruits of these reforms will not be ripe until the system of health centres has had time to grow and that growth would be gradual even if lack of bricks and mortar did not inhibit it at the start.

. . . One must think of the health service as a huge natural organism in process of growth, not as a creation of magic called out of the void by the wand of the Minister of Health.

5 July 1948 *p.3*

MR. BEVAN'S BITTER ATTACK ON CONSERVATIVES
No 'Free for All' Policy Under Labour

'The eyes of the world are turning to Great Britain. We now have the moral leadership of the world and before many years are over we shall have people coming here as to a modern Mecca learning from us in the twentieth century as they learned from us in the seventeenth century,' said Mr. Aneurin Bevan, Minister of Health, at a Labour rally in Manchester.

. . . The Labour Party, he said, would win the 1950 election because successful Toryism and an intelligent electorate were a contradiction in terms.

Poverty generally speaking was a consequence of bad social organisation and his own experiences ensured that no amount of cajolery would eradicate from his heart a deep burning hatred of the Tory Party. 'So far as I am concerned they are lower than vermin,' he went on. 'They condemned millions of people to semi-starvation. I warn you, young men and women, do not listen to what they are saying, do not listen to the seductions of Lord Woolton. They have not changed or if they have they are slightly worse than they were.'

MR. BEVAN DEFENDS SECURITY FOR THE INDIVIDUAL
Eliminating Fears Which Check Initiative

Mr. Aneurin Bevan, the Minister of Health, yesterday chose Lancashire as the area in which to demonstrate publicly the nation's succession to its inheritance of the health services. He visited a hospital at Davyhulme and later spoke to a representative gathering at Preston. . . .

Mr. Bevan said that the conception behind the five great Acts that had just come into force was one to which people of all parties had made their contribution. 'Since 1848 the health services of the country have undergone adaptation, extension, and improvement, until to-day I think we can say we have the best organised system of social security in the world,' he declared. Some said it was a mistake to put individual security so much to the fore, that in making the individual too secure some vital element was sucked out of life, that the spirit of adventure and the uncertainties that were the spur of original thought would be retarded. There was, however, no spirit of adventure in a mother being unable to give proper attention to her child, or in inefficient social services. The fear that was now eliminated undermined individual initiative.

Discussing the structure of the service, Mr. Bevan said, 'You might say that a man of my temperament would find it difficult to obtain universal agreement, but I sometimes wonder whether a less belligerent personality would have started the scheme at all.' A certain amount of aggressiveness was necessary, Mr. Bevan went on, and he could claim there had been no political bias in the selection of people to take part in the voluntary machinery. He had achieved that universal measure of disagreement that was evidence of complete impartiality, and already a team spirit had grown up.

MR. BEVAN SORRY
The 'Vermin' Speech a Political One

Mr. Aneurin Bevan, the Minister of Health, replied in a letter received by Mr. Lionel Heald, K.C., to questions about his speech in Manchester on Sunday in which he referred to the Conservative party as 'lower than vermin.'

Mr. Heald, who recently accepted the Minister's invitation to serve for a further period of two years as a governor of the Middlesex Hospital, wrote to Mr. Bevan's secretary about reports of the speech and asked: 'If he was correctly reported, how can he honestly accept the services of any Tory for voluntary work in connection with the National Health scheme?'

Mr. E.J.S. Clarke, private secretary to Mr. Bevan, replied as follows:

'I have shown Mr. Bevan your letter to me of July 5. He is sorry that you and others have taken remarks made upon a political platform so much amiss. No doubt you have seen reports of his speech the next day in Preston when as Minister of Health he made it quite clear that he had not allowed any political bias to affect the selection of people invited by him to take part in the running of the new health services and that he had been glad to observe the strength of the team spirit which had already grown up.

'These remarks are reflected in all the recent appointments which have been made irrespective of party in the sole desire to secure the services of those most fitted by their experience and outlook to administer the service and make it a success.

'This remains Mr. Bevan's attitude and he hopes that you will continue your work as a governor of the Middlesex Hospital in this spirit.'

12 July 1948   *p.3*

MR. CHURCHILL'S RETORT TO HEALTH MINISTER

Discussing Mr. Bevan's recent reference to Tories as lower than vermin, Mr. Churchill at Woodford (Essex) on Saturday said one would have thought that a man who had been only a burden in the years of storm and who received high office in the days of victory would have tried to turn over a new leaf and redeem his past. Instead he had chosen the moment of bringing the National Health Service into being to speak of at least half of the British nation as 'lower than vermin' and to give vent to the 'burning hatred' by which his mind was seared.

'We speak of the Minister of Health,' said Mr. Churchill, 'but we ought rather to say Minister of Disease, for is not morbid hatred a form of mental disease. . . . Indeed I can think of no better step to signalise the inauguration of the National Health Service than that a person who so obviously needs psychiatric attention should be among the first of its patients.'

Just one week after the inauguration the 'Guardian' published the first letter of complaint about the health service.

HEALTH SERVICE

To the Editor of the Manchester Guardian

Sir,—We have been waiting a long time for the benefits which are supposed to come to us under the new health service, but my own experience of the first working of it has been far from happy. My wife has been for some weeks under the doctor's care as a private patient. This week, for the first time, she goes to him as a patient under the new health service. The doctor tells her that he can no longer supply the same medicine as he gave her privately, explaining that certain ingredients in the medicine previously supplied could not be prescribed under the new health service.

We have, therefore, to accept a service which is admittedly inferior, although we have been given to understand that no discrimination would be made by accepting the new service. Surely if a certain treatment was necessary before the Act it is necessary now, and either (1) the doctor is trying to keep private patients, or (2) there is something wrong with the Act.—Yours &c.,

H.R.
July 8.

THE HEALTH SERVICE
21,300 Doctors Applied by July 5

More than 21,300 doctors throughout Great Britain had applied to take part in the National Health Service when it started on July 5, it was officially stated yesterday, but it is not expected that the final total, which will not be known until executive councils have completed the examination of their lists, will be as high, because duplication of names may have occurred in some instances. The provisional figure of doctors for England and Wales was 19,006 and for Scotland 2,245, but the Scottish total comprises applicants only up to July 3.

It is estimated that when the service started more than 36,700,000 persons in Great Britain had been accepted by doctors taking part. Of this total more than 14,300,000 were new applications.

The provisional number of dentists in England and Wales who had applied by July 5 to take part in the new service was 4,560, and there has since been a steady increase. More than 550 had applied in Scotland by the same date, with returns still outstanding from several of the largest executive councils.

10 September 1948   *p.8*

B.M.A. CALLS FOR EXPERIMENTAL HEALTH CENTRES
Avoiding Overlap of Present Services

From our London Staff

The importance of co-ordinating the work of family practice with that of clinics is one of the chief points made in the interim report of health centres presented by the Council of the British Medical Association. In April the B.M.A. appointed a special committee to investigate and report on existing forms of group practice, including partnerships and other forms of collaboration between general practitioners, and to relate this and other experience to health centre development.

The committee's findings on the conception of the health centre and the general problems arising from it are based on the results of an extensive field inquiry which is the first of its kind to be carried out in this country. The report gives examples of lack of co-ordination that results when two unrelated but overlapping services, the general practitioners and the clinics, exist side by side.

OVERLAPPING SERVICES

It cites ante-natal clinics where expectant mothers are examined by medical officers who never conduct a confinement, while midwives needing medical help send for a doctor who has not seen the patient beforehand, or health visitors who visit the homes of young babies and others who are being attended simultaneously by their family doctors. The two agencies could be complementary and extremely helpful to each other were there any organised co-operation between them. Lacking it, they often 'confuse an anxious parent and exasperate each other.'

The report states that some way must be found of uniting the work of family practice with that of the clinics. It is not enough to conduct infant welfare, ante-natal and other clinics in the same premises, or even to arrange in addition that the work of the clinics is conducted by general practitioners. What is wanted is assimilation not merely liaison. A group of doctors, housed in a well-equipped building, could carry out in a co-ordinated way all the work at present done by general practitioners and clinical medical officers. The working place of such a group of doctors might be called a 'Health Centre.'

248

RANGE OF WORK

The report visualises such a centre having its own staff of nurses and mid-wives so that the work of doctors and nurses might be co-ordinated. The minimum range of work would include general medical service, care of mothers and young children, care of school children, vaccination and immunisation, ante and post natal examinations, health visiting, home nursing, and health education. The administration of the centre should be in the hands of a joint committee representing all the professional elements, doctors, nurses, dentists, pharmacists, and the medical officer of health or his nominee. In areas where it is impossible to provide premises it should still be possible to experiment with the health centre method to some extent.

11 September 1948   *p.6*

HEALTH CENTRES
Problem of the Private Patient

Local doctors may refuse to serve in the experimental health centre which Birmingham is building at Stechford unless the Ministry of Health's ruling that private patients cannot be treated there is withdrawn. 'The local doctors feel they could not take service in the centre if this were among the required conditions,' states the 'Lancet.' Their objection has been received sympathetically by the local executive council, which has approved a report by its general purposes committee declaring that adherence to this ruling would be detrimental to the Health Service.

The doctors' case for treating private patients at the health centre, as argued by the 'Lancet' is that by treating private cases in their own surgeries they lay themselves open to the charge that they are offering two standards of service. In addition, their consulting hours will have to be duplicated for the two types of patient, and one of the 'vaunted attractions' of the health centre – the freedom offered to the doctors household – would be lost if consulting-rooms had still to be maintained there. Furthermore, if the centre offers a better standard of practice, the private patient would be denied some of the advantages which he – as a ratepayer – was helping to provide. . . .

SUGGESTED WAY OUT

As a way of solving the problem, the early establishment of experimental centres is suggested. If experiment showed that private practice in the centre was incompatible with the successful conduct of the centre's other functions, this sanction could be withdrawn before wider health centre provision was embarked upon.

2 October 1948 *p.6*

A 'REVOLUTION' IN MEDICINE

Sir William Gilliatt, the gynaecologist, described the new national health service as a measure which had revolutionised the organisation of medicine when he spoke at the annual dinner of the Royal College of Obstetricians and Gynaecologists, in London last night.

'This council,' he said, 'has felt that it has always been its duty to give such advice to the Ministry as would maintain or raise the standards of obstetrics and gynaecology in this country. In the last eighteen months, however, we have seen our principles gradually abandoned.'

Sir William referred to the advent of the new committee which would be appointed to advise the Minister. 'It is for our college and its representatives to continue to press so that gynaecology and the maternity services shall not be allowed to drift backwards, but shall be maintained and raised,' he said.

MR. BEVAN'S WARNING

Mr. Aneurin Bevan, Minister of Health, said at Folkestone last night that the health service would break down unless the people of the country use it intelligently, sparingly, and prudently.

'There was a great demand at the beginning but I believe it will ease down and the whole thing will find its proper level,' he said. 'There is as much need for prudence on the part of the medical profession as a whole in giving the benefits of the service to the population in the claiming of those benefits. If the population and profession co-operate intelligently, then before very long we shall have a health service of which we can be exceedingly proud.'

17 December 1948 *p.8*

NATIONAL HEALTH

In the House of Commons yesterday, Mr. Aneurin Bevan (Minister of Health) told Colonel M. Stoddart-Scott (C.–Pudsey and Otley) that the total amounts paid out of public funds between July 5 1948, and November 30 1948, in respect of hospital, general medical, pharmaceutical, general dental and ophthalmic services were:

Hospital services	53,000,000
General medical services	7,982,944
Pharmaceutical services	5,438,709
General dental services	5,541,658
Ophthalmic services	4,047,568

The total liability incurred in that period could not be stated. All the Regional Hospital Boards had submitted estimates for the financial year 1949-50. Total gross expenditure shown in the estimates received was £157,680,000, of which £10,236,000 represented capital expenditure. Income was given as £9,021,000.

31 December 1948   *p.3*

DOCTORS' PROTEST
M.P.'s 'Partisan Attitude'

The 'British Medical Journal' complains that the chairman of the Central Health Services Council, Mr. Fred Messer (Labour M.P. for Tottenham), has adopted 'a highly partisan attitude' to medical men and their work. In a recent speech, Mr. Messer is reported to have said: 'In the days before the new Act the people were only allowed to be ill at certain times during the day – the times set down on the brass plate in front of the doctor's door.'

'What kind of confidence can the medical profession have in the chairman of the Health Service Council,' asks the journal, 'if he makes such ill-judged, inaccurate, and unjust remarks – remarks directed at men and women who, after a hard day's work, have to be ready to get up at any time of the night in response to a call for help?'

Mr. Messer is also alleged to have said: 'Now, for the first time, the Health Service as a whole will have a master mind behind it.' The journal asks, 'Does he mean the mind of the chairman of the Central Health Services Council, or the unco-ordinated mind of an endless series of Ministers of Health?' The article concludes: 'Our new administrators have yet to learn the lesson of humility, the humility of the man who minds the machine created by men who understand how it works.'

Education

In education the themes remained fairly constant, as did the extra-parliamentary nature of the debate. Thus secondary education dominated, along with teachers' conditions of service, and these were discussed in the teaching unions' conference. Towards the end of the year proposals were unveiled for more generous grants to students in higher education.

3 March 1948   *p.4*

Leader   **THE COMPREHENSIVE SCHOOL**

 The National Association of Labour Teachers is a champion of the 'Comprehensive School' against the 'tripartite system' of grammar, technical and modern secondary schools favoured by the Ministry of Education and has just stated its case in a pamphlet. The comprehensive school is defined as 'taking all children who are not subnormal, from the age of eleven'. It does not divide them into distinct 'sides' or streams. As they grow older they will take various 'special studies' in accordance with their abilities and aptitudes and for these they will be regrouped: but they will remain members of their unselected class for which there will be a 'common core curriculum'. This is in fact the system on which the London County Council has decided to work. The pamphlet discerns in the tripartite theory taken over by the Ministry from the findings of the Norwood Committee a persistence of 'the habit of thinking of education in terms of class.' This is perhaps less than fair to the Ministry. To distinguish children by their type of mind is not the same thing as to distinguish them by their degree of ability and both are far removed from the time-honoured custom of distinguishing them by their parents' incomes. But the tripartite theory has obvious flaws in practice even if it could be shown that children fall neatly into the three main types which it postulates. It still remains to be shown that they can be distinguished at the age of eleven. A good many education authorities have already submitted development plans on tripartite lines but the shortage of building materials will make the construction of the new schools a slow business and give time for further reflection, experiment, and research.

30 March 1948   p.5

TEACHERS' ATTITUDE TO SCHOOL MEALS
Demand for Release from All but Supervisory Duties

From our Special Correspondent

Douglas (Isle of Man), Monday.

The part teachers ought to play in the school meals service was the subject of a warm debate at to-day's conference of the National Union of Teachers. A resolution calling for a fully staffed ancillary service which would release teachers from the job of supervising meals, and demanding that the Education Act of 1944 should be amended accordingly, met with strong opposition from the executive.

Mr. W. Oldroyd (South Shields) said teachers already supervised games, drama, gardening, and a host of school activities from cinema clubs to pig-sties, and they wanted to know by what right they were condemned to sacrifice their dinner-time too. Such duties would clearly grow: it was quite likely that school dinners would be followed by school breakfasts and even school boarding. . . .

SIZE OF CLASSES

Miss A.M. Edwards, of the Executive, moved that a reduction in the size of classes was education's most imperative need. She argued that none should be bigger than 30. At present there were 34,490 schools with more than 40 children in a class, 2081 with more than 50, and 47 with more than 60.

Tired of 'pious declarations,' Mr. L. Davison (Reading) moved that a day should be fixed for this reform. A still more forthright motion from Heston and Isleworth, ruled out of order, called on teachers to refuse to teach a class of more than 30 after April 1, 1953. The debate on the subject will be continued today.

TEACHING OF BOYS
Schoolmasters Claim it as a Man's Job

The National Association of Schoolmasters unanimously decided at its conference in Scarborough yesterday that the teaching of boys is a man's job, not a woman's. Mr. D.N. Thomas, of London, said women were in charge of 3,217 boys' classes. 'These avaricious hordes of women have already staked their claim in our field,' he added, 'and the sooner they are smoked out of that field the better it will be for the boys of this country.'

Mr. W.S. Buckley, Liverpool, moving a protest against the Burnham scale of salaries, declared that it afforded opportunities to unscrupulous head teachers of enlarging their schools at the expense of others. Assistant teachers have reported, he said, that heads of grammar schools in the South of England were persuading boys of 17 to stay at school to take the scholarship examination against the advice of assistant masters who knew the lads had no chance of success. Mr. Buckley alleged that head teachers were persuading boys to stay at school so as to get the extra ten BUs.

His motion, which declared that the salaries of men teachers under the new scale were too low, the incremental period too long, and the method of assessing head teachers' salaries unsatisfactory, was carried by a large majority.

UNSUITABLE SCHOOL PREMISES
Education Committees' Recommendation to Minister

From our Special Correspondent

Llandudno, Thursday.

School holidays, school premises, and the multilateral school were discussed at the conference of the Association of Education Committees to-day. . . .

The West Riding Education Committee sought to commit the conference to the view that the multilateral school was to be preferred educationally. Councillor W.M. Hyman, chairman of the West Riding Committee, arguing the case from the social angle, said we had divided the nation into two classes – those who attended grammar schools or a few rich schools and those who remained in the modern schools. When Tom and Mary won scholarships to the grammar schools, he said, they became different from other members of their family. Secondary school masters and mistresses led different social lives from their colleagues in the elementary schools. Did head masters and head mistresses of grammar schools, he asked, ever enter an elementary school?

An amendment from Surrey and Bristol urged that full autonomy be left to each authority to determine its scheme for organising secondary schools in its area. Mr. R. Beloe considered the resolution a dangerous one. It claimed that the multilateral school could provide a flexible curriculum, adapted to the varying needs of all its students. 'We don't know whether it can or not,' he said, 'and that is the whole point of the amendment.'

Alderman F.C. Williams (Bristol) thought it unwise at this time of day to attempt to 'iron out' to one pattern all the schools of the country.

The amendment was carried by a large majority.

1 July 1948   *p.4*

Leader   **PROGRESS REPORT**

The raising of the school-leaving age to fifteen on April 1, 1947, brought into operation the first of the major reforms of the Education Act of 1944. The report published to-day by the Ministry of Education shows what has been done over the past year towards solving the main material problems raised by the change. The need to provide more teachers and more school accommodation has been aggravated by what the Minister has called the 'bulge in the birth-rate,' and the report estimates that the number of pupils at maintained and assisted primary and secondary schools in England and Wales, which was 5,034,275 in January 1947, will go up by about a million by 1952. During 1947 the number of full-time teachers in these schools increased from 188,399 in January to 193,313 in October, but although there were some 500,000 fewer pupils than in 1938 the size of classes remained a serious problem. The report expects that the figures for 1947, when they are available will show that the fall in the ratio of pupils to teachers during 1946 will have been maintained; but it rightly admits that the situation affords 'no cause for complacency,' for we are still a long way off even the 'standard maxima' (by no means in themselves 'final desiderata') of thirty pupils for senior classes and forty for junior. The provision of buildings received a setback owing to the fuel crisis, and a good deal of the progress reported is still in the planning stage. But among the 400 new schools whose plans have been approved is the first county boarding school, which the Surrey education authority hopes to open next September.

'LIP SERVICE TO EDUCATION'
Teachers' Criticism

Warning that the Education Act might be jettisoned unless progressive sections moved swiftly in its defence was given by Miss M. Holmshaw, of Manchester, in her presidential address to the National Federation of Class Teachers, whose conference opened in Manchester yesterday.

No sooner was the Act on the statute book than the forces of reaction and of despondency began to work against it. Apart from the raising of the leaving age to 15 there had been no educational advance of the extent envisaged in it. The blame rested mainly with the Government, which, although paying lip service to education, allowed it to languish.

There were two essentials to the realisation of the Act – teachers and buildings. A serious shortage of women teachers in infants' and junior schools had been allowed to develop and though the Ministry's plans shown in Circular 174 would eventually relieve the situation in infants' schools in general they meant little more than a return to the position before the war. Miss Holmshaw advocated a greater use of prefabricated buildings and the maintenance of the emergency training scheme for both sexes, coupled with a recruiting campaign.

PLAN FOR MORE UNIVERSITY SCHOLARSHIPS
Working Party's Recommendations

A wide expansion of university scholarships and a marked improvement in the value of the awards are proposed by the Working Party on University Awards whose report to the Minister of Education is published to-day (Stationery Office, 9d.).

It is suggested that about 11,000 students of a total of some 18,000 entering English and Welsh universities each year should receive aid from public funds. This would mean increasing the number of State scholarships from 800 to about 2,000; increasing the number of entrance scholarships and exhibitions which qualify for supplementation from the Ministry from 1,200-1,500 to 2,000, and increasing the number of awards made by local authorities from 4,000 to a minimum of 7,000 a year.

Under the new schemes proposed, the Minister would be responsible for assisting students whose academic gifts could be tested by examination alone; the local education authorities would select other students who have qualities likely to carry them to success at the university or in their careers. In addition to the 11,000 awards which may be made by the Ministry and by local education authorities there would be about 7,000 more places to be filled annually. These would go to students from overseas, to those with grants from other bodies, and to students who can afford a university education without financial help.

Another suggestion is that in selecting candidates for university awards from among National Service men, the machinery used by the Civil Service Selection Board should be adopted. It is also proposed that State scholarships should be tenable at the universities within the Commonwealth and in foreign countries.

To meet the needs of industry for advanced technologists the report recommends that postgraduate awards should be available for students who have taken a university degree course and spent a period in industry. It is also proposed that there should be more undergraduate awards for students who have left full-time education and have taken up employment.

Changes are proposed in the value of the awards and in the method of their assessment. At present the grant normally payable does not include any allowance towards the student's keep in vacations, but in future the normal rates of grant would cover the full calendar year. It is recommended that the maximum of the existing scale for calculating the contribution expected from the student's parents should be raised from £1,500 to £2,000. Under existing arrangements no grants are payable when the income of the parents after certain deductions have been made is above the maximum of the income scale, but the report recommends that a fixed sum of £30 should be paid to holders of all awards without regard to financial circumstances. Moreover, the allowances for children and the cost of their education, which are deducted from the parents' income before applying it to the income scale, would be greatly increased.

In a foreword to the report the Minister says it goes a long way towards establishing equality of opportunity in the highest stages of education.

8 December 1948   *p.4*

Leader   **SCHOLARSHIPS**

Many anomalies and irritations in the present system of awarding State and local scholarships to the universities will disappear if the authorities concerned accept the recommendations, published to-day, of the Working Party on University Awards. Three in particular may be mentioned. At present a student may gain provisional admission to the university he prefers and win a State scholarship tenable only at another. He must then forgo either his preference or his scholarship. The Working Party say: 'It is unlikely that all State scholars will be able to go to the universities of their choice, but it is felt that they should be allowed to hold their scholarships at any university to which they may gain entry.' Second (as our correspondence columns have shown), the present 'means test' for State scholars bears hardly on many middle-class families who get next to no relief from the award. The Working Party would raise from £1,500 to £2,000 the income level above which a parent has to pay the whole of a State scholar's expenses, with proportionate concessions for lower incomes. Third, some young people have to leave school at fifteen but keep on with part-time study, and are well worth sending to a university later; but they are at an obvious disadvantage in the ordinary written entrance examination. The report suggests in such cases a selection procedure 'similar in principle to that used by the Civil Service Selection Board.' The Working Party think that there should be about 4,000 open and State, and about 7,000 local authority, scholarships. This estimate may be compared with a plan to be presented to President Truman by the National Education Association for 20,000 scholarships supported by Federal grants and tenable at any American university.

Social Security and Welfare

In the area of social security and welfare two features stand out: the introduction of the Children Act and the inauguration of the social insurance scheme on 5 July. In both cases there was widespread political support and very little debate was engendered at this stage.

21 January 1948   *p.8*

NEW SOCIAL SERVICE SCHEMES TO START ON JULY 5
Administration of the Hospitals

From our Political Correspondent

Westminster, Tuesday.

The first legal notices fixing July 5 as the start of the new social service schemes have been issued to-day by the Minister of National Insurance and relate to the operation of the National Insurance Act and of the National Insurance (Industrial Injuries) Act.

The insurance schemes are so completely bound up with the national health service that there should no longer be any question of the postponement of the service. Mr. Bevan said on Saturday that he would stick to July 5, and all that is needed now is an official notice naming it as the appointed day.

The Minister of Health has in fact laid before Parliament to-day rules governing the functions of the regional hospital boards, hospital management committees, and of the boards of governors of the hospital services. The administrative processes for the establishment of the new health service are being applied as though Mr. Bevan had no dispute of moment with anybody.

PENSIONERS' BENEFITS

Two statutory instruments embody the decision of the Minister of National Insurance and have been laid before Parliament. One

259

of them (No. 53 of 1948) fixes July 5 as the appointed day for the operation of the National Insurance (Industrial Injuries) Act, and the other (No. 54 of 1948) fixes the same appointed day for the operation of the National Insurance Act. From July 5, therefore, not only will the National Insurance scheme start working fully (some of the pension provisions are already in force) but the present National Health and Unemployment Contributory Pension, and Workmen's Compensation Acts will be repealed.

The repeal of these Acts has a bearing on the controversy between Mr. Bevan and the doctors. There has been a tendency for some doctors to argue that even if their objections to the national health service caused a postponement of the appointed day, nobody would suffer since the 'panel' would still go on. In fact, the panel, as now authorised, will be ended under Mr. Griffith's statutory instruments, and the new health service must take its place.

Mr. Griffiths has also laid before Parliament to-day regulations which will provide increased benefits to some 300,000 pensioners from July 5. The new regulations are only the first instalment of those to be made under section 65 of the National Insurance Act to ensure continuity between old schemes and the new. About 150,000 men now drawing contributory old-age pensions of 26s. a week will be eligible from July 5 for an increase of 16s. a week for a dependent wife under the age of 60. From the same date some 10,000 men and women will be entitled to an increase of 7s. 6d. a week for a child in the pensioner's family.

Some 140,000 widows under 60 with children, or with some infirmity which prevents them from supporting themselves, will similarly benefit. Men who propose to claim for a dependent wife will be able to get application forms, from January 26, at local offices of the Assistance Board and of the Ministry, but not from post offices.

HOSPITAL SERVICES

Mr. Bevan's new regulations do not lay down the method of administering the health service, but deal with the division of functions between the Minister and the various regional and local bodies. The regulations confer on regional hospital boards, acting as the Minister's agents, the power needed to enable them to guide the planning, conduct, and development of the services in their area. Hospital management committees, acting as agents of the regional boards, are empowered to administer the hospitals and services under their control. Boards of governors of teaching hospitals, acting as agents of the Minister, are also given the powers they need.

The regional hospital boards were appointed by the Minister of Health last June and they will be appointing management committees during the coming weeks. The Minister himself will shortly appoint the boards of govenors of teaching hospitals.

CHILD-CARE PLANS
Government's Bill

SAFEGUARDS FOR HOMELESS

From our Political Correspondent

The Government's plans for the care of some 125,000 homeless children in England and Wales and 13,500 in Scotland, have been published to-day in the Children Bill, with an explanatory White Paper (Cmd. 7306, price 2d.). The bill is based on the principal findings of the reports of the Curtis and Clyde committees, and also continues the care of those children who, through the ending of the Poor Law, would otherwise have been unprotected.

The Children Bill carries out the policy announced by Mr. Attlee in the House of Commons on March 24, but it does not touch the law of adoption, although both the Curtis and Clyde committees recommended changes in it. These, states the White Paper, 'have been noted for consideration in connection with appropriate legislation.' The Government claims, however, that the new bill deals with the main problem of child care.

County and county borough councils will be given the duty of taking into their care any child in their area under the age of 17 who has no parents or guardians, or has been abandoned or lost, or whose parents or guardians are prevented in some way from giving him proper accommodation and maintenance, and upbringing. It must appear to the local authority that its intervention is necessary in the interests of the child. No local authority will be allowed to evade its duty because the child normally lives in the area of a second authority, but the second authority may either assume responsibility for the child or pay the first authority for his upkeep.

LOCAL AUTHORITY AS PARENT

Normally a local authority will maintain a child until he is 18, but he may be returned to the care of parents or guardians if that is thought to be consistent with his welfare. It is intended that 'the local authority should stand as a parent to the child and should interest themselves in his welfare as long as his need of their care continues. . . . A local authority will be under obligation to make such use of facilities and services available for children living with their parents as is reasonable in his case.'

'Protected' children who may go to secondary schools or the university are not to be handicapped by the lack of the equipment (blazers, for example) ordinarily used by their fellows.

The children are to be accommodated in various ways: with foster-parents, or in homes or hostels to be provided by the local authorities, or in voluntary homes. The Home Secretary asks for power to make regulations to secure the welfare of children accommodated by voluntary organisations. When the bill comes into force, which will be not later than July 5 next – the start of the National Health Service scheme – all voluntary homes will have to be registered, and a month's notice will have to be given to the Home Secretary by anybody proposing to open a new voluntary home.

Local authorities will be obliged to appoint a children's committee to administer the new provisions unless the Home Secretary is satisfied that special circumstances make this unnecessary. Children's committees will be given a life of three years, after which the administration of the scheme may be reviewed. The Government holds that there is a greater certainty of bringing child welfare before the notice of councils if a separate committee (rather than a sub-committee of, say, the education committee) exists and reports. Similarly, each local authority will have to appoint a children's officer who will be the executive of the children's committee and who is not to be used in any other way without special permission.

28 May 1948   p.4

THE CHILDREN BILL

To the Editor of the Manchester Guardian

Sir,–The Children Bill is now in the committee stage, and it is not yet too late for suitable amendments to bring it somewhat farther down from the realms of theory to common earth.

It seems to be the intention of the bill as it stands that the new children's officer shall not only care for the deprived child but shall deal with all the functions of the local authority under the Children and Young Persons Act, 1933, with the exception of those under Part II. That means in effect that the welfare work of the local education authority is for the most part taken from it, and in particular it is no longer to be allowed to give (through its school attendance and welfare department) information to the juvenile courts concerning the homes of children brought before these courts as delinquent.

The reports given by the school attendance and welfare officers are the sum of long years of visiting at all sorts of times and for many different reasons; these officers have seen the families of delinquents years before delinquency developed; they know the parents, the children, and the way of life of the folk concerned.

Reports given by children's officers, on the other hand, will be the result of one visit paid to a home which is expecting it, just because one of the children is 'in trouble.' And 'one-visit' reports can scarcely have the same value as those which are the result of years of observation.

The bill as it stands may be administratively tidy, but my association feels that the function of the children's officer should be that which was originally proposed – the care of deprived children. Let existing officers of knowledge and experience continue to guide the courts. – Yours &c.,

F.G.C. ELWICK, Public Relations Officer,
Education Welfare Officers' National Association,
Nottingham.

29 June 1948   *p.4*

Leader   **NEGLECTED CHILDREN**

The Children Bill, which had its third reading in the Commons yesterday, should do much to improve the lot of those 'deprived of a normal home life,' who were the subject of the Curtis Report. It deals with those who have lost, permanently or temporarily, the one thing that all children need for full and happy development. Many of them in institutions, schools, or with foster-parents have come from homes not fit to live in, where health and morals alike are in danger from neglect or cruelty. 'The Neglected Child and his Family,' a study made by the Women's Group on Public Welfare, is an illuminating report on this serious problem, for it deals with the stage before the child has to be removed from home. In the introduction Mr. J.B. Priestley points out that the average type of mother guilty of grave neglect is not a 'thoroughly bad sort,' but she is often, as the instances here show, a victim of poor health, mental dullness, poverty, fatigue, and finally apathy; and it is the mother, rather than the father, who gives the 'temper' to the family. If such 'problem families' could receive practical, personal help and encouragement to get a grip on their responsibilities, the increasing social services might do more good. It is important that this study mentions the work of the Pacifist Service Units, who did excellent pioneer work in Liverpool and Manchester and are now extending it in the Family Service Units. They attack the core of the problem. Another sound scheme is at 'Brentwood' in Lancashire, where such mothers, with the children, may both recuperate and learn some home management. These are only beginnings, but work of this kind does show a way in which some standards of decency and self-respect can be restored so that the children may stay in their own homes.

JULY 5

. . . The new system of social security under the Ministry of
National Insurance [also] comes into operation today. The impact
of this, unlike that of the National Health Service, will make itself
felt at once to many people in the disagreeable form of a higher
rate of weekly insurance contributions, to others by a demand for
contributions previously not paid at all. Most of the benefits will
not be experienced until the need for them arises and many people
will wait long enough for that. Yet it too is a great step forward and
recalls the surge of enthusiasm with which the Beveridge Report
was greeted. To millions of people below the minimum income level
security is almost as tangible a thing as money itself. To know that
bad luck will not mean acute poverty is to be free of the most
persistent and stabbing anxiety which afflicts the wage earner.

THE INSURANCE SCHEME

Most people familiar with the difficulties of social
administration have been pleased and surprised to see how
peacefully the new National Insurance Scheme has passed through
the first month of its existence. The National Health Service has
had a far rougher time largely because the Ministry of Health was
far less ready than the Ministry of Insurance to take the plunge on
July 5. But it may prove later that the appearance of relative calm
in the insurance sector has been deceptive.

Many hundreds of thousands of people who think they have
solved the conundrum of the value of the stamp they should have
on their cards, of who should pay what and whether any national
insurance stamp is required at all will find in due course that their
decision was wrong – particularly if their decision was that they
needed no stamp and no card. Not one married woman in ten
thousand can possibly have mastered the fifty or more provisions
in the Married Women's Regulations. It is said that not even the
Ministry's officials themselves understand them all yet. And what
about the million or so part-timers and casual workers and those
who work for five or more employers in the week – for example
cleaners?

. . . The technicalities affecting qualifications for benefits and
pensions have not been really tested yet – notably the
contributory qualifications required of the newly insured classes.
Meanwhile it is interesting to hear that of the two million or so

inquiries at the newly opened local offices of the Ministry of National Insurance over 50 per cent ask something about the National Health Service, with which these offices are not officially concerned.

Major Political Figures

Addison Christopher: 1st Viscount of Stallingborough (1945). Secretary of State for Commonwealth Relations 1945–47. Paymaster General 1948–49, Lord Privy Seal 1947–51.

Attlee Clement Richard (Lab Limehouse). Deputy Prime Minister in war time coalition, 1942–45. Prime Minister 1945–51, Minister of Defence 1945–46.

Bevan Aneurin: (Lab Ebbw Vale) Minister of Health 1945–51.

Beveridge Sir William (Lord Beveridge 1946): Liberal MP for Berwick-on-Tweed 1944–45, Chairman of Inter-Departmental Committee on Social Insurance and Allied Services 1941–42.

Bevin Ernest: (Lab Central Wandsworth) Minister of Labour and National Service 1940–45, Secretary of State for Foreign Affairs 1945–61.

Butler Richard Austen: (Con, Saffron Walden) Minister of Education 1941–45, Minister of Labour June–July 1945.

Churchill Winston: (Con, Woodford) Prime Minister and Minister of Defence 1940–5, Leader of the Opposition 1945–51.

Chuter-Ede James: (Labour, South Shields) Parliamentary Secretary Ministry of Education 1940–45, Home Secretary 1945–51.

Cripps Stafford: (Lab East Bristol) Minister of Aircraft Production 1942–45, President of Board of Trade 1945, Minister of Economic Affairs 1947, Chancellor of the Exchequer 1947–50.

Curtis Myra: Principal Newnham College Cambridge, Chairman of Interdepartmental Committee on Children Deprived of a Normal Home Life 1945–46.

Dain Sir H. Guy: General Medical Practitioner, Chairman British Medical Association 1942–48.

Davies Clement: (Lib Montgomeryshire) Leader of Parliamentary Liberal Party.

Eden Anthony: (Con Warwick and Leamington) Secretary of State for Foreign Affairs 1940–45, Leader of the House of Commons 1942–45, Deputy Leader of the Opposition 1945–51.

Greenwood Arthur: (Lab Wakefield) Lord Privy Seal 1945–47, Paymaster General 1946–7.

Griffiths James: (Lab Llanelly) Minister of National Insurance 1945–50.

Hastings Somerville Dr: (Lab Barking) President of Socialist Medical Association.

Henderson of Ardwick, Lord of the Treasury 1945–50.

Hill Charles Dr, "Radio Doctor", Secretary of the BMA.

Hirst Francis W.: Hon Fellow Wadham College Oxford, Governor of LSE, prolific academic writer.

James Eric Dr: Headmaster Manchester Grammar School.

Jowitt Sir William: (Lab Ashton-U-Lyne), First Minister of National Insurance 1944–45, Lord Chancellor 1945–51.

Key Charles William: (Lab Bow and Bromley) Parliamentary Secretary Minister of Health 1945–47, Minister of Works 1947–50.

Laski Harold J.: Professor of Political Science in the University of London, Member of the Executive Committee of the Labour Party 1936–49, Chairman of the Executive 1945–46.

Llewellin of Upton, elevated to House of Lords 1945, J.J. Lewellin (Unionist 1929–45)

Little Sir Eric Graham (Ind University of London) Eminent physician and MP.

Moran Lord: President Royal College of Physicians.

Morrison Herbert: (Lab South Hackney 1935–45, East Lewisham 1945–51) Home Secretary and Minister of Home Security 1940–45, Deputy Prime Minister, Lord President of Council and Leader of the House of Commons 1945–51.

Rathbone Eleanor: (Independent Combined Universities), Chairman Family Endowment Society. Vigorous campaigner for Family Allowances.

Reith Lord: First Director General of BBC, served as Minister of Information. Transport and Works during the war. Member of New Towns Committee 1946.

Sandys Duncan: (Con Norwood) Minister of Works 1944–45.

Silkin Lewis: (Lab Peckham) Minister of Town and Country Planning 1945–51.

Tomlinson George: (Lab Fernworth) Parliamentary Secretary Ministry of Labour 1941–45, Minister of Works 1945–47, Minister of Education 1947–51.

Webb-Johnson Sir Alfred: President Royal College of Surgeons.

Wilkinson Ellen: (Lab Jarrow) 1945 Minister of Education. Died Feb 1947.

Willink Henry: (Con Croydon) Minister of Health 1943–45.

Woodburn Arthur: (Lab Clackmannon and East Stirling) Parliamentary Secretary Ministry of Supply 1945–47, Secretary of State for Scotland 1947–50.

Woolton Lord: Member of War Cabinet 1943–45 (Minister of Reconstruction), Lord President of Council 1945, Chairman of Conservative Party Central Office.